THE CROSS IN CANADA

The Cross In Canada

EDITED BY
JOHN S. MOIR

INTRODUCTION BY JOHN WEBSTER GRANT

THE RYERSON PRESS TORONTO

PRINTED AND BOUND IN CANADA BY THE RYERSON PRESS TORONTO

A GRANT FROM THE CENTENNIAL COMMITTEE OF THE UNITED CHURCH
OF CANADA MADE PUBLICATION OF THIS BOOK POSSIBLE

FOREWORD

This collection of documents illustrating the influence of the Christian Church in the Canadian story will fill an immediate need. I should think that this publication will be one of the more useful achievements in the marking of one hundred years of Confederation, and The United Church of Canada, through its Centennial Committee, is honoured to sponsor the work.

We are reminded in these pages of how influential religious sentiment has been in the founding of the Canadian nation. From the earliest exertions of the explorers, through the labours of the pioneers both east and west, a considerable part in the settlement of this land was inspired and maintained by the Christian faith and by the institutions it created. The records made available within will enable us to remember the actors and the occasions.

A collection of such documents illustrating Canadian church history has been frequently projected but not undertaken. We are grateful to John S. Moir and John Webster Grant for investing their experience and knowledge in the volume now before us. Their choice of selections has been done with such imagination and competence as to make the whole collection attractive to the general reader of Canadian history.

C. M. NICHOLSON

The Centennial Committee

THE UNITED CHURCH OF CANADA

Canada was not founded like New England as an experiment in government by the godly, nor was it colonized to any great extent by religious enthusiasts. Most of our ancestors were attracted here by such tangible assets as fish, furs, gold or wheat, or came here in desperation to escape famine or unemployment or—more rarely—oppression. Their subsequent relations with each other have been determined in large measure by the resources and communications of the country to which they came and by the languages and political loyalties they brought with them. Hence it has been possible to tell the Canadian story without much reference to the presence of the churches, and many writers have done so. The influence of the Christian Church is a hypothesis of which, apparently, the Canadian historian has felt little need.

From earliest times, however, representatives of the church have been staking claims in Canadian soil. Jacques Cartier did so literally in 1534 when he planted a cross at Gaspé on the Gulf of St. Lawrence. Many others have done so less dramatically but more effectively in the years since. Some of the staking has been done by agents of the church consciously engaged in a missionary task, some by administrators whose motives were perhaps more political than religious, and some by settlers who brought their faith with them. The main effort was an integral part of the missionary thrust that took representatives of western Christendom into every corner of the earth. Its eventual result was to make Canadians one of the most church-conscious peoples in the world and to involve them in their turn in witness in many lands.

New France, first developed as an outpost of the fur trade, was soon discovered by the fervent piety that characterized the Roman Catholic Church in the seventeenth century. Enthusiasts prayed for the colony, had visions about its future and discovered vocations that led them to consecrate their lives to it. In the remote wilderness of what is now Ontario, missionaries of the Jesuit order offered their lives and their deaths for the conversion of the vanishing Huron nation. In Quebec City Bishop Laval sought to enforce holy living, while a succession of dedicated women set an example of austerity and strenuous spiritual discipline. Montreal, founded in response to direct revelation, was conscious from the first of its mission as a beleaguered outpost of the faith. This sacred concern lavished on the infant colony did not make French Canadians docile followers of their priests, as many Protestants still suppose, but it gave them an almost apocalyptic sense of destiny that persists in a secularized form even today. No one can understand the separatist movements that have appeared recently in Quebec who has not learned to appreciate the intimate connection between the ethnic self-assurance of today and the awareness of a supernatural mission that was built into the fabric of New France centuries ago.

In the English-speaking colonies the infusion of Christian significance into an enterprise originally economic and strategic lacked this romantic flair but was almost equally thorough. Immigrant pastors like James MacGregor in Nova Scotia and Bishop Alexander Macdonnell in Glengarry worked among their exiled flocks, fanning the embers of old-world piety and giving them new life in the new world. American saddlebag preachers, ignoring political boundaries, carried the techniques of frontier evangelism into Upper Canada and changed a motley assortment of "backsliders" into devout members of Methodist societies and bands. Prophets like Henry Alline, arising as if from nowhere among the settlers themselves, gathered congregations of enthusiasts that grew in respectable denominations. In time, as visitors from abroad have frequently remarked, religious affiliation overtook place of origin and even political allegiance as the primary badge of personal identity and as the chief source of social contacts. Knowing what church a Canadian belonged to furnished until recently the most useful clue to where he stood in his community and where he found his friends. A Canadian belonging to no church was so rare that it was not found necessary to instruct census-takers how to classify him.

This deep penetration of religion into the fabric of Canadian society was the result of a programme that extended far beyond the explicitly religious aspects of life. The churches took to themselves, and to some extent had thrust upon them, the role of confessors and guides to the emerging nation in its formative years. They were the founders of universities, and even institutions that were technically undenominational sought out their ministers as presidents. Religious journals like the *Christian Guardian* composed a significant portion of the reading matter available in Canadian homes, and some of the country's most influential newspapers, such as the Toronto *Globe*, were really unofficial denominational organs. Moral guidance was a recognized function of the churches. Temperance movements were sponsored, first by the Roman Catholic Church in New France, later by Protestant groups, and character-building was the theme of many sermons and prayer-meeting addresses. Theoretically most of the churches avoided direct political action, but politics was always narrowly defined. Prohibition, the observance of the Lord's Day and the suppression of prostitution were widely regarded as such clear moral issues that the churches could not be silent about them, and education was classed as an essentially religious matter. When such questions were at stake ministers did not hesitate to urge the election of particular candidates from the pulpit, and the Methodist leader Egerton Ryerson has been credited with changing the course of an election fought over educational policy. The pattern of life and thought we now call Victorian was in large measure implanted in Canadians by their churches, with an effectiveness that is demonstrated by the violence of the reaction against it in some quarters today.

Those who planted the church in Canada brought with them their inherited doctrinal standards and forms of church government, and controversial pamphlets expounding the advantages of one or another abounded. In a frontier land of great distances, however, the chief emphasis had to be on the extension of the church and the shaping of a Christian character rather than on the exploration of ideas. The widespread involvement of the churches in education saved Canada in its early days from the extreme anti-intellectualism that took root in the "Bible Belt" of the United States, but the tendency was to leave speculative matters to the universities and theological colleges and to get on with jobs that obviously seemed to need doing. Greatly as the churches differed in their inherited doctrines and policies, they all found themselves confronted with the same urgent challenges and met them in remarkably similar ways. The great enemy was the roughness of the frontier, which expressed itself in profanity, rowdiness, carelessness about accepted moral standards and, above all, drunkenness. The remedies were preaching, education and eventually legislation. Religious groups differing widely in class background and in traditions of behaviour naturally responded in varying ways, but a close look shows that each denomination was compelled to find its own way of taming the frontier spirit.

Similar as the churches of nineteenth-century Canada may appear to students of another era, contemporaries were most aware of the differences. The early mission to Canada was consciously conceived as so many separate missions to Canada, intersecting only at points of mutual irritation. It is actually possible to read the journals of some early missionaries without suspecting that any others were at work in the same region, for Canadian life outside the sphere of God's chosen emissaries is described to us in terms of complete spiritual destitution. Denominational conflict seemed to be the primary phenomenon, while the underlying unity of purpose was sensed only by a few leaders in moments of unusual clarity.

The great drawback of religious rivalry, in the eyes even of many Canadians who were loyal members of their own denominations, was that it prevented the emergence of that sense of community required for stable government and even for tolerable co-existence. The disunity of Christians, expressing itself in disruptions within denominations, in contests over church privilege and in the Orangemen's denunciations of papacy, not only contributed a Donnybrook atmosphere to Canadian politics but seriously threatened the influence of the Christian Church. More and more Canadians desired religious peace, and the non-sectarian public school came to be one of the chief symbols of their point of view. The failure of Canadian historians to give more space to the churches may well be the result not of a conspiracy of silence but of a tendency to dismiss them as mere disrupters of the peace.

A similar situation in the United States had led to the acceptance, by church and state alike, of a concept of complete separation. The First Amendment to the American Constitution decreed in 1791 that there should be no national establishment of religion, and this was later extended to the individual states and interpreted as forbidding any form of government aid to projects under church sponsorship. The existence of separate denominations, usually regarded in the old world as a temporary anomaly that would be overcome in the future, came to be accepted in the new world as the normal state of the church. In line with the philosophy of free enterprise, the general public came to think of the churches as competing institutions offering religious consumers a variety of marginally differentiated products. Basic to the whole arrangement was the assumption that the sphere of the churches' concern is limited to the private lives of their members and need not therefore interfere with that of the state.

The extension to Canada of this method of dealing with sectarian differences was hindered by several factors in the situation. One of the most important of these was the position of the Roman Catholic Church in Quebec. With its long tradition of public involvement, its deep roots in popular loyalties and its sheer numerical strength, it could only with the greatest difficulty be regarded merely as one voluntary body among many. Another factor was the determination of the British authorities in early days to prevent a recurrence of the American Revolution in the remaining colonies by transplanting the English system of aristocracy, complete with an established church. The scheme was destined from the beginning to failure, but it left behind a residue of special privileges that would trouble colonial politics for decades and raised among Anglicans expectations of national status that would not quickly be forgotten.

Even the more distinctly Protestant churches were by no means unanimously opposed to some form of state connection. Canadian Methodists and Presbyterians maintained closer ties with Britain than did their American counterparts and were therefore more familiar with the European tradition of church-state alliance. Those who traced their origins to the Scottish Kirk or Free Church or to the English Wesleyans even favoured such an alliance. In the pluralistic society of Canada such pressures could not prevent the virtual separation of church and state, but the churches were never able to conceive of themselves as mere private corporations after the American pattern. While abandoning claims to the privileges of establishment, they remained national in conception.

Movements towards church union in Canada arose in various and sometimes obscure ways, for which there is no single, all-inclusive explanation. The ultimate spur towards union was theological, rooted in the New Testament conception of the presence of the Holy Spirit in the church as a pledge of the final reconciliation of all creation in Christ. Every disruption of the church has struck Christians as scandalous and thereby called forth new attempts to find a satisfactory basis of reunion. Throughout the nineteenth century, especially during its later years, proposals for union were constantly on the agenda of churches in every English-speaking country.

Nevertheless, it is impossible to doubt the close connection between the pioneering role that Canada has taken in the union enterprise and the peculiar problems of Canadian nationhood. The complicated relations of church and state that made it impossible for Canadians to bypass the problems created by sectarianism forced them to attack them frontally, and the alternative to a "you-go-to-your-church-and-I'll-go-to-mine" philosophy seemed to be some form of union. It is surely no mere coincidence that the first serious proposal of union in 1886 came from representatives of the Church of England, which for historical reasons took most seriously its potential role as the religious embodiment of the nation, and that those who ultimately came together in The United Church of Canada expressed the hope that their work would eventually issue in a church that might "fittingly be described as national." Their aim was not an established church after the European pattern but a united fellowship that would fulfil the same role of conscience and guide to the nation that all churches had found themselves playing separately within their limited spheres.

Despite these incentives to union, the churches might in time have worked out a relatively stable pattern of inter-denominational relations if Canada itself had remained static. Instead, a series of crises of expansion prevented each tentative equilibrium from becoming permanent. On at least three occasions it seemed that Canada might have evolved an enduring denominational balance, but each time a new explosive factor quickly made it obsolete. The first of these occasions was about 1820 when the earliest wave of frontier revivalism was dying down, sects were becoming churches and each was beginning to find its constituency as large as it could handle. Then followed forty years of large-scale immigration from the British Isles that radically changed the composition of the population and inspired intense competition for members among British missionary agencies and between them and indigenous churches already occupying the ground. Gradually immigrants and old settlers fused into a new Canadian amalgam. Politically the result was Confederation, ecclesiastically the consolidation of denominational sub-groups into strong self-confident communions. The process can be demonstrated most graphically in the case of the Presbyterians and Methodists, who had each been divided into several segments, but other denominations developed functioning national organizations during the same period.

The applecart was upset again, and radically, by the opening of the West that followed the purchase of the Hudson's Bay Company territories in 1869 and was speeded up by immigration from overseas after the election of the Laurier administration in 1896. The initial response of the churches was again to intensify competition as each rushed to pre-empt desirable sites in towns along the western railways or in the rapidly growing cities of the east. Now, it was the Canadian churches themselves that took the initiative in expansion, although still with considerable help in men and money from Britain. By about the turn of the century Canadians were becoming excited about their new national status and soberly aware of the problems lurking in the new cosmopolitan cities. Soon the inhabitants of the West were stridently conscious of their importance within the Canadian nation and eager to weld their numerous ethnic groups into a single community. From this period dates the movement that led to the union of Methodists, Presbyterians and Congregationalists in 1925 to form The United Church of Canada.

The last-minute strength shown by a predominantly eastern section of the Presbyterian Church in Canada that declined to enter the union may indicate that by 1925 the country was again entering a period of resurgent denominationalism. In any event there were no further gestures towards union during the rest of the 1920s and the depression years of the 1930s, while new radical Protestant groups appeared in the West and in the cities. Another period of expansion was begun by the creation of wartime industries, however, and extended by the long post-war prosperity. The churches, no longer dependent on overseas aid, rushed as was their custom to stake their claims in suburban subdivisions while disclaiming any desire to compete for members. In this situation second thoughts have been more sobering than ever, for the issue is not a mere problem of church extension beyond the resources of individual denominations but the existence of a complex, highly technical society that will not take conflicting sectarian claims seriously.

It is scarcely surprising that proposals for greater unity have been in the air again. The Canadian Council of Churches was formed in 1941 by major Protestant, Anglican and Orthodox groups. Conversations between the United and Anglican churches, begun in 1943, have recently issued in a proposed statement of Principles of Union. Even the traditional Orange curtain separating Protestants from Roman Catholics in Canada has not been impregnable to the new ecumenical spirit, and friendly dialogue is bridging the great linguistic divide at the very time when secular conversations are becoming strained. In these discussions, too, there is a new depth of theological concern, for the problems posed to the church are no longer ones that can be solved by the exercise of a little frontier ingenuity. It is impossible to predict where they will lead, only that the circumstances giving rise to them will not quickly disappear.

In the texture of Canadian church history one can distinguish two constant strands—a warp of expanding witness and service to follow a shifting frontier, a woof of consolidation and union to equip the church for its mission. If this survey has pointed to some elements of continuity in the varied events of this history, it has served its purpose. No historical summary can reproduce the kaleidoscope colours of Canadian church life as reflected in the camaraderie of rural bazaars or in the discarded crutches at Brother André's shrine, nor can it afford glimpses of pioneer missionaries enduring hardship for Christ, of ministers engaged in the undramatic but essential routines of preaching and pastoral work, or of laymen trying to be Christian in a strange land. For this more intimate view of the witness of the church one most naturally turns to accounts of individual episodes from our past. Of such vignettes the text of this book is made.

JOHN WEBSTER GRANT

CONTENTS

THE COMING OF THE CROSS

JACQUES CARTIER PLANTS THE CROSS

Perhaps the first Christian to reach Canada, and for that matter North America, was Leif the Lucky. About A.D. 1000 he was blown off course on his way to Greenland. Legend has it that Leif had been sent to carry the gospel to the Greenland settlers at the order of St. Olaf, King of Norway. In 1006 the Christian Viking, Thorvald Ericksson, died after an encounter with the native "Skraelings" of Vinland and was buried at his own wish on the headland he called "Crossness," or Cross Point.

Probably the next Christians to visit the territory of Canada were unnamed Portuguese fishermen who began to fish in and around Newfoundland about the same time that Columbus was making his epic discovery in the West Indies. But the first certain evidence of the cross in Canada came from Jacques Cartier, the Mariner of St. Malo, who described his first voyage into the Gulf of the St. Lawrence in 1534.

On [Friday] the twenty-fourth of the said month [of July], we had a cross made thirty feet high, which was put together in the presence of a number of the Indians on the point at the entrance to this harbour [Gaspé], under the cross-bar of which we fixed a shield with three *fleurs-de-lys* in relief, and above it a wooden board, engraved in large Gothic characters, where was written, LONG LIVE THE KING OF FRANCE. We erected this cross on the point in their presence and they watched it being put together and set up.

1

And when it had been raised in the air, we all knelt down with our hands joined, worshipping it before them; and made signs to them, looking up and pointing towards heaven, that by means of this we had our redemption, at which they showed many marks of admiration, at the same time turning and looking at the cross.

When we had returned to our ships, the chief, dressed in an old black bear-skin, arrived in a canoe with three of his sons and his brother; but they did not come so close to the ships as they had usually done. And pointing to the cross he [the chief] made us a long harangue, making the sign of the cross with two of his fingers; and then he pointed to the land all around about, as if he wished to say that all this region belonged to him, and that we ought not to have set up this cross without his permission. And when he had finished his harangue, we held up an axe to him, pretending we would barter it for his fur-skin. To this he nodded assent and little by little drew near the side of our vessel, thinking he would have the axe. But one of our men, who was in our dinghy, caught hold of his canoe, and at once two or three more stepped down into it and made the Indians come on board our vessel, at which they were greatly astonished. When they had come on board, they were assured by the captain that no harm would befall them, while at the same time every sign of affection was shown to them; and they were made to eat and to drink and to be of good cheer. And then we explained to them by signs that the cross had been set up to serve as a land-mark and guide-post on coming into the harbour, and that we would soon come back and would bring them iron wares and other goods; and that we wished to take two of his [the chief's] sons away with us and afterwards would bring them back again to that harbour. And we dressed up his two sons in shirts and ribbons and in red caps, and put a little brass chain around the neck of each, at which they were greatly pleased; and they proceeded to hand over their old rags to those who were going back on shore. To each of these three, whom we sent back, we also gave a hatchet and two knives at which they showed great pleasure. When they had returned on shore, they told the others what had happened. About noon on that day six canoes came off to the ships, in each of which were five or six Indians, who had come to say good-bye to the two we had detained, and to bring them some fish. These made signs to us that they would not pull down the cross, delivering at the same time several harangues which we did not understand.

From H. P. Biggar, *The Voyages of Jacques Cartier* (Ottawa: Public Archives of Canada, 1924), pp. 64-67.

MAYSTER WOLFALL

Sir Martin Frobisher pioneered in the search for a northwest passage to China before joining forces with Sir Francis Drake in the Caribbean. Frobisher's three voyages of exploration—in 1576, 1577 and 1578—carried him to the shores of Baffin Island, and it was probably on that island that the first Protestant communion was celebrated during his third voyage.

"Mayster" Wolfall was apparently a clergyman of high repute and one devoted to his calling, for he left the green and pleasant English countryside to join a hazardous expedition to the Arctic when he became chaplain to Frobisher's fleet of fifteen ships. The reunion of the fleet after it had been scattered and damaged by a "greate Storme" was the occasion for Wolfall's service of thanksgiving as described by Frobisher himself.

Heere every man greatly rejoysed of their happie meeting, and welcomed one another after the sea manner, with their great ordinance, and when eache partie hadde reaped up their sundrie fortunes and perils past, they highlye praised God, and altogither uppon their knees gave hym due, humble and harty thanckes, and Mayster Wolfall, a learned man, appoynted by hir Majesties Councell to be theyr minister and preacher, made unto them a godly sermon, exhorting them especially to be thankefull to God for theyr strange and miraculous deliverance in those so dangerous places, and putting them in mynde of the uncertainetie of mans life, willed them to make themselves alwayes ready as resolute men to enjoy and accept thankefully whatsoever adventure his divine Providence should appoynt. This Mayster Wolfall being well seated and setled at home in his owne countrey, with a good and large living, having a good honest woman to wife, and very towardly children, being of good reputation among the best, refused not to take in hand this paynefull voyage, for the only care he had to save souls, and to reform those infidels if it were possible to Christianitie; and also partly for the great desire he hadde that this notable voyage, so well begun, might be brought to perfection, and therefore he was contented to stay there the whole yeare, if occasion had served, being in every necessary action as forward as the resolutest men of all. Wherfor in this behalfe he may rightly be called a true pastor and minister of Gods word, which for the profite of his flocke spared not to venture his owne life.

● ● ●

The thirtith of August [1578] the *Anne Frances* was brought aground, and had viij great leakes mended, whiche she had received by means of the rocks and ise. This daye the masons finished a house whiche Captaine Fenton caused to be made of lyme and stone upon the Countesse of Warwickes Ilande, to the ende we mighte prove against the nexte yeare, whether the snow coulde overwhelm it, the frosts break uppe, or the people dismember the same. And the better to allure those brutish and uncivill people to courtesie, againste other times of our comming, we lefte therein dyvers of our countrie toyes, as bells, and knives, wherein they specially delight, one for the necessarie use, and the other for the great pleasure thereof. Also pictures of men and women in lead, men a horsebacke, lookinglasses, whistles, and pipes. Also in the house was made an oven, and breade left baked therein, for them to see and taste.

We buried the timber of our pretended forte, with manye barrels of meale, pease, griste, and sundrie other good things, which was of the provision of those whych should inhabite, if occasion served. And insteede therof we fraight oure ships full of ore, whiche we holde of farre greater price.

Also here we sowed pease, corne, and other graine, to prove the fruitfulnesse of the soyle against the next yeare.

Mayster Wolfall on Winters Fornace preached a godly sermon, which being ended, he celebrated also a communion upon the lande, at the partaking whereof was the capitaine of the *Anne Frances*, and manye other gentlemen and soldiours, marriners and miners wyth hym. The celebration of divine mistery was yᵉ first signe, seale, and confirmation of Christes name, death and passion ever knowen in all these quarters. The said M. Wolfall made sermons, and celebrated the communion at sundrie other times, in severall and sundrie ships, bicause the whole company could never meet togither at any one place.

From Richard Collinson (ed.), *The Three Voyages of Martin Frobisher in Search of a Passage to Cathaia and India by the North-West, A.D. 1576-78* (London: Hakluyt Society, 1867), Ser. I, Vol. XXXVIII, pp. 252, 272-273.

THE CALL OF THE NEW WORLD

Marc Lescarbot, lawyer, settler and historian of the earliest French settlement in Acadia shared the religious enthusiasm of De Poutrincourt, Acadia's founder. His account of their difficulties in getting religious support for their venture reflected the still widespread image of Canada as a forbidding wilderness holding little attraction for Europeans. Distressed but undaunted by the reluctance of the clergy to undertake the risky voyage to Acadia, Lescarbot tried in vain to reinstate a custom of the early church to provide the sacrament for travellers to a distant land.

And since I am undertaking to write a narrative of events in the manner in which they took place, I will say that it is a shame to our religion that the Protestant ministers of La Rochelle pray to God daily in their meetings for the conversion of these poor savage tribes, and also for our own safety, and that our Church-men do not the like. In truth we asked neither the one nor the other to do so, but in this the zeal of each is manifest. At length, shortly before our

departure, I took thought to ask Monsieur le Curé or the
Vicar of La Rochelle, if one of his colleagues could not be
found who would be willing to come with us; which I hoped
could easily be done, for there were plenty of them about,
and furthermore, as we were in a seaport town, I thought
they would have been glad to sail the billows. But I could
get nothing out of them, and was given as excuse that none
would go on such a voyage, unless impelled by great zeal
and piety, and that I would do well to address myself to
the Jesuit Fathers. This we could not then do, since our
vessel was almost loaded. In this connexion, I remember
having frequently heard M. de Poutrincourt say, that when
he was at Court after his first voyage, a court Jesuit asked
him what hopes could be cherished for the conversion of
the tribes of New France, and whether they were numerous.
To this he replied that one might win one hundred thousand
souls for Jesus Christ, giving a definite number in place of
speaking vaguely. This good father, making light of the
number, thereupon exclaimed with wonder, "Is that all?"
as if such a matter was not worth one man's time.

Seeing that I had made no progress by asking for some one
in orders to administer to us the sacraments, whether during
our journey, or after we had landed, I bethought me of the
ancient custom of the Christians on their journeys, who
took with them the blessed bread of the Eucharist; and this
they did because they did not everywhere find priests to
administer this sacrament to them, since the world was at
that time still full of paganism or of heresy. In so much that
it was well called the Viaticum, the provision for the way,
since when they went on their way, they carried it with
them; and yet I agree that this term is to be understood
spiritually. And considering that we might be brought to
this necessity, since only one priest had remained in the
plantation of New France (and his death was announced to
us on our arrival), I asked if they would not do unto us as
to the ancient Christians, who were not less wise than we.
But I was told that this was done in those days for considerations which no longer exist. I pointed out that

Satyrus, the brother of St. Ambrose, when on a sea-voyage, made use of this spiritual medicine (as we read in the funeral oration pronounced by the said Saint Ambrose), which he carried *in orario*, which I take to mean in a cloth of linen or taffeta; and well for him that he did, for when shipwrecked he escaped on a broken plank of his vessel. But herein I was put off, as in everything else. This gave me cause for wonder, and it seemed to me to show great rigour to put us in worse condition than the early Christians. For the Eucharist is in no way different to-day from what it was then, and if they held it precious, we did not intend in asking for it to pay it less regard.

From W. L. Grant and H. P. Biggar (eds.), Marc Lescarbot, *History of New France* (Toronto: Champlain Society, 1907-1914), Vol. II, pp. 292-294.

CONVERSION IN ACADIA

Lescarbot left us a penetrating account of the first baptisms among the Indians of Acadia in which he pointed out the very practical problem of such conversions—was the Christianity of the newly baptized natives more than skin-deep? Lescarbot advised using free food to attract the Indians' interest in the white man's faith but warned his readers plainly against the danger of creating thereby a group of what the twentieth century would call "rice Christians."

The first care of the said gentleman [de Poutrincourt] was to have the land tilled and made ready to receive the seeds of grain for the following year. When this was done he was unwilling to neglect spiritual things, and what he regarded as the chief end of his journey thither, to bring about the salvation of these poor savage and barbarous tribes. When we were there previously we had sometimes given them good beginnings of the knowledge of God, as may be seen in the account of our voyage and in my Adieu to New France. On the return of the said gentleman he taught them once more what he had formerly told them, doing so by means of his son the Baron de Saint Just, a young nobleman of great hopes, who gives himself up entirely to navigation, whereof in two years he has acquired great experience. After the necessary instructions had been given, on St. John the Baptist's Day, June 24th, 1610, they were baptized to the number of 21, to each of whom was given the name of some great man or notable personage of our country. Thus Membertou was named Henry after the name of the King, who was believed to be still alive. His eldest son was named Louis after the name of our young King who now reigns, whom I pray God to bless. His wife was named Mary after the name of the Queen Regent, and the others in succession . . . .

●　　●　　●

Membertou, the chief sagamos of these parts, driven on by a religious zeal but without knowledge, says that he will declare war on all who refuse to become Christians. This must be taken in good part from him, but could not be received from another, for it is certain that religion will not come by compulsion, and by this method one will never become a good Christian.

●　　●　　●

The best method of attracting the tribes of which we are speaking is to give them bread, to assemble them together, to teach them the Christian doctrine and the arts, which cannot be done all at once. The men of to-day are not wiser than the apostles. But I would not charge their minds with so many things which depend on man's institution, seeing that our Lord has said: "My yoke is easy, and my burden is light." The apostles have left for simple folk the *credo* for belief and the *paternoster* for prayer, first teaching the meaning of both that men may not believe and pray a thing which they do not understand. What is over and above is for the more instructed, who may wish to make themselves capable of instructing others. Let this be said by way of advice and counsel to those who shall form the first colonies, for I do not think that it is less allowable for me to say it by writing than by word of mouth, which I would do if I were there.

The pastor who accomplished this masterpiece of Christian piety is M. Jessé Fleché, a priest of the diocese of Langres, a man of good life and good learning, sent by my lord the Nuncio Robert Ubaldini, though in my opinion the commission of a French bishop would certainly have been at least as good as that of one who is a foreign bishop. He gave him by his letters patent, which I have copied from the original, permission to hear in those parts the confessions of all persons, and to absolve them from all sins and crimes not expressly reserved for the apostolic see, and to enjoin on them penitences according to the character of the sin. Further, he gave him power to consecrate and bless chasubles and other sacerdotal vestments and the fittings of altars, except monstrances, chalices, and censers. This is in brief the power contained in his commission.

●　　●　　●

On the report of what had taken place on the day of St. John the Baptist many savages had come thither that they too might receive holy baptism. To this they were admitted, and many others after them, but perchance too soon and by too ardent a zeal. For although it had indeed been fitting to baptize Membertou and his family, who were resident at Port Royal, there is not the same reason in the case of the others, who dwell far off and have no pastors to hold them to their duty. But what was M. de Poutrincourt to do in that regard: for he was importuned by the savages, who would have felt themselves scorned had he refused. In truth their zeal was such that there was one of them, all skin and bone with no flesh on him, who with great difficulty dragged himself to three cabins searching for the patriarch, as they called the pastor, to be instructed and baptized.

Another living at St. Mary's Bay, more than twelve leagues away, feeling ill, sent hastily to tell the said patriarch that he was ill, and desired to be baptized for fear of dying without becoming a Christian. This was granted him.

Another, formerly called Acouanis but now Loth, also feeling ill, hastily sent his son from more than twenty leagues off to recommend him to the prayers of the Church and say that if he died he wished to be buried with the Christians.

One day when M. de Poutrincourt had gone to the breaking up of a stag killed by Louis the son of Henry Membertou, on his return, as each one was drifting about in the harbour of Port Royal, it befell that the wife of the said Louis brought forth a child, and the savages seeing that the child had but a moment to live, cried out "Tagaria, tagaria"—"Come here, come here." They went, and the child was baptized.

This may be given as one of many proofs in witness of the zeal of this poor people, who are not, I confess it, sufficiently instructed in points of religion, but are more fit to possess the kingdom of heaven than those who know much and do the works of darkness; for they believe and carefully practise what is told them, while in these parts we see in men nought but infidelity. And if one reproaches them for their ignorance, the same reproach must be brought against the greater part of us here, who are Christians only in name. In short, I shall set down here in Latin the saying of St. Augustine: "Surgunt indocti, et rapiunt caelos, nos cum scientia nostra mergimur in infernum"— "The ignorant rise up and take the kingdom of heaven by violence; we with our knowledge are plunged into hell."

I shall add here an instance of the simplicity of a neophyte named Martin of Port La Have, who when ill of the disease whereof he died, on being told of the celestial paradise, asked if he should eat pasties there as good as those which had been given him to eat. In reply he was told that there were better things, and that he would be content there. A few days afterwards he died and was buried with the Christians, though not without debate, the savages wishing to bury him with his fathers . . . as he himself had so desired.

From W. L. Grant and H. P. Biggar (eds.), Marc Lescarbot, *History of New France* (Toronto: Champlain Society, 1907-1914), Vol. III, pp. 37, 40-44.

VOLUNTEERS FOR A HOLY VOYAGE

Samuel de Champlain, the "Father of New France," was a sincere and devout Christian, anxious for the salvation of the natives whom he encountered in Acadia and along the

St. Lawrence. From the time that he established the French post at Quebec in 1608 he had cherished an ambition to interest some religious order in missionary work among the Indians. With the help of a high-ranking court official he finally obtained a promise of help from the Récollets, a branch of the Franciscans.

But first it is fitting to state that having observed on my previous voyages that in some places there were settled tribes with a taste for tillage of the soil, but without faith or law, living without God and without religion like brute beasts, I thereupon concluded in my private judgment that I should be committing a great sin if I did not make it my business to devise some means of bringing them to the knowledge of God. And to attain this end I exerted myself to find some good friars, with zeal and affection for the glory of God, whom I might persuade to send or come themselves with me to this country to try to plant there the faith, or at least to do what was possible in the way of their calling, and while doing this to note and see whether some good fruit could not be gathered there; and, because to attain this object would require an expenditure beyond my means, and for other reasons, I neglected this matter for a time, in view of the difficulties in obtaining what would be requisite and necessary in such a matter, as is customary in such voyages. Moreover no persons offered to contribute to it. Nevertheless, while I was still searching and in communication with many people, a man of honourable character with whom I was on terms of ordinary acquaintance presented himself, named the Sieur Hoüel, the King's Secretary and controller-general of the salt works at Brouage, a man of pious habits, and inspired with a great zeal and love for the honour of God and for the extension of His religion, who gave me some information which was very acceptable to me, to wit, that he knew some good fathers of the Récollet order, of whom he felt assured, having so intimate an acquaintance and such confidence in them, that he could easily induce them to agree to undertake the voyage, and as to the equipment necessary for three or four friars that might be sent out, there would be no lack of worthy people who would give them what they needed, offering for his own part to assist them to the utmost of his power; and in fact he wrote about it to Father Du Verger, who liked the idea and took the matter up very warmly, and following the suggestion of the Sieur Hoüel communicated and spoke with some of his brethren on the subject, who, burning with charity, all offered themselves freely to undertake this holy journey.

From H. P. Biggar (ed.), *Works of Samuel de Champlain* (Toronto: Champlain Society, 1922-1936), Vol. III, pp. 15-18.

THE FIRST MISSIONARIES IN NEW FRANCE

Champlain's appeal to the Récollets bore its first fruit in 1615 when four friars accompanied him to Quebec. The zeal of these missionaries for their chosen work in the new world was soon evident when Le Caron eagerly left the tiny outpost of French settlement to live among the Indians themselves. This act of courage—for the hardships Le Caron would endure were beyond any reasonable call of duty—set the pattern for later missionaries to carry the gospel to the Indians rather than wait for them to come to the missionaries.

Now the Fathers appointed and chosen for this sacred undertaking were Father Denis as commissary, Jean Delbeau, Joseph Le Caron and Pacifique Du Plessis, each of whom was moved by a holy zeal; and they burned to make the voyage, through God's grace, in order to see if they could produce some good fruit and set up in these regions the standard of Jesus Christ, with the determination to live and die for His holy name, should it be necessary, and should the occasion present itself. When everything was ready, they provided themselves with the Church ornaments, and we with the things necessary for the voyage.

I left for Paris on the last day of February to meet our partners at Rouen and make known to them the wishes of my lord the Prince; among others, his desire that these good Fathers should make the voyage, in recognition of the fact that the affairs of the country could with difficulty reach any completeness or advancement if, first of all, services were not paid to God. Our associates were well pleased with this, and promised to assist the said Fathers to the utmost and thenceforward to keep them in provisions.

On the twentieth of March following these Fathers arrived at Rouen, where we remained some time, and thence we went to Honfleur to embark, where we also remained some days, waiting for our vessel to be fitted out and laden with the things necessary for such a long voyage. Meanwhile we made ready our consciences, by each of us examining himself and being cleansed from his sins by repenting and confessing them, in order to receive the sacrament and put himself in a state of grace, so that afterwards, our consciences being relieved, we might expose ourselves in God's keeping to the mercy of the waves of this great and perilous ocean.

This done, we embarked in the vessel of the company, which was of 350 tons' burden, called the *Saint-Etienne*, commanded by the Sieur du Pont-Gravé, and set out from the said Honfleur on the twenty-fourth day of August [April] in the said year. We set sail with a very favourable wind and made the voyage without encountering ice or other dangers, thanks be to God, and in a short time arrived, on the twenty-fifth of May, off the place called Tadoussac, where we returned thanks to God for having guided us so seasonably to this haven of safety.

Afterwards we began to set the men to work to fit up our long-boats in order to go to Quebec, the place of our settlement, and to the great St. Louis rapid, where was the meeting-place of the savages who come there to trade.

When the boats were fitted up we embarked with the aforesaid Fathers, one of whom, called Father Joseph, wanted without stopping or making any stay at Quebec to go straight to the great Rapid, where on his arrival he saw all the savages and their mode of life. This prompted him to go and pass the winter in their country, more particularly in that of the tribes who have a fixed abode, both to learn their language and to see what hopes there were of their being brought to Christianity. Having made this decision he returned to Quebec on the twentieth of June to get a few Church ornaments and other things for his needs. Meanwhile I had remained at Quebec to arrange matters relating to the settlement, both for the quarters of the Fathers and for Church ornaments and for the construction of a chapel in which to celebrate mass, and also to set others to work to clear the land. I embarked to go to the said Rapid* along with Father Denis, who had arrived that same day from Tadoussac with the Sieur du Pont-Gravé.

As to the other friars, to wit, Fathers Jean and Pacifique, they remained at Quebec to fit up their chapel and to put their quarters in order. They were greatly encouraged at seeing the place quite different from what they had imagined, and this increased their zeal.

From H. P. Biggar (ed.), *Works of Samuel de Champlain* (Toronto: Champlain Society, 1922-1936), Vol. III, pp. 22-27.

A BIT OF OLD FRANCE

However far the missionaries might travel into the forests to reach the pagan Indians, there was always in Quebec a refuge and place of rest after their journeys. Gabriel Sagard, a Récollet who reached Canada in 1623, left a full account of his journey into the Huron Indian country around Georgian Bay as well as a description of the tiny monastery at Quebec that was both a headquarters for the Récollets and a touching reminder of their homeland in France.

QUEBEC, THE RESIDENCE OF THE FRENCH AND
OF THE RECOLLET FATHERS

From the island of Orleans we see Quebec full in front of us built on the banks of narrows in the great St. Lawrence river, which at this spot is only about a good quarter-league in breadth, at the foot of a mountain, on the summit of which is the small wooden fort built for the defence of the country and of Quebec or the merchants' house. The latter is at present quite a fine dwelling, surrounded by a wall in

*The Lachine Rapids.

the form of a square, with two small turrets at the angles which have recently been added for the safety of the place.

● ● ●

It is in our little river that the savages catch an immense numbers of eels in the autumn, and the French kill the game-birds which come to it in quantity. The little meadows which border it are bespangled in summer with many small flowers, particularly with what we call cardinals,* and matagon lilies,** bearing a number of blossoms on one stalk, nearly six, seven, or eight feet high; the savages eat the bulb, roasting it in the ashes, and it is quite good. We brought some to France, along with some cardinal plants, as rare flowers, but they did not succeed nor come to perfection as they do in their own climate and native soil.

Our orchard-garden is also very fine, with a good bottom soil, for all our herbs and roots do well, better than in many gardens we have in France. If it were not for the countless number of mosquitoes and midges there, as there are everywhere in Canada during the summer, I do not know that one could find a pleasanter abode; for besides the beauty and fertility of the countryside and the fine air, our dwelling is very convenient for those it shelters, yet it resembles rather the house of one of our rural nobility than a monastery of Friars Minor. We have been forced to build it in that fashion as well because of our poverty as to defend ourselves in any event against the savages, if they should try to turn us out. The building is in the middle of the court-yard, like a keep; the curtain walls and ramparts are of wood, with four little bastions of the same material at the four corners, raised from twelve to fifteen feet above the level of the ground, in which little gardens have been planted and arranged. The gate has a square tower above it built of stone, which serves us as a chapel, and a fine natural moat surrounds the house and adjoining garden and the rest of the enclosure, which covers about six or seven acres, or rather more in my judgment. The raspberry-bushes round about attract so many turtle-doves at the fruit season that it

---

*The scarlet lobelia.
**The tiger-lily.

is delightful to see trees quite filled with them; moreover the Frenchmen of the habitation often come to pick the fruit, as is is the best place and involves least trouble. If our brethren wish to go to Quebec, or people of Quebec to come to us, there is a choice of ways, by land or by water, according to the weather and the season; and this is no small convenience, of which the savages also avail themselves to come and see us and to receive instructions from us concerning the way to Heaven and the knowledge of a God made man, as to whom they have hitherto been in ignorance. It is calculated that this place Quebec is in latitude 46 and a half degrees, nearly two degrees farther south than Paris, and yet the winter is longer and the country colder, partly because of a wind from the north-west which brings frightful cold when it blows, and partly because the country is almost uninhabited and uncultivated, and this through the negligence and lack of interests of the merchants who hitherto have been satisfied to get furs and profit out of it without having been willing to make any outlay for cultivation, settlement, or progress of the country.

• • •

But if they will do nothing more than in the past Antarctic France will always be a name of fancy, and ourselves an imaginary possession in others' hands. Also the conversion of the savages will be always incomplete, for it can only be accomplished through the aid of some settlements of good and virtuous Christians, together with the teaching and example of the good monks.

From G. M. Wrong (ed.), G. Sagard, *Long Journey to the Country of the Hurons* (Toronto: Champlain Society, 1939), pp. 50-53.

THE BROTHERS FROM DIEPPE

A mission field as vast as Canada soon proved itself too much for the Récollets to handle alone and in 1625 they got help from the wealthy and powerful Society of Jesus. With the Jesuits on the scene the great missionary endeavour in

*New France began to grow rapidly, and permanent mission
posts were established. But the work was brought to a
sudden halt by the English capture of Quebec in 1629.*

*Taking advantage of a war between France and England,
some London merchants combined forces under the leadership of Jarvis Kirke, a merchant who had spent much of his
life in Dieppe, in an attempt to take the rich fur trade of
Canada away from Champlain and his French supporters.
An expedition by Kirke's four sons in 1628 failed to oust
Champlain from Quebec but the following year that post
was surrendered to the English because the garrison was
starving. Champlain left us a detailed description of the
English take-over by David Kirke and his brother Louis,
both of them French-born but Anglicans, and of the strained
relations between conquered and conqueror when some of
Champlain's men turned traitor.*

*Ironically the Kirkes had captured Quebec after a peace
treaty had been signed by France and England, but the
profits of the fur trade were so attractive that the brothers
from Dieppe defied the kings of both countries and refused
to hand Quebec back to Champlain until 1632. Champlain
and the French never got compensation for the loss of furs
and damage to property caused by the English occupation,
but David Kirke was knighted and made governor of Newfoundland by England's Merry Monarch, Charles I.*

I asked Louis Kirke to give me soldiers to prevent any
ravaging of our chapel, or of the quarters of the Reverend
Jesuit and Récollet Fathers, or of the house of the widow
Hébert and her son-in-law. This he did, stationing them
also in some other places where they were needed. Then
he landed some 150 armed men, proceeded to take possession of the factory . . . .

●　　　●　　　●

Louis Kirke advanced to the fort to take possession of it.
I wished to vacate my quarters there, but he would not hear
of my doing so until I should be leaving Quebec entirely.
And every kind of courtesy that he could think of he showed
me. I asked him for permission to have a celebration of the

Mass, which he granted to our Fathers. I begged him also to give me a certificate of all that was in the fort and the factory, to which he consented in the most kindly manner.

● ● ●

They took possession also of a number of things belonging to the Reverend Jesuit and Récollet Fathers, of which they declined to give any list, saying, "If they have to be given back (which I do not believe), nothing will be lost; and it is not worth while putting them down on paper, or making any enquiry about them. As to the provisions that we are finding, no ink or paper will be wasted over them; but we are not sorry for that; for we prefer to assist you with ours." —"We thank you very much," I said; "the only drawback is that you make us pay very dearly for them without our being able to dispute your account."

On the following day he had the English flag hoisted on one of the bastions, ordered the drums to beat to assemble the soldiers, whom he placed in order on the ramparts; he then had a salute fired from the ships as well as with the five brass guns at the fort, the two small falconets at the factory, and some iron mortar-pieces; after which he made all his soldiers fire volleys of musketry—the whole in sign of rejoicing.

The next day he went to the house of the Jesuit Fathers, who showed him some books, pictures, and church ornaments, and offered to give him some of these books and pictures, if he cared for them. He took what he wanted of those that seemed the finest, as also three or four pictures. The English minister also got some books which he asked the Fathers to give him; and then, having seen the house and all their cultivated land, which was very fine, he went to see the Récollet Fathers, and thence returned to the settlement.

On the night following, Le Baillif took from the under-clerk, Corneille, a hundred livres in gold and silver, with a silver cup, some silk stockings, and other small articles that were in his chest. He was also suspected of having taken from the Chapel a gilded silver chalice worth over a hundred livres, concerning which complaint was made to Louis Kirke, who made some search in connection with the matter; but nobody would acknowledge having committed this act of sacrilege, detestable before God and in the sight of men. This Le Baillif, accustomed as he was to deny and blaspheme the name of God at every turn, swore hard enough to clear himself; but he is without either faith or morals, though he calls himself a Catholic, as do the three others, who have no objection to eating meat on either Friday or Saturday—thinking thus to curry favour with the English, who, on the contrary, blamed them for it. And they did many other licentious and culpable things. I pointed out clearly to him the blame and reproach which would some day befall him, but of this he took little heed, as he did not expect ever to return to France. All the evil turns that he could do to the French he did. We had every kind of courtesy from the English; but from this wretch, only injury. I will leave him for what he is worth, awaiting the time when God will punish him for his oaths, blasphemies, and impieties.

From H. P. Biggar (ed.), *Works of Samuel de Champlain* (Toronto: Champlain Society, 1922-1936), Vol. VI, pp. 62, 64, 66-69.

THE QUALIFICATIONS OF A MISSIONARY

Jean de Brébeuf, a towering six feet, four inches in his moccasins, had just returned from Huronia to Quebec in 1629 when the Kirke brothers arrived. Of all the missionaries Brébeuf was the best acquainted with the hardships of the long voyage to the Huron country and with the sacrifices demanded by the crude surroundings of the mission itself. The following instructions, written by Brébeuf in 1637, could at best be only a partial warning to new missionaries of the privations they must suffer.

INSTRUCTIONS FOR THE FATHERS OF OUR SOCIETY WHO SHALL BE SENT TO THE HURONS
By Father Jean de Brébeuf

You must have sincere affection for the Savages,—looking upon them as ransomed by the blood of the son of God, and as our Brethren with whom we are to pass the rest of our lives.

To conciliate the Savages, you must be careful never to make them wait for you in embarking.

You must provide yourself with a tinder box or with a burning mirror, or with both, to furnish them fire in the daytime to light their pipes, and in the evening when they have to encamp; these little services win their hearts.

You should try to eat their sagamité or salmagundi in the way they prepare it, although it may be dirty, half-cooked, and very tasteless. As to the other numerous things which may be unpleasant, they must be endured for the love of God, without saying anything or appearing to notice them.

It is well at first to take everything they offer, although you may not be able to eat it all; for, when one becomes somewhat accustomed to it, there is not too much.

You must try and eat at daybreak unless you can take your meal with you in the canoe; for the day is very long, if you have to pass it without eating. The Barbarians eat only at Sunrise and Sunset, when they are on their journeys.

You must be prompt in embarking and disembarking; and tuck up your gowns so that they will not get wet, and so that you will not carry either water or sand into the canoe. To be properly dressed, you must have your feet and legs bare; while crossing the rapids, you can wear your shoes, and, in the long portages, even your leggings.

You must so conduct yourself as not to be at all troublesome to even one of these Barbarians.

It is not well to ask many questions, nor should you yield to your desire to learn the language and to make observations on the way; this may be carried too far. You must relieve those in your canoe of this annoyance, especially as you cannot profit much by it during the work. Silence is a good equipment at such a time.

You must bear with their imperfections without saying a word, yes, even without seeming to notice them. Even if it be necessary to criticize anything, it must be done modestly, and with words and signs which evince love and not aversion. In short, you must try to be, and to appear, always cheerful.

Each one should be provided with half a gross of awls, two or three dozen little knives called jambettes (pocket-knives), a hundred fish-hooks, with some beads of plain and coloured glass, with which to buy fish or other articles when the tribes meet each other, so as to feast the Savages; and it would be well to say to them in the beginning, "Here is something with which to buy fish." Each one will try, at the portages, to carry some little thing, according to his strength; however little one carries, it greatly pleases the savages, if it be only a kettle.

●　　●　　●

Be careful not to annoy anyone in the canoe with your hat; it would be better to take your nightcap. There is no impropriety among the Savages.

Do not undertake anything unless you desire to continue it; for example, do not begin to paddle unless you are inclined to continue paddling. Take from the start the place in the canoe that you wish to keep; do not lend them your garments, unless you are willing to surrender them during the whole journey. It is easier to refuse at first than to ask them back, to change, or to desist afterwards.

Finally, understand that the Savages will retain the same opinion of you in their own country that they will have formed on the way; and one who has passed for an irritable and troublesome person will have considerable difficulty afterwards in removing this opinion. You have to do not only with those of your own canoe, but also (if it must be so stated) with all those of the country; you meet some today and others tomorrow, who do not fail to inquire, from those who brought you, what sort of man you are. It is almost incredible, how they observe and remember even the slightest fault. When you meet Savages on the way, as you cannot yet greet them with kind words, at least show them a cheerful face, and thus prove that you endure gayly the fatigues of the voyage. You will thus have put to good use the hardships on the way, and have already advanced considerably in gaining the affection of the Savages.

This is a lesson which is easy enough to learn, but very difficult to put into practice; for, leaving a highly civilized community, you fall into the hands of barbarous people who care but little for your Philosophy or your Theology. All the fine qualities which might make you loved and respected in France are like pearls trampled under the feet of swine, or rather mules, which utterly despise you when they see that you are not as good pack animals as they are. If you could go naked, and carry the load of a horse upon your back, as they do, then you would be wise according to their doctrine, and would be recognized as a great man, otherwise not. Jesus Christ is our true greatness; it is He alone and His cross that should be sought in running after these people, for, if you strive for anything else, you will find naught but bodily and spiritual affliction. But having found Jesus Christ in His cross, you have found the roses in the thorns, sweetness in bitterness, all in nothing.

From R. G. Thwaites (ed.), *The Jesuit Relations and Allied Documents* (Cleveland: Burrows, 1896-1901), Vol. XII, pp. 117-123.

THE TWO ENEMIES

Of the many remarkable women who came to New France in the early days to work for the Christian faith, probably the most famous and interesting was Mère Marie de l'Incarnation. Born at Tours in 1599 of a merchant family, Marie Guyart was at the age of nineteen a widow with an infant son. Eleven years later her son was placed in a Jesuit school and Marie was finally free to fulfil the goal of her mystical nature—to seek solitude and spiritual exercise as a nun. In 1631 she entered an Ursuline convent and took the name Marie de l'Incarnation. At the nunnery she was deeply moved by the Jesuits' call for volunteers to build a Christian colony in New France. Another woman who felt the same call was Mme de La Peltrie, a pious but haughty person, also widowed at an early age. In order to finance a school and orphanage at Quebec, Mme de La Peltrie went through the forms of a second marriage so that she could claim her dowry.

With Mme de La Peltrie and two other Ursulines Marie de l'Incarnation arrived at Quebec in 1639 and began the teaching of Indian girls. School attendance was small but the Ursulines found themselves feeding hordes of Indian visitors and acting as an overflow hospital during a small-pox epidemic. For a while Mme de La Peltrie transferred her interests and her fortune to the mission work at Montreal. Throughout her life Marie de l'Incarnation corresponded with her son in France, and her letters were a revealing account of life in the young colony and of

*Marie's religious mysticism. The following excerpt from
a modern biography of Marie de l'Incarnation depicts some
of the difficulties that the Ursulines, "the most adventurous
of nuns", faced in their early years in New France.*

Cold and dirt were the two antagonists encountered by the
nuns; the cold being provided by Nature, and the dirt being
apparently inseparable from little Indian girls. "They have
lived like young animals in the woods," avowed Mère
Marie, "and they care no more for cleanliness than if they
were four-footed. Their filthy habits give us many a rude
shock." In this regard, however, the nuns were a thousand
times better off than were the missionaries. They could
stay, and they did stay, in their own convent, with soap and
water at their command. The priests were compelled to
visit the Indian lodges, where they were stifled by the smoke,
nauseated by the stench, overrun by naked children and
mangy dogs, tormented by fleas, and devoured by lice. As
it would have been a deadly affront to have appeared in-
commoded by these things, or to have shortened a visit
because of them, their social duties were a daily martyrdom.
The worst that could happen to the nuns was a fresh inroad
of never-to-be-discouraged vermin, a fresh scrubbing where
all had been thought clean, or the finding of an old mocca-
sin in the soup pot. This last mishap suggests a very unusual
sense of humour on the part of a misguided Indian child.

As for the cold, it seems to have amazed Mère Marie
more than it distressed her. A lifetime spent in the heart of
France had done little to prepare her for such an experience. If she and her sisterhood could have gone outdoors
and braved the buffeting wind, they might have warmed
their frozen blood, and rejoiced in defying the elements.
But caged in their little house, they could do nothing but
hug the fire. "Do not suppose," wrote their superior to the
convent in Tours, "that we could live long without returning again and again to the fire place. Even I, who have
never wanted to warm myself, am now reluctant to leave
it." To pray in the freezing chapel was impossible. The
rosary was recited and the office read in the community
room, which was a community room only when it was not

needed for a dozen other purposes. Private devotions were deferred until the tired and sleepy nuns were in bed. Mère Marie considered with Saint Theresa that acute physical discomfort was incompatible with absorption in prayer.

From Agnes Repplier, *Mère Marie of the Ursulines* (New York: Doubleday & Company, 1931), pp. 82-83.

THE CITY OF MARY

The Jesuit Relation of 1635 described the island of Montreal in glowing terms as a strategic site for an Indian mission. While reading this Relation Jérôme de La Dauversière, a pious tax collector of La Flèche, received a divine command to found an order of nursing nuns to operate a mission hospital at Montreal. In Paris at the same time a heavenly voice ordered Father Jean-Jacques Olier to organize a body of priests to serve there.

The two men met providentially, and their mystical zeal resulted in the formation of the priestly community of Saint-Sulpice and the Society of Our Lady of Montreal. Just six years later Paul de Chomedey de Maisonneuve, an experienced and intensely religious soldier, led the first party of settlers of the Society of Montreal ashore on the island to found Ville-Marie, the city dedicated to Mary.

On the seventeenth of May, 1642, Maisonneuve's little flotilla—a pinnace, a flat-bottomed craft moved by sails, and two row-boats—approached Montreal; and all on board raised in unison a hymn of praise. Montmagny was with them, to deliver the island, in behalf of the Company of the Hundred Associates, to Maisonneuve, representative of the Associates of Montreal. And here, too, was Father Vimont, Superior of the missions; for the Jesuits had been prudently invited to accept the spiritual charge of the young colony. On the following day, they glided along the green and solitary shores now thronged with the life of a busy city, and landed on the spot which Champlain, thirty-one years before, had chosen as the fit site of a settlement. It was a tongue or triangle of land, formed by the junction of a rivulet with the St. Lawrence, and known afterwards as Point Callière. The rivulet was bordered by a meadow, and beyond rose the forest with its vanguard of scattered trees. Early spring flowers were blooming in the young grass, and birds of varied plummage flitted among the boughs.

Maisonneuve sprang ashore, and fell on his knees. His followers imitated his example; and all joined their voices in enthusiastic songs of thanksgiving. Tents, baggage, arms, and stores were landed. An altar was raised on a pleasant spot near at hand; and Mademoiselle Mance, with Madame de la Peltrie, aided by her servant, Charlotte Barré, decorated it with a taste which was the admiration of the beholders. Now all the company gathered before the shrine. Here stood Vimont, in the rich vestments of his office. Here were the two ladies, with their servant; Montmagny, no very willing spectator; and Maisonneuve, a warlike figure, erect and tall, his men clustering around him,—soldiers, sailors, artisans, and laborers,—all alike soldiers at need. They kneeled in reverent silence as the Host was raised aloft; and when the rite was over, the priest turned and addressed them:—

"You are a grain of mustard-seed, that shall rise and grow till its branches overshadow the earth. You are few, but your work is the work of God. His smile is on you, and your children shall fill the land."

The afternoon waned; the sun sank behind the western forest, and twilight came on. Fireflies were twinkling over the darkened meadow. They caught them, tied them with threads into shining festoons, and hung them before the altar, where the Host remained exposed. Then they pitched their tents, lighted their bivouac fires, stationed their guards, and lay down to rest. Such was the birth-night of Montreal.

Is this true history, or a romance of Christian chivalry? It is both.

From F. Parkman, *The Jesuits in North America* (Boston: Little, Brown, 1922), pp. 301-303.

A GIRL OF CHARACTER

The same fervent piety that inspired La Dauversière, Olier and Maisonneuve in the founding of Montreal also led a remarkable young woman, Jeanne Mance, to offer herself for His service. In that far-distant outpost of Christianity Jeanne Mance established the Hôtel-Dieu hospital and was the first secular nurse in North America. Her devotion and self-sacrifice at Ville-Marie from its beginnings in 1642 to her death in 1673 is commemorated today by several Canadian hospitals named in her honour.

Father Francis Dollier de Casson arrived in 1666 to join the other Sulpicians and wrote the first history of the City of Mary, recording its early connection with Jeanne Mance whom he knew personally.

They had need of one thing they could not find and which their purses could not buy them, a girl or a woman of character sufficiently heroic and of determination sufficiently masculine to come to this country and take charge of all the supplies and merchandise while at the same time acting as nurse to the sick and wounded. Yet whilst money could not buy this, Providence which had helped them thus far, and which since 1640 encouraged them strongly in this work, had, unknown to them, taken care to provide the person they needed, bringing her at the proper time from the heart of Champagne to the place of embarkation, just when they realized the great need they had of such a person and the impossibility of finding her. This was no small matter, and too well deserves a place in this history for me not to recount it at length.

We must begin with the first stirrings of the call experienced by this good girl in Langres, about mid-April 1640, through a canon of that place, who in talking enthusiastically of New France gave most fervent praise to Our Lord in that it was His will to be served there now by both sexes. He added that a short time since a lady of quality, Mme. de la Peltrie, had introduced the Ursulines there, that Mme. d'Aiguillon had established the Hospital Nuns and that, in short, to all appearance God willed there to be specially honoured. These words provoked the first impulse that Mlle. Mance felt on behalf of this country (this is the name of the girl that the Lord of the Universe had chosen to come and work in this new vineyard). As she heard these words her heart surrendered itself to the deepest and strongest operations of grace, which took entire possession of her heart, bearing it, despite herself, across to Canada in wish and hope. Astounded to find herself in such a state she began to consider the weakness of her health and her former illnesses, trying to provide herself with reasons for exemption from these divine impulsions. But the more she drew back, the more she was disturbed at the thought of being false to these heavenly signs. Her native land became a prison to her, her heart was full of doubts, and though she tried to get rid of them by revealing them to her director, they still remained so numerous and so deep-seated that after much labour he abandoned all hope of getting the better of them. He therefore, after calling upon the Holy Spirit, advised her to go to Paris the Wednesday after Pentecost, and there to apply to Father Charles Lalemant who had the care of Canadian affairs, taking as spiritual guide the head of the Jesuit establishment nearest to the place where she lodged.

With this advice she came to Paris to carry out the divine will, making the pretence at home that she wished merely to visit her relations: she did indeed stay with them near to the Jesuit novices' quarters. Without loss of time she found her way to Father Charles Lalemant, who at her second visit gave her great encouragement, related to her the wondrous purposes of God for New France, and told her that he was about to go to Lyons on a matter of the utmost importance for that country. It was indeed for the negotiation of Montreal of which we have spoken, though he did not tell her so, as there was no need to do so at that time.

From R. Flenley (ed.), Dollier de Casson, *History of Montreal* (Toronto: J. M. Dent, 1928), pp. 75-77.

THE CAPTAIN OF THE DAY

As the first missionary to return to Huronia after the departure of the Kirkes from Quebec, Brébeuf discovered that the Indians had moved from the old village site where his mission had stood. He has given us a glimpse of everyday life in the new mission, built near Penetanguishene but later deserted in favour of fortified Sainte-Marie which the Jesuits established just east of Midland, Ontario.

Having, therefore, determined to stay where we are, the question of building a cabin arose. The cabins of this country are neither Louvres nor Palaces, nor anything like the buildings of our France, not even like the smallest cottages. They are, however, somewhat better and more commodious than the hovels of the Montagnais. I cannot better express the fashion of the Huron dwellings than to compare them to bowers or garden arbors,—some of which, in place of branches and vegetation, are covered with cedar bark, some others with large pieces of ash, elm, fir, or spruce bark; and, although the cedar bark is best, according to common opinion and usage, there is, nevertheless, this inconvenience, that they are almost as susceptible to fire as matches. Hence arise many of the conflagrations of entire villages. There are cabins or arbors of various sizes, some two brasses* in length, others of twenty, of thirty, of forty; the usual width is about four brasses, their height is about the same. There are no different stories; there is no cellar, no chamber, no garret. It has neither window nor chimney, only a miserable hole in the top of the cabin, left to permit the smoke to escape. This is the way they built ours for us.

The people of Oënrio and of our village were employed at this by means of presents given them. It has cost us much exertion to secure its completion, we were almost into October before we were under cover. As to the interior, we have suited ourselves; so that, even if it does not amount to much, the Savages never weary of coming to see it, and seeing it, to admire it. We have divided it into three parts. The first compartment, nearest the door, serves as an antechamber, as a storm door, and as a storeroom for our provisions, in the fashion of the Savages. The second is that in which we live, and is our kitchen, our carpenter shop, our mill, or place for grinding wheat, our Refectory, our parlor and our bedroom. On both sides, in the fashion of the Hurons, are two benches which they call *Endicha*, on which are boxes to hold our clothes and other little conveniences; but below, in the place where the Hurons keep their wood, we have contrived some little bunks to sleep in, and to store

---

Brasse: a linear measure, of five old-French feet, or 1.82 metres, equivalent to 5.318 English feet.

away some of our clothing from the thieving hands of the Hurons. They sleep beside the fire, but still they and we have only the earth for bedstead; for mattress and pillows, some bark or boughs covered with a rush mat; for sheets and coverings, our clothes and some skins do duty.

The third part of our cabin is also divided into two parts by means of a bit of carpentry which gives it a fairly good appearance, and which is admired here for its novelty. In the one is our little Chapel, in which we celebrate every day holy Mass, and we retire there daily to pray to God. It is true that the almost continual noise they make usually hinders us, and compels us to go outside to say our prayers. In the other part we put our utensils. The whole cabin is only six brasses long, and about three and a half wide. That is how we are lodged, doubtless not so well that we may not have in this abode a good share of rain, snow and cold. However, they never cease coming to visit us from admiration, especially since we have put on two doors, made by a carpenter, and since our mill and our clock have been set to work. It would be impossible to describe the astonishment of these good people, and how much they admire the intelligence of the French.

●　　●　　●

No one has come who has not wished to turn the mill; nevertheless we have not used it much, inasmuch as we have learned that our Sagamités* are better pounded in a wooden mortar, in the fashion of the Savages, than ground within the mill. I believe it is because the mill makes the flour too fine. As to the clock, a thousand things are said of it. They all think it is some living thing, for they cannot imagine how it sounds of itself; and when it is going to strike, they look to see if we are all there, and if some one has not hidden, in order to shake it.

They think it hears, especially when, for a joke, one of our Frenchmen calls out at the last stroke of the hammer,

---

*Sagamité: a word derived by Maurault from sôgmôipi, "the repast of chiefs." The most common form in which Indians prepared maize as food; termed "samp" or "hominy" by the English. The corn, usually pounded into meal, was boiled in water, with the addition of meat, fish, or oil, when they had such, to enrich and flavor it.

"That's enough," and then it immediately becomes silent. They call it the Captain of the day. When it strikes they say it is speaking; and they ask when they come to see us how many times the Captain has already spoken. They ask us about its food; they remain a whole hour, and sometimes several, in order to be able to hear it speak. They used to ask at first what it said. We told them two things that they have remembered very well; one, that when it sounded four o'clock of the afternoon, during winter, it was saying, "Go out, go away that we may close the door," for immediately they arose, and went out. The other, that at midday it said, *yo eiouahaoua*, that is, "Come, put on the kettle"; and this speech is better remembered than the other, for some of these spongers never fail to come at that hour, to get a share of our Sagamité. They eat at all hours, when they have the wherewithal, but usually they have only two meals a day, in the morning and in the evening; consequently they are very glad during the day to take a share with us.

From R. G. Thwaites (ed.), *The Jesuit Relations and Allied Documents* (Cleveland: Burrows, 1896-1901), Vol. VIII, pp. 105-113.

DEATH AT THE STAKE

Caught in the mortal struggle between Hurons and Iroquois for control of the rich fur trade, the Jesuits and their missions were doomed to go down with the weaker Huron nation to whom they were so closely connected. Despite the obvious warning signs that the end of Huronia was fast approaching, the devoted missionaries stuck doggedly to their posts until the Iroquois tide rolled over them in 1648. In less than two years the bloody onslaught scattered the Hurons like chaff and destroyed the missions completely.

Of the seven Jesuits who won martyrs' crowns at the merciless hands of the Iroquois, two—Gabriel Lalemant, nephew of the Superior of the Missions, and Jean de Brébeuf, the beloved giant—were captured and tortured to death at Saint-Ignace, near Coldwater, Ontario.

Christophe Regnaut, a donné *or lay servant at Sainte-Marie, reported the details of their terrible end as he heard them from Christian Hurons, details which he verified the morning after the martyrdom by a personal examination of the mangled bodies.*

"The Iroquois came, to the number of twelve hundred men; took our village, and seized Father de Bréboeuf and his companion; and set fire to all the huts. They proceeded to vent their rage on those two Fathers, for they took them both and stripped them entirely naked, and fastened each to a post. They tied both of their hands together. They tore the nails from the fingers. They beat them with a shower of blows from cudgels, on the shoulders, the loins, the belly, the legs and the face—there being no part of their body which did not endure this torment." The savages told us further, that, although Father de Bréboeuf was overwhelmed under the weight of these blows, he did not cease continually to speak to God, and to encourage all the new Christians who were captives like himself to suffer well, that they might die well, in order to go in company with him to Paradise. While the good Father was thus encouraging these good people, a wretched Huron renegade,—who had remained a captive with the Iroquois, and whom Father de Bréboeuf had formerly instructed and baptized,—hearing him speak of Paradise and Holy Baptism, was irritated, and said to him, "Echon," that is Father de Bréboeuf's name in Huron, "thou sayest that Baptism and the sufferings of this life lead straight to Paradise; thou wilt go soon, for I am going to baptize thee, and to make thee suffer well, in order to go the sooner to thy Paradise." The barbarian, having said that, took a kettle full of boiling water, which he poured over his body three different times, in derision of Holy baptism. And, each time that he baptized him in this manner, the barbarian said to him, with bitter sarcasm, "Go to Heaven, for thou art well baptized." After that, they made him suffer several other torments. The first was to make hatchets red-hot, and to apply them to the loins and under the armpits. They made a collar of these red-hot hatchets, and put it on the neck of this good Father. This is the fashion in which I have seen the collar made for other prisoners: They make six hatchets red-hot, take a large withe of green wood, pass the 6 hatchets over the large end of the withe, take the two ends together and then put it over the neck of the sufferer. I have seen no torment which more moved me to compassion than that. For you see a man, bound naked to a post, who, having this collar on his neck, cannot tell what posture to take. For, if he lean forward, those above his shoulders weigh the more on him; if he lean back, those on his stomach make him suffer the same torment; if he keep erect, without leaning to one side or the other, the burning hatchets, applied equally on both sides, give him a double torture.

After that they put on him a belt of bark, full of pitch and resin, and set fire to it, which roasted his whole body. During all these torments, Father de Bréboeuf endured like a rock, insensible to fire and flames, which astonished all the blood-thirsty wretches who tormented him. His zeal was so great that he preached continually to these infidels, to try to convert them. His executioners were enraged against him for constantly speaking to them of God and of their conversions. To prevent him from speaking more, they cut off his tongue, and both his upper and lower lips. After that, they set themselves to strip the flesh from his legs, thighs and arms, to the very bone; and then put it to roast before his eyes, in order to eat it.

While they tormented him in this manner, those wretches derided him, saying, "Thou seest plainly that we treat thee as a friend, since we shall be the cause of thy Eternal happiness; thank us, then, for these good offices which we render thee,—for, the more thou shalt suffer, the more will thy God reward thee."

Those butchers, seeing that the good Father began to grow weak, made him sit down on the ground; and one of them, taking a knife, cut off the skin covering his skull. Another one of those barbarians, seeing that the good Father would soon die, made an opening in the upper part of his chest, and tore out his heart, which he roasted and ate. Others came to drink his blood, still warm, which they drank with both hands,—saying that Father de Bréboeuf had been very courageous to endure so much pain as they had given him, and that, by drinking his blood, they would become courageous like him.

● ● ●

Father de Bréboeuf was captured on the 16th day of March, in the morning, with Father Lalemant, in the year 1649. Father de Bréboeuf died the same day as his capture, about 4 o'clock in the afternoon. Those barbarians threw the remains of his body into the fire; but the fat which still remained on his body extinguished the fire, and he was not consumed.

From R. G. Thwaites (ed.), *The Jesuit Relations and Allied Documents* (Cleveland: Burrows, 1896-1901), Vol. XXXIV, pp. 27-31, 33.

JESOUS AHATONHIA

The deaths of Brébeuf and Lalemant gave to the Catholic Church and to all Canadians an inspiring legacy of fortitude and sacrifice. But Brébeuf also left something more concrete to future generations—the first carol written in Canada, and probably the first written in the New World.

The words of "Jesous Ahatonhia", now called simply the "Huron Carol", were composed by Brébeuf probably about 1641 or 1642, and were sung by the Christian Hurons each Christmas until the Iroquois invasion of 1649. Some Hurons escaped to Lorette near Quebec City and carried Brébeuf's carol with them.

The tune was taken from a fifteenth-century carol, "A Young Maiden." About 1750 another Jesuit missionary translated Brébeuf's Huron verses into French, and in 1926 the Canadian poet J. E. Middleton wrote the English words, which are not a literal translation but an interpretation of the carol's message.

> 'Twas in the moon of winter time
>   When all the birds had fled,
> That mighty Gitchi Manitou
>   Sent angel choirs instead;
> Before their light the stars grew dim
> And wond'ring hunters heard the hymn:
>   "Jesus your King is born,
>   Jesus is born: In excelsis gloria!"

Within a lodge of broken bark
    The tender Babe was found
A ragged robe of rabbit skin
    Enwrapped His beauty 'round;
And as the hunter braves drew nigh
The angel song rang loud and high:
    "Jesus your King is born,
    Jesus is born: In excelsis gloria!"

The earliest moon of winter time
    Is not so round and fair
As was the ring of glory on
    The helpless Infant there.
The chiefs from far before Him knelt
With gifts of fox and beaver pelt.
    "Jesus your King is born,
    Jesus is born: In excelsis gloria!"

O children of the forest free,
    O sons of Manitou,
The Holy Child of earth and heaven
    Is born today for you.
Come kneel before the radiant Boy
Who brings you beauty, peace, and joy.
    "Jesus your King is born,
    Jesus is born: In excelsis gloria!"

Chrétiens, prenez courage,
    Jésus Sauveur est né!
Du malin les ouvrages
    A jamais sont ruinés
Quand il chante merveille,
    A ces troublants appas
Ne prêtez plus l'oreille:
    "Jésus est né: In excelsis gloria!"

Oyez cette nouvelle,
    Dont un ange est porteur!
Oyez! âmes fidèles,
    Et dilatez vos coeurs.

La Vierge dans l'étable
Entoure de ses bras
L'Enfant-Dieu adorable.
"Jésus est né: In excelsis gloria!"

Voici que trois Rois Mages
Perdus en Orient,
Déchiffrent ce message
Ecrit au firmament:
L'astre nouveau les hante.
Ils la suivront là-bas,
Cette étoile marchante:
"Jésus est né: In excelsis gloria!"

Jésus leur met en tête
Que l'Etoile en la nuit
Qui jamais ne s'arrête
Les conduira vers Lui.
Dans la nuit radieuse
En route ils sont déjà,
Ils vont l'âme joyeuse.
"Jésus est né: In excelsis gloria!"

Pour l'Enfant qui repose
Dans un petit berceau
Humblement ils déposent
Hommages et cadeaux.
Comme eux, l'âme ravie,
Chrétiens, suivons ses pas,
Son amour nous convie,
"Jésus est né: In excelsis gloria!"

FIRST STANZA IN HURON

Estennialon de tsonoue
Jesous ahatonhia
Onnaouateoua d'oki
N'onouandaskouaentak
Ennonchien skouatrihotat
N'onouandilonrachatha
Jesous ahatonhia.

From Edith Fowke and Richard Johnston, *Folk Songs of Canada* (Waterloo: Waterloo Music Company, 1954), pp. 130-132, *The Huron Carol*, J. Middleton (trans.), used by permission of the Frederick Harris Music Co. Ltd., Oakville.

THE CHURCH IN THE ROYAL
COLONY

A VISIT TO NEW ENGLAND

*Rivals for empire in the New World, the English and French
seldom met except as enemies on the field of battle. A
remarkable exception to this state of perpetual war was the
visit of Father Gabriel Dreuillettes to New England in
1650 as the ambassador of the Abenaki Indians in Acadia.*

*The Jesuit missionary proposed a union of the French
and the Puritans of eastern New England against the men-
ace of the aggressive Iroquois. Though no lasting agreement was reached, Dreuillettes reported his kind reception
by John Winslow, leader of the Plymouth colony, and for a
brief moment in history Puritan and Jesuit expressed their
common interest as Christians in furthering Christ's kingdom in the new world.*

The Agent, named John Winslau, a merchant and a citizen
of the Plimouth colony, who has a very kindly disposition,
as we shall relate hereinafter, answered: "I love and respect
the patriarch," this is the name they use on this river, and
on all the coast of Acadia, in speaking of me; "I will lodge
him at my house, and will treat him as my own brother; for
I know very well the good that he does among you, and the
life which he there leads." This he said because he has a
special zeal for the Conversion of the Savages, as also has
his brother Edward Winslow,—agent for this New England
before the parliament of old England,—who is trying to
institute a brotherhood to train and instruct the Savages,
just as is practiced with the poor by the charity of London.

● ● ●

37

Contrary winds prevented us from reaching Kepane, which forms the Cape of the great bay of Boston, until the fifth of December; for the same reason, we were compelled to go partly by land and partly by boat, in order to cross over the great bay to Charleston; we there crossed the river which separates it from Boston, where we arrived on the eighth. The principal men of Charleston, knowing that I came on behalf of the Sieur governor, went ahead to give notice to Major-General Gebin, so that he might be present at my entrance into his abode.

His agent, John Winslow,—whom I shall henceforth call my pereira, on account of the friendliness which he ever showed me,—having made his report to Sieur Gebin regarding the occasion of my journey, he received me as a veritable ambassador on the part of the Sieur governor. He also gave me a key to an apartment in his house, where I could with complete liberty offer my prayer, and perform my religious exercises; and begged me to take no other lodgings while I should sojourn at Boston.

The next day, the eighth, Sieur Gebin, accompanied by [blank space], conducted me [blank space] from boston to a village named Rogsbray, where at that time was Sieur Dudley, Governor of Boston, to whom I presented my credentials on the part of the Sieur governor,—which, having opened, he commanded an interpreter to translate from french into english.

He was told that this man came to speak on behalf of Nouel and the Christians of Scillery, as also of the Abnaquiois Catechumens, who had made me their ambassador to him. He then appointed a day to hear me,—on the following Tuesday, the thirteenth of December,—giving orders that the magistrates should be notified to betake themselves to Boston on that day.

On the thirteenth, the Sieur Governor of Boston and the Magistrates invited me to dine, and, at the close, gave me audience. Besides the Magistrates and the Secretary, there was present a man deputed by the people, whom they call a "representative."

I made a special entreaty on behalf of the Abnaquiois who had been killed by the Irocquois,—this is in the letter written to father Lejeune, in the eighth clause,—after which I was told to withdraw. Later, I was invited to supper, after which they gave me the answer which is in the other letter, in the clause before mentioned.

In regard to the character which I assumed of ambassador for my Catechumens of the Kenebec, they told me that Boston took no interest therein, and that I must address myself to Plimouth.

I left boston on the twenty-first of that month, December, for plimouth, where I arrived on the morrow, with my [*blank space*] who lodged me with one of the five farmers of Koussinoc, named padis. The governor of the place, named John Brentford, received me with courtesy, and appointed me an audience for the next day; and he invited me to a dinner of fish, which he prepared on my account, knowing that it was Friday. I found considerable favor in this settlement, for the farmers—and among others the captain, Thomas Willets—spoke to the governor in advocacy of my negotiation; and afterward we had discussions,

. . . .

24th. I left on the twenty-fourth, and returned to boston by land, in company with the son and the nephew of my [*blank space*], who paid for me during the journey. I arrived at Rosqbray, where the minister, named Master heliot, who was teaching some savages, received me at his house, because night was overtaking me; he treated me with respect and kindness, and begged me to spend the winter with him.

The next day, the twenty-ninth, I arrived at boston, and proceeded to the Sieur major-general guebin's.

On the thirtieth of the said month, I spoke to Sieur Ebens, one of the magistrates, who assured me that he was very glad that the governor of Plimout was willing to grant aid against the Irocquois. He said that it was very reasonable to succor one's Christian brethren, even if of another religion,—and especially against a pagan persecutor of the Christians. He presented to me the answer of the Sieur governor of boston and of the magistrates, to those of monsieur the governor.

On the last of the said month, I returned to Rosquebray to ask permission from Sieur Dudley, the Governor, that

safe-conduct might be inserted in the letter for the passage
of the french who might wish to go through boston against
the Irocquois; and, grasping my hand, he said to me:
"Assure Monsieur your governor that we wish to be his
good friends and servants, whatever war there may be between the crowns. I am very glad that the governor of
plimout is willing to further the assistance that you desire
against the Irocquois: I will aid him with all my power."

From R. G. Thwaites (ed.), *The Jesuit Relations and Allied
Documents* (Cleveland: Burrows, 1896-1901), Vol. XXXVI,
pp. 85-93.

MARQUETTE ON THE MISSISSIPPI

*Under the ambitious eye of Governor Frontenac the
influence and territory of France in the new world was
pushed steadily westward and southward during the last
decades of the seventeenth century. Eventually the lily-flag
of France flew from Quebec to Lake Superior, and from
Lake Superior to the Gulf of Mexico. The Church was
naturally interested in the new mission fields being opened
up by the joint forces of exploration and the fur trade, but
it seldom had enough clergy to serve the settled parishes
along the St. Lawrence, much less send missionaries to the
vast interior of the continent. Perhaps because the presence
of the Church in explorations made his grandiose schemes
more acceptable in France, Frontenac attached priests to
such expeditions whenever he could. In any case the missionaries were useful as translators because of their training
in Indian languages. Such a translator-missionary-explorer
was Father Jacques Marquette who shared with Louis Joliet
the honour of discovering the Mississippi River in 1673.*

The feast of the IMMACULATE CONCEPTION of the
BLESSED VIRGIN—whom I have always Invoked since I
have been in this country of the outaouacs, to obtain from
God the grace of being able to visit the Nations who dwell
along the Missisippi River—was precisely the Day of which
Monsieur Jollyet arrived with orders from Monsieur the

Count de frontenac, Our Governor, and Monsieur Talon, Our Intendant, to accomplish This discovery with me. I was all the more delighted at This good news, since I saw that my plans were about to be accomplished; and since I found myself in the blessed necessity of exposing my life for the salvation of all these peoples, and especially of the Ilinois, who had very urgently entreated me, when I was at the point of st. Esprit, to carry the word of God to Their country.

We were not long in preparing all our Equipment, although we were about to Begin a voyage, the duration of which we could not foresee. Indian Corn, with same smoked meat, constituted all our provisions; with these we Embarked—Monsieur Jollyet and myself, with 5 men—in 2 Bark Canoes, fully resolved to do and suffer everything for so glorious an Undertaking.

Accordingly, on the 17th day of may, 1673, we started from the Mission of st. Ignace at Michilimakinac, where I Then was. The Joy that we felt at being selected for This Expedition animated our Courage, and rendered the labor of paddling from morning to night agreeable to us. And because We were going to seek Unknown countries, we took every precaution in our power, so that, if our Undertaking were hazardous, it should not be foolhardy. To that end, we obtained all the Information that we could from the savages who had frequented those regions; and we even traced out from their reports a Map of the whole of that New country; on it we indicated the rivers which we were to navigate, the names of the peoples and of the places through which we were to pass, the Course of the great River, and the direction we were to follow when we reached it.

Above all, I placed our voyage under the protection of the Blessed Virgin Immaculate, promising her that, if she granted us the favor of discovering the great River, I would give it the Name of the Conception, and that I would also make the first Mission that I should establish among Those New peoples, bear the same name.

●　　●　　●

Here we are at Maskoutens. This Word may, in Algonquin, mean, "the fire Nation,"—which, indeed, is the name given to this tribe. Here is the limit of the discoveries which the french have made, For they have not yet gone any further.

• • •

No sooner had we arrived than we, Monsieur Jollyet and I, assembled the elders together; and he told them that he was sent by Monsieur Our Governor to discover New countries, while I was sent by God to Illumine them with the light of the holy Gospel. He told them that, moreover, The sovereign Master of our lives wished to be known by all the Nations; and that in obeying his will I feared not the death to which I exposed myself in voyages so perilous. He informed them that we needed two guides to show us the way; and We gave them a present, by it asking them to grant us the guides. To this they very Civilly consented; and they also spoke to us by means of a present, consisting of a Mat to serve us as a bed during the whole of our voyage.

On the following day, the tenth of June, two Miamis who were given us as guides embarked with us, in the sight of a great crowd, who could not sufficiently express their astonishment at the sight of seven frenchmen, alone in two Canoes, daring to undertake so extraordinary and so hazardous an Expedition.

We knew that, at three leagues from Maskoutens, was a River, which discharged into Missisipi. We knew also that the direction we were to follow in order to reach it was west-southwesterly. But the road is broken by so many swamps and small lakes that it is easy to lose one's way, especially as the River leading thither is so full of wild oats that it is difficult to find the Channel. For this reason we greatly needed our two guides, who safely Conducted us to a portage of 2,700 paces, and helped us to transport our Canoes to enter That river; after which they returned home, leaving us alone in this Unknown country, in the hands of providence.*

*Reference is here made to the Fox-Wisconsin portage. The name "Meskousing" is but one of the numerous variants of "Wisconsin."

Thus we left the Waters flowing to Quebec, 4 or 500 Leagues from here, to float on Those that would thenceforward Take us through strange lands. Before embarking thereon, we Began all together a new devotion to the blessed Virgin Immaculate, which we practised daily, addressing to her special prayers to place under her protection both our persons and the success of our voyage; and, after mutually encouraging one another, we entered our Canoes.

The River on which we embarked is called Meskousing. It is very wide; it has a sandy bottom, which forms various shoals that render its navigation very difficult. It is full of Islands Covered with Vines. On the banks one sees fertile land, diversified with woods, prairies, and Hills. There are oak, Walnut and basswood trees; and another kind, whose branches are armed with long thorns. We saw there neither feathered game nor fish, but many deer and a large number of cattle. Our Route lay to the southwest, and, after navigating about 30 leagues, we saw a spot presenting all the appearances of an iron mine; and, in fact, one of our party who had formerly seen such mines, assures us that The One which We found is very good and very rich. It is Covered with three feet of good soil, and is quite near a chain of rocks, the base of which is covered by very fine trees. After proceeding 40 leagues on This same route, we arrived at the mouth of our River, and, at 42 and a half degrees of latitude, We safely entered Missisipi on the 17th of June, with a Joy that I cannot Express.

From R. G. Thwaites (ed.), *The Jesuit Relations and Allied Documents* (Cleveland: Burrows, 1896-1901), Vol. LIX, pp. 89-93, 101, 105-107.

THE FIRST TEMPERANCE MEETING

New France depended for its life on the fur trade, and the fur trade in turn depended on brandy—so the traders said. The disastrous results of brandy on the morals and the health of the Indians became apparent very early, and for decades the Church tried to use its influence to stem the tide of fire-water that was destroying their efforts to christianize and civilize the Indians.

Francis Parkman, the American historian who popularized the dramatic history of New France, has told the story of Canada's first temperance meeting. When such voluntary efforts to curb the brandy trade failed the church turned to the government in France demanding total prohibition. The government was never able to decide between the claims of the church and the pleas of the traders who said the furs would go to the English in exchange for rum if the brandy trade was banned.

In the summer of 1648, there was held at the mission of Sillery a temperance meeting; the first in all probability on this continent. The drum beat after mass, and the Indians gathered at the summons. Then an Algonquin chief, a zealous convert of the Jesuits, proclaimed to the crowd a late edict of the governor imposing penalties for drunkenness, and, in his own name and that of the other chiefs, exhorted them to abstinence, declaring that all drunkards should be handed over to the French for punishment. Father Jérôme Lalement looked on delighted. "It was," he says, " the finest public act of jurisdiction exercised among the Indians since I have been in this country. From the beginning of the world they have all thought themselves as great lords, the one as the other, and never before submitted to their chiefs any further than they chose to do so."

There was great need of reform; for a demon of drunkenness seemed to possess these unhappy tribes. Nevertheless, with all their rage for brandy, they sometimes showed in regard to it a self-control quite admirable in its way. When at a fair, a council, or a friendly visit, their entertainers regaled them with rations of the coveted liquor, so prudently measured out that they could not be the worse for it, they would unite their several portions in a common stock, which they would then divide among a few of their number, thus enabling them to attain that complete intoxication which, in their view, was the true end of all drinking. The objects of this singular benevolence were expected to requite it in kind on some future occasion.

A drunken Indian with weapons within reach, was very dangerous, and all prudent persons kept out of his way.

This greatly pleased him; for, seeing everybody run before him, he fancied himself a great chief, and howled and swung his tomahawk with redoubled fury. If, as often happened, he maimed or murdered some wretch not nimble enough to escape, his countrymen absolved him from all guilt, and blamed only the brandy. Hence, if an Indian wished to take a safe revenge on some personal enemy, he would pretend to be drunk; and, not only murders but other crimes were often committed by false claimants to the bacchanalian privilege.

In the eyes of the missionaries, brandy was a fiend with all crimes and miseries in his train; and, in fact, nothing earthly could better deserve the epithet infernal than an Indian town in the height of a drunken debauch. The orgies never ceased till the bottom of the barrel was reached. Then came repentance, despair, wailing, and bitter invective against the white men, the cause of all the woe. In the name of the public good, or humanity, and above all of religion, the bishop and the Jesuits denounced the fatal traffic.

Their case was a strong one; but so was the case of their opponents. There was real and imminent danger that the thirsty savages, if refused brandy by the French, would seek it from the Dutch and English of New York. It was the most potent lure and the most killing bait. Wherever it was found, thither the Indians and their beaver-skins were sure to go, and the interests of the fur trade, vital to the colony, were bound up with it. Nor was this all, for the merchants and the civil powers insisted that religion and the saving of souls were bound up with it no less since, to repel the Indians from the Catholic French, and attract them to the heretic English, was to turn them from ways of grace to ways of perdition. The argument, no doubt, was dashed largely with hypocrisy in those who used it; but it was one which the priests were greatly perplexed to answer.

In former days, when Canada was not yet transformed from a mission to a colony, the Jesuits entered with a high hand on the work of reform. It fared hard with the culprit caught in the act of selling brandy to Indians. They led him, after the sermon, to the door of the church; where, kneeling on the pavement, partially stript and bearing in his hand the penitential torch, he underwent a vigorous flagellation, laid on by Father Le Mercier himself, after the fashion formerly practised in the case of refractory schoolboys. Bishop Laval not only discharged against the offenders volleys of wholesale excommunication, but he made of the offence a "reserved case"; that is, a case in which the power of granting absolution was reserved to himself alone. This produced great commotion, and a violent conflict between religious scruples and a passion for gain. The bishop and the Jesuits stood inflexible; while their opponents added bitterness to the quarrel by charging them with permitting certain favored persons to sell brandy, unpunished, and even covertly selling it themselves.

From Francis Parkman, *The Old Régime in Canada* (Boston: Little, Brown, 1922), p. 386-390.

HIGH FASHION

Paris fashions were just as much the vogue in New France three hundred years ago as they are in Canada today. Ladies eagerly awaited news each year of the latest styles adopted by the court of the "Sun King," Louis XIV, and if they could not afford the luxury of imported dresses they remodelled last year's clothes to keep abreast of the changing times. Off-the-shoulder gowns might be all the rage at Versailles, but the church in New France—and especially Bishop Laval and the Jesuits—had very different views on womens' fashions.

MANDEMENT
AGAINST THE LUXURY AND VANITY OF WOMEN AND GIRLS IN CHURCH

François, by the grace of God and the Holy See, first Bishop of Quebec.

If the fathers and doctors of the Church inveighed with so much force against the luxury and vanity of women and girls who forget the promises of their baptism, appearing dressed and ornamented in Satan's pomp which they have so solemnly renounced, it is for us to make known the extreme horror that God has for such a disorder, which renders those who are guilty so much more criminal before him, that wishing to be pleasing in the eyes of men they become the captives and instruments of the demon who uses this luxury to make them, and those who see them in this state, commit an infinity of sins. That is why God declares often in the Holy Scripture that he will punish severely those worldly women who parade thus the marks and livery of his enemy. . . . If these vain fineries displease God so strongly, and if he takes such rude vengeance, of what crime are they not guilty and what punishment must not attend those who carry this pompous apparel even into our churches appearing in these consecrated places at prayers and confession in indecent dresses, showing scandalous nudities of arms, shoulders, and throat, being content to cover them with a transparent veil which serves more often to give greater lustre to these disgraceful nudities, the head uncovered, or covered only with a transparent net and the hair curled in a manner unworthy of a Christian, offending the holiness of these places against the express prohibition of the Blessed Apostles Saint Peter and Saint Paul. . . .

The zeal we must have for the honour of the house of God and for the salvation of the flock that it has pleased the Divine Providence to confide to us, obliges us to employ every means within our jurisdiction and authority to drive out entirely from the churches of our diocese an abuse so pernicious and which was introduced there several years ago. . . .

In this cause we prohibit very expressly all girls and women of whatever quality and fortune from approaching the Sacraments, presenting the consecrated bread, going to the offering and making the collection in the churches in the indecent manner that we have just specified in our present *mandement,* and all the *curés* of our diocese from receiving them there in this state; instead we wish that when they come to church that they dress with the decency and modesty which is demanded by Christian holiness and humility. We forbid, likewise, all other priests of our diocese, seculars as well as regulars, from receiving at the

sacraments the said girls and women in this state, and finally
that no one pretends ignorance, we order that, at the diligence of our Grand Vicars, our present *mandement* will be
immediately sent to all the *curés* of our diocese and everywhere it is needed, to be read there and published in the
sermon and affixed to the door of the church.

Given at Quebec the 26th day of February, 1682.

FRANCOIS, Bishop of Quebec.

From H. Têtu and C. O. Gagnon, *Mandements, lettres pas-
torales et circulaires des Evêques de Québec* (Quebec, 1887),
Vol. I, pp. 106-108. S. D. Clark (trans.), *Social Development
of Canada* (Toronto: University of Toronto Press, 1942).

ADVICE FOR A GOVERNOR

*Bishop Laval was determined to make New France into a
God-fearing, church-attending colony. No one was exempt
from his criticisms—not even the governor, the brave and
honest Marquis de Denonville, and his pious wife who received the following gratuitous directions on how to behave
as leaders of Christian society soon after their arrival in
New France in 1685.*

ON FEASTS

One: When the Governor and his wife are invited to eat
with someone it is proper that it be for dinner rather than
for supper in order to avoid extended evenings and dangerous pastimes and other vexatious habits which arise at
banquets and night assemblies.

Two: They should declare themselves unhappy, be un-
civil, and even dismiss for ever their hosts, should the meal
which is given to them be too sumptuous and magnificent.
In this way, finding themselves at meals that are frugal, they
will accustom, bit by bit, their hosts to the avoidance of too
sumptuous feasts which are not only inconvenient to the
families but opposed to temperance and wound Christian
modesty and decorum.

Three: They should never suffer these feasts to be accompanied by dances or balls, and several other dangerous and

licentious recreations. Their presence at these divertissements would cause great harm as past experience has shown.

ON BALLS AND DANCES

Balls and dances, in themselves, are harmless by nature,
nevertheless they are dangerous because of the environ-
ment they provide, and the evil, and almost inevitable consequences that follow . . . it is best not to find oneself at
balls or dances unless one is absolutely obliged, in which
cases they should season these divertissements with great
modesty, good intentions, dignity, and Christian consideration and pious sentiments, so that one may preserve oneself
from corruption. . . .

• • •

As the age and vivacity of their daughter necessitates a
few diversions and recreations one may deign to permit her
a few honest and moderate dances but only with people of
her own sex and in the presence of her mother for fear that
none too decent words and songs are used, and never in the
presence of men and boys, for this mixing of sexes, frankly
speaking, is the cause of the inconveniences and disorders
of balls and dances.

ON COMEDIES AND OTHER PLAYS

We do not believe that Christian decorum permits the representation of comedies, or to appear before an audience as
an actress declaiming verses, no matter how holy the subject
matter. And less still should we suffer that boys declaim
with girls. . . .

From H. Têtu and C. O. Gagnon, *Mandements, lettres pas-
torales et circulaires des Evêques de Québec* (Quebec, 1887),
Vol. I, pp. 169-172. Cameron Nish (trans.), *Canadian Historical Documents Series* (Toronto: Prentice-Hall, 1965), Vol.
I, pp. 76-77.

TUMULT AT THE BISHOP'S FUNERAL

*Jean-Baptiste de La Croix de Chevrières de Saint-Vallier,
Laval's successor as bishop of New France, was an aristo-
crat by nature, but lacked all sense of compromise. His*

abitrary actions brought him into conflict with officials of both church and state, including King Louis XIV himself. Saint-Vallier even in his old age seemed to be a natural centre of strife, and at his death the religious tensions that he had caused in Quebec broke out in the open with a most unseemly quarrel over the bishop's burial.

Events at the funeral of Saint-Vallier read like a chapter from a mediaeval chronicle. He died just after midnight on December 21, 1727, in the fine General Hospital, a house for the poor which he had built on the banks of the St. Charles. He had prepared a tomb in the neighbouring parish church of Notre-Dame-des-Anges and his reputation for saintliness made it seem likely to the faithful that there miracles would occur. Perhaps with this in view the canons of the Quebec cathedral took prompt action. They planned that the emaciated body of the prelate should be carried in succession to each of the Quebec churches and then to the cathedral for elaborate funeral rites, and the suspicion spread that the canons intended to keep it there in what might become a wonder-working shrine. In making their plans the canons claimed authority in the diocese until instructions should come from Monseigneur de Mornay, the new bishop. But he was in France; he might, indeed, be dead; it was mid-winter and months must elapse before word could come from him, and so the cathedral chapter must rule meanwhile. The rights claimed by the canons were promptly disputed. The Archdeacon Lothbinière insisted that he was acting head of the Church and proceeded to carry out the bishop's plan for his own burial.

At this stage the state intervened in the person of the Intendant Dupuy. He had arrived in 1725 with the new governor, the Marquis de Beauharnois, and had been so quick to verify the long tradition of strife between governor and intendant that Beauharnois wrote to the court: "If ever there was an impossible man he [Dupuy] is one. If I say white he is sure to say black. He thinks himself general, bishop and intendant all in one." So assertive was he of his dignity that he required two soldiers with muskets at the shoulder to accompany him to his seat in church. Now he took up warmly the side of the archdeacon and ordered the canons to appear before the Superior Council on January 2. When they failed to obey he went to the General Hospital and gave orders that the burial should take place at once. The archdeacon and other clergy present hastily put on their surplices, the nuns were summoned and, as night fell, the body was carried to the church with what pomp was possible in such haste, and was buried in the prepared grave.

The news went quickly to Quebec and there created a sensation. That evening the tocsin sounded; rumours spread that the Hospital was on fire; and the canons hurried thither followed by a crowd. They found at the door of the church an armed guard which tried but failed to prevent their entrance. There was a threat of exhuming the body already placed under a heavy stone. Though wiser counsels prevailed, during the following months the Superior Council fumed against the canons and they retorted in kind. At last the governor intervened and rebuked both sides; orders came from the new bishop in France denying the claims of the canons; and the king recalled the intendant because of his unwise handling of the matter.

From G. M. Wrong, *The Rise and Fall of New France* (Toronto: The Macmillan Company, 1928), Vol. II, pp. 655-656.

THE TIPSY SISTERS

After the Age of Laval the Church settled into a comfortable pattern of parish life. Small villages crowded the water's edge along the St. Lawrence, each village a knot of modest buildings clustered like a brood of chickens around their mother, the local church whose tall spire and shining roof proclaimed visibly the central place of religion in the life of New France. Quebec, capital and bishop's seat, grew in elegance as new and imposing government and church structures rose above the sky-line of Cape Diamond. But it was Montreal, marketplace for the fur trade of half a continent, that typified the colony's perpetual contact with the frontier.

Sprawling, boisterous Montreal was the scene of riotous behaviour every time the coureurs de bois *and Indians of the fur brigades arrived from the west. Between these disorderly bouts the City of Mary relapsed into relative calm. Yet even in those periods of calm Montreal bore social scars as evidence of its double life. Painfully conscious of the presence of the needy, sick and aged, Marguerite d'Youville, pious widow of a liquor merchant, gathered three other devout women in 1737 in a project to open their homes and their purses to the sufferers of Montreal. From this modest beginning grew a great Order devoted to charitable work among the less fortunate, but the first appearances of these good women in the streets of Montreal earned them the peculiar nickname, "tipsy sisters", that in time became their proud title, the Grey Nuns.*

The four associates, on December 31, agreed to spend the following year in gradually putting their plans into execution. They would continue to live in their own homes for the present, but would work together as much as possible, taking care of the poor persons whom Madame d'Youville would receive. She could not receive many, however; her rooms were too small and too few. But the lease for this house on the Market Place would not expire until the first of November. Perhaps by that time they could rent a house in a more suitable locality, a house large enough for themselves and their poor, and then they would live in common.

In the meantime, they would all contribute to the general revenue from their earnings. Catherine Cusson and Catherine Demers, skilled in sewing, already had many clients whom they would continue to serve; and Louise Thaumur could help them. Perhaps in time they could sew for the King's stores in the Market Place. Then their income would indeed be assured for the future.

Finally these four courageous women, united more closely than ever through their eager planning, agreed to keep secret as much as possible the great work to which they had consecrated themselves.

Before many weeks, however, their close and unusual association began to excite comment. It was now known that blind Françoise Osseau was being cared for in Madame d'Youville's home; her husband in the General Hospital had spoken gratefully of her relief and contentment. Would more destitute persons be taken? Who was going to take care of them? It was impossible now to deny or to hide the truth.

Some relatives and friends were surprised and even shocked. This was a new thing indeed! Were not the poor sufficiently cared for in their own homes by the good members of the Confraternity? Who was the widow of François d'Youville to collect the destitute persons of Montreal in her house and then get other people to take care of them? Was it true that they were aiming to take over the General Hospital in time? And how did they propose to support themselves and their poor?

Some questioners with particularly long memories subtly wondered if the liquor traffic would provide revenue, as once it had, in this very house too.

Already the sinuous stirrings of curiosity were beginning to arouse suspicion and blind antagonism—not among the poor who would profit by the heroic self-sacrifice of a few good women, but among excellent people not quite virtuous enough to resist envy of a good work which they were not themselves inspired to perform.

Mere words, however, could not deter brave women dedicated to deeds. In the noise about them they kept silent and continued their work.

As spring passed into early summer they realized even more sharply that the house in the Market Place would soon have to be abandoned. It stood in the very centre of all the agitation that was ever aroused in Montreal. Drunken Indians from the woods often stumbled into the store or lounged on the steps outside, as they had done in summers past; for even to the red men Madame d'Youville was a friend. But lately loud and ominous remarks from passers-by had reached her ears as she attended to her affairs at the counter.

"Look at those Indians! Where did they get their fire-water this time?"

"Maybe the widow d'Youville sold it to them in secret, just as old You and his son—"

A coarse laugh covered up the words as the men passed on.

The ugly comments grew. Madame d'Youville's associates, passing in and out of her home, frequently met a barrage of jeers. Already the suspicious questionings of relatives and friends had degenerated into the gibes and insults of the common mob that thronged the Market Place in the summer time. Somehow the sight of the quiet women, plainly dressed, intent on something far removed from the noisy confusion around them, irritated the careless idlers into malicious mockery.

"Voilà! Les soeurs!"

"Les soeurs grises!"

The rabble took up the taunt. *Les soeurs grises!* The tipsy nuns!

Without a word, but with burning cheeks and swiftly beating hearts, the brave women went on. Sensitive, kind-hearted, they could not be totally indifferent to the cruel experience which they had suffered. And yet, were they not called *nuns*? For the infinite honor of this term, could they not endure the adjective?

From Sister Mary Pauline Fitts, G.N.S.H., *Hands to the Needy: Mother d'Youville, Apostle to the Poor* (New York: Doubleday, 1950), pp. 93-95.

CONQUEST AND COMPROMISE

THE SCARS OF WAR

The British siege of Quebec lasted throughout the summer of 1759. Batteries of heavy artillery, poised at Lévis on the opposite shore, rained tons of iron on the city. After the decisive battle on the Plains of Abraham the victorious British army marched into a city so scarred by months of bombardment that it was only a shell of its former self. The grand church buildings of Quebec had suffered most heavily —the body of the French General Montcalm was buried first in a shell crater in the floor of the Ursuline convent's chapel.

The historian Francis Parkman described the ravages that war had wrought on a once proud and beautiful city, and the chaos that followed its capture.

The fleet was gone; the great river was left a solitude; and the chill days of a fitful November passed over Quebec in alternations of rain and frost, sunshine and snow. The troops, driven by cold from their encampment on the Plains, were all gathered within the walls. Their own artillery had so battered the place that it was not easy to find shelter. The Lower Town was a wilderness of scorched and crumbling walls. As you ascended Mountain Street, the Bishop's Palace, on the right, was a skeleton of tottering masonry, and the buildings on the left were a mass of ruin, where ragged boys were playing at see-saw among the fallen planks and timbers. Even in the Upper Town few of the churches and public buildings had escaped. The Cathedral was burned to a shell. The solid front of the College of the Jesuits was pockmarked by numberless cannon-balls, and the adjacent church of the Order was woefully shattered. The Church of the Récollets suffered still more. The bombshells that fell through the roof had broken into the pavement, and as they burst had thrown up the bones and skulls of the dead from the graves beneath. Even the more distant Hôtel-Dieu was pierced by fifteen projectiles, some of which had exploded in the halls and chambers.

The Commissary-general, Berniers, thus describes to Bourlamaque the state of the town: "Quebec is nothing but a shapeless mass of ruins. Confusion, disorder, pillage, reign even among the inhabitants, for the English make examples of severity every day. Everybody rushes hither and thither, without knowing why. Each searches for his possessions, and, not finding his own, seizes those of other people. English and French, all is chaos alike. The inhabitants, famished and destitute, escape to the country. Never was there seen such a sight."

From F. Parkman, *Montcalm and Wolfe* (Boston: Little, Brown, 1922), Vol. II, pp. 340-341.

THE FIRST PROTESTANT SERVICE

A few days after the battle on the Plains of Abraham the Reverend Eli Dawson, chaplain of the Sterling Castle, *held a thanksgiving service for the British soldiers and sailors. The exact date is uncertain—it may have been September 27 or October 4. Mr. Dawson took his text from Psalm xviii, 49: "Therefore will I give thanks unto thee, O Lord, among the heathen, and sing praises unto thy name." Ironically his pulpit in the Ursuline chapel stood only ten feet from Montcalm's temporary grave.*

Although Protestants had been officially banned from New France for one hundred and thirty years, John Knox, an ensign in the Black Watch Regiment, noted in his diary the presence of several Huguenots at this, the first recorded Protestant church service held in Quebec.

4th. [October]—Moderate weather these two days: in consequence of orders for this purpose, to-day has been dedicated to Divine service and a solemn thanksgiving for the success of his Majesty's arms, in the reduction of this fortress; the troops were excused all duties of labour and fatigue, and, about eleven o'clock, the several regiments marched to the church of the Ursulines, preceded by our General Officers, where they heard an excellent sermon suitable to the *occasion*; several French merchants, said to be of the Reformed religion, and commonly called Hugonots, attended, though unacquainted with our language.

From John Knox, *An Historical Journal of the Campaigns in North America* (Toronto: Champlain Society, 1914), Vol. II, pp. 229-230.

THE COMPLIMENT OF THE HAT

With the departure of their fleet from Quebec the British began to settle in for a long winter. The French still controlled the rest of the colony outside of the city, so the army of occupation had to remain on the alert for possible attacks or for subversive activities within the city itself. The relations of French and English that winter were a model of mutual respect and charity. The nuns of Quebec nursed the wounded with tender care and the soldiers shared their meagre rations with the civilians as together they faced severe famine.

The second set of Standing Orders issued in November, 1759, detailed the relations to be observed between victor and vanquished and imposed a strict discipline on each.

It is the duty of every British subject to inform the Governor of every thing that happens derogatory to those orders, and every other circumstance they may discover, inconsistent with the good of his Majesty's service and the prosperity of the nation: if it is required and necessary, the informers shall not only be concealed, but rewarded handsomely, in proportion to the importance of the intelligence. No French inhabitants to be allowed to work upon the batteries or ramparts at any time, nor are they to be in the streets, after it is dark, without a lanthorn; after tattoo-beating all French inhabitants, found in the streets, are to be made prisoners; and, notwithstanding the proclamations issued to the citizens, inforcing these orders, the Commanding Officers of corps will direct their Quarter-Masters to repeat them in their respective districts, that none may plead ignorance. As the regiments will have a number of creepers, snowshoes or rackets, and mogosans delivered to them, they will take care to keep them properly fitted, that they may be come at for use on the shortest notice; the snow-shoes to be kept hung up, to prevent the rats and mice from eating them. Each regiment will likewise have a number of snow-shovels, to clear away within their own districts, and to keep open communications. All chimnies are to be swept once a fortnight. The Quarter-Masters to attend the magazines, when the regiments are served with provisions or wood; and to march their men regularly to and from thence. The French inhabitants of Quebec by the capitulation being intitled to the possession of their effects, and his Majesty's proclamation for the free exercise of their religion, it is determined to punish all robbing and plundering, or insult offered to their persons, in an exemplary manner; and, when any of their processions are made in the public streets, *it is ordered that the Officers pay them the compliment of the hat,* because it is a civility due to the people who have chosen to live under the protection of our *laws; should this piece of ceremony be repugnant to the consciences of any one, they must retire, when the procession approaches.*—As the honour of the nation and this army is concerned in a strict discipline being kept up, all officers are to take notice of every disobedience of orders, or neglect of duty, they may observe in the men of any regiment. It is hoped this garrison will consider themselves as one corps, zealously and unanimously in promoting his Majesty's service, and preserving that reputation which they have so justly acquired.

N.B. *These orders to be read to the men once a month.*

From John Knox, *An Historical Journal of the Campaigns in North America* (Toronto: Champlain Society, 1914), Vol. II, pp. 259-260.

A CAPTIVE CHURCH

When no relief force reached New France from old France in 1760, the French army at Montreal surrendered just a year after the fall of Quebec. In 1762 General Murray, senior military governor during the occupation, prepared a long report on the condition and prospects of the colony, including a detailed account of the state of the Roman Catholic Church. At a time when Roman Catholics were politically and legally second-class citizens in Britain, Murray showed his breadth of understanding and humanity by recommending toleration for the Roman Church in New France. Like most people in Britain and in the occupied colony, the general assumed that the return of peace would see Catholic New France become a permanent part of George III's Protestant empire.

CHURCH GOVERNMENT

The Bishop

When the Bishoprick of Quebec was first established in 1674, the See was endowed by Louis the 14th with the Revenues of two Abbacies, those of Benevent and L'Estrees; about 30 Years ago the Bishop then finding it difficult, considering the distance, to recover the revenues of them by consent of Louis the 15th resigned the same to the Clergy of France, to be united to a particular revenue of theirs stiled the *Aeconomats* applied to the augmentation of small livings. In consideration of which the Bishop of this See has ever since received 8,000 Livres out of the said Revenues. A few Years before the late Bishops death, the Clergy of France granted him for his life only a further pension of 2000 Livres. The Bishop had no estate whatsoever, except his palace in Quebec destroyed by our Artillery, a Garden and the Ground rent of two or three houses adjoining it and built upon some part of the land.

● ● ●

The Chapter of Quebec

The Chapter consists of a Dean and twelve Canons. Their revenue consisted of an Abbacy in France which brought them in about 4000 Livres and a pension from the King of Eight Thousand paid out of the Domaine. The whole was divided into fourteen shares of which the Dean had two.

There is one vacancy in the Chapter, the present Dean the Abbé de la Corne, a Canadian and five of the Canons are in France.

•   •   •

Parish of Quebec

The Town and Suburbs form but one parish which is very extensive and is served by a Curé and two Vicars under him. The Church is Parochial as well as Cathedral, no part of it is left standing but the bare walls; a Chapel of ease in the lower Town was likewise burnt during the Siege. The people at present perform their devotions in the Chapels of the several religious communities.

•   •   •

The Jésuites

They possess a large commodious House, a handsome Chapel and a spacious Garden within the upper Town, the House and Chappel suffer'd a good deal from our artillery, but might be easily repaired; no other place in the Town being so proper, it has and is still made use of as a Magazine of Provisions. For this reason it was necessary to dislodge the Fathers the first Winter, less their turbulent and intriguing genius should prompt them to play some trick which might have proved fatal in the critical situation of affairs and which they could perhaps have easily compassed had they been suffer'd to reside in the House. After the capitulation of Montreal they were readmitted and conveniently lodged in one wing of it and have freely consented to His Majesty making use of the remainder.

Their particular province is the instruction of Youth and the Missions of the Savages, the King allow'd them on account of the latter, 13,300 Livres.

•   •   •

The Récollets

This is an order of Mendicant Friars who possess nothing of their own but a House and Garden in the upper Town.

They had a piece of ground in the suburb of St. Rock on which they formerly had a house and church, which has been abandoned for some Years. A small part of the Intendants buildings is erected upon a piece of this Land, in consideration of which under the French Government they were paid fifty Louis a Year from the Marine by way of charity as they can receive no rents. They acted as Chaplains to the Army, and at the several Forts or posts and in failure of regular Clergy served the vacant Curés.

● ● ●

Seminary of Quebec

These are Secular Clergy: Their institution is to educate the Youth and fit them for the priesthood. They have a large House and Chapel in the City of Quebec, both in a ruinous condition ever since the siege of 1759.

● ● ●

Convent of the Hôtel-Dieu of Quebec

This is a community of women, particularly instituted for the care of the Sick; They had been in good circumstances but their House having been entirely consumed by Fire, a few Years ago, they are considerably indebted for the rebuilding of it.

● ● ●

Convent of the Ursulines at Quebec

This is likewise a community of Women, their institution is for the education of Young Girls.

● ● ●

The General Hospital near Quebec

This is a community of Women, they have a Foundation for taking care of Thirty Invalids, Idiots or Incurables, which they are at present in no condition to fulfil, their revenues being no way equal to the expence, and as a large sum is owing them by the King of France for the sick of his army. In the time of the French they were allowed rations for as many of the above as they took in and a pension of 2,000

Livres. The Ladies of this community are of the best
Families in Canada and by the presents they were continually receiving from them they were chiefly enabled to
subsist; That revenue is now at an end, as the Gentry in
general are at present in the most distressed circumstances.

They owe a very large debt contracted in a good measure
for the support of the sick Officers and Soldiers of the
French Army. The French King owes them a large sum,
sufficient to discharge it, but they must be reduced to the
utmost beggary and distress if he does not; The sale of all
their houses and Lands will scarce be sufficient to satisfy
their Creditors.

● ● ●

Les Filles de la Congregation

This was an institution for teaching Young Girls to read
and write; they take the vows but are not cloister'd and go
abroad about their affairs. They are poor. However besides
what they possess in the other two Governments they had
a House in the lower Town destroy'd by our Artillery, one
at Point au Tremble and one with a small Farm at St.
Famille in the Island of Orleans.

Their number at present in this Government [Quebec city
and vicinity]—4.

● ● ●

Observations

1st The Canadians are very ignorant and extremely
tenacious of their Religion, nothing can contribute so much
to make them staunch subjects to his Majesty as the new
Government giving them every reason to imagine no alteration is to be attempted in that point.

2 ... Care was taken under the former Government to
keep up a great part of the Clergy French, especially the
dignified part: To prevent the further importation of these,
it would be necessary to encourage the natives to engage in
the profession, which cannot be so well done, except the See
is filled up, as without a Bishop there can be no ordination:
some difficulty will attend this, as it is unendow'd tho' hereafter means may be found of making up this deficiency.

3d . . . A like difficulty occurs in relation to the Chapter, their number indeed might be reduced by letting the vacancies lye dormant, if some provision cannot be made for them as will hereafter be proposed.

4th . . . An expedient to assist the people in rebuilding their great Church, would much ingratiate their new Masters with them.

5th . . . The Jesuites are neither loved nor esteemed in general, and this order may be easily removed whenever the Government shall think proper without giving offence, out of part of their Estate provision might be made for the Bishoprick, and Chapter which would ease the Crown of further expences on that head.

6th The Recollets is an order of Mendicants, as they depend upon charity for subsistence, they are careful not to give offence; probably should they find the Inhabitants upon the present change, cool towards their Order, they will of themselves seek a better living somewhere else.

7th The Seminary educates the Youth, and fits them for Orders, it will be necessary to preserve and encourage this House on that account, and it is to be observed, this was the only Religious House or order, that heretofore did not participate of the French King's Bounty.

8th As to the communities of Women they are much esteemed and respected by the People, the narrowness of their circumstances will probably prevent their being filled up so easily as in former times; when the Canadians become a little more reconciled to British customs and Government, it may not be amiss under colour of serving those communities in their distressed situation, to restrict the admission of any under a certain sum; this regulation with another fixing a certain age, under which no vows to be taken, would probably soon reform the worst abuses of such institutions.

9th . . . There are some few French Protestants in this Country who no doubt will be willing to remain, it would be a great comfort to these, if a Church was granted for their use, and some French Clergyman of sound sense and good Character, with a tolerable salary, was invited to settle among them, such an establishment may be attended with the further good consequences of enticing many of their Brethren in France, to come and enjoy that religious liberty, after which they so ardently sigh, amidst a people sprung from the same origin, speaking the same language, and following the same Customs. It may likewise be conducive towards bringing about a Reformation, by slow degrees and must at least prove to the Canadians there is nothing in our Holy Religion repugnant to Virtue or Morality.

From Adam Shortt and A. G. Doughty (eds.), *Documents Relating to the Constitutional History of Canada, 1759-1791* (2nd. ed.; Ottawa: Department of Public Printing and Stationery, 1918), pp. 66-72.

WE HAVE A BISHOP!

Before Quebec's fall Bishop Henri de Pontbriand had fled to Montreal. Before Montreal surrendered Bishop Pontbriand had died there. Without a bishop no more priests could be ordained and no believers confirmed. Without a bishop the Roman Catholic Church seemed doomed to die out in Canada, for George III was pledged by his coronation oath to uphold the Protestant religion and oppose Roman Catholicism. Legally the King and his advisers could not permit the papacy to appoint a bishop for any part of the Protestant empire. What could be done, what should be done, for the religion of the sixty thousand new subjects of the King in Canada?

The compromise solution to this dilemma was largely the work of General Murray. At his suggestion Jean-Olivier Briand was allowed to go to France for consecration while the British government looked the other way. The importance of Bishop Briand's consecration was fully understood by the faithful Roman Catholics who welcomed him back to Quebec—their church would now live on, thanks to the practical toleration of their conquerors.

QUEBEC GAZETTE, 3 July 1766

[*Saturday, 28 June, General Murray embarked on the* LITTLE WILLIAM *for England at 11 a.m.; it passed the* COMMERCE *in the river*]

The same Day, at 11 o'Clock at Night, arrived in this City from London, on board the Commerce, Capt. Johnson, Mr. *Briand*, Bishop of Quebec, for the Roman Catholicks, who manifested on this Occasion all their Affection for what concerns their Religion. On the Day following, at 5 o'Clock in the Morning, the Bells of all their Churches announced his Arrival to the whole City, which gave such general Satisfaction to the Canadians, that many of them were seen to shed Tears thro' Joy. It was really affecting to see them congratulate each other wherever they met, and to hear them incessantly say one to another, "It is then true that we have a Bishop; God hath taken Pity on us:" And to see them afterwards run in Crowds to the Parish Church to see this Bishop, whom them look upon as the Support of their Religion, and as a Pledge of the King's Paternal Goodness to them. In Fact, at the same Time that they publickly bless the Lord for having given them a Bishop, they loudly proclaim their Gratitude to His Majesty for having attended to their Requests: It is likely that this Favour confer'd on the Canadians by the King, will effectually attach them to the British Government. It is also very pleasing to them, to have received on this Occasion the Congratulations of several Persons of Note of our Nation, who indeed seemed to partake of their Joy. And we doubt not, but that the Canadians, who appear to be very susceptible of Gratitude, will by those Means more firmly unite to us.

From *Quebec Gazette*, July 3, 1766.

A CHARTER OF LIBERTIES

The peace treaty of 1763 that made Canada a part of the British empire also promised religious freedom to the Roman Catholic population. The consecration of Bishop Briand ensured the survival of the Church as an institution. The Quebec Act of 1774 confirmed not only that religious freedom but also the ancient rights of the Catholic Church in the colony, such as collecting the tithe and holding property. As the only institution of New France to survive the Conquest intact the Roman Catholic Church became, with

*the British government's support, the living embodiment of
French-Canadian culture, and the* QUEBEC ACT *formed the
Magna Carta of the people and of the Church.*

And, for the more perfect Security and Ease of the Minds
of the Inhabitants of the said Province, it is hereby declared,
That His Majesty's Subjects, professing the Religion of the
Church of *Rome* of and in the said Province of *Quebec*,
may have, hold, and enjoy, the free Exercise of the Religion
of the Church of *Rome*, subject to the King's Supremacy,
declared and established by an Act, made in the First Year
of their Reign of Queen *Elizabeth*, over all the Dominions
and Countries which then did, or thereafter should belong,
to the Imperial Crown of this Realm; and that the Clergy
of the said Church may hold, receive, and enjoy, their
accustomed Dues and Rights, with respect to such Persons
only as shall profess the said Religion.

Provided nevertheless, That it shall be lawful for His
Majesty, His Heirs or Successors, to make such Provision
out of the rest of the said accustomed Dues and Rights, for
the Encouragement of the Protestant Religion, and for the
Maintenance and Support of a Protestant Clergy within the
said Province, as he or they shall, from Time to Time, think
necessary and expedient.

Provided always, and be it enacted, That no Person, professing the Religion of the Church of *Rome*, and residing in
the said Province, shall be obliged to take the Oath required
by the said Statute passed in the First Year of the Reign of
Queen *Elizabeth*, or any other Oaths substituted by any
other Act in the Place thereof; but that every such Person
who, by the said Statute is required to take the Oath therein
mentioned, shall be obliged, and is hereby required, to take
and subscribe the following Oath before the Governor, or
such other Person in such Court of Record as His Majesty
shall appoint, who are hereby authorized to administer the
same; *videlicet,*

I, A. B. *do sincerely promise and swear, That I will be
faithful, and bear true Allegiance to His Majesty King*
GEORGE, *and him will defend to the utmost of my Power,
against all traiterous Conspiracies, and Attempts whatso-*

ever, which shall be made against His Person, Crown and Dignity; and I will do my utmost Endeavour to disclose and make known to His Majesty, His Heirs and Successors, all Treasons, and traiterous Conspiracies, and Attempts, which I shall know to be against Him, or any of Them; and all this I do swear without any Equivocation, mental Evasion, or secret Reservation, and renouncing all Pardons and Dispensations from any Power or Person whomsoever to the Contrary.

SO HELP ME GOD.

And every such Person, who shall neglect or refuse to take the said Oath before mentioned, shall incur and be liable to the same Penalties, Forfeitures, Disabilities, and Incapacities, as he would have incurred and been liable to for neglecting or refusing to take the Oath required by the said Statute passed in the First Year of the Reign of Queen *Elizabeth.*

From Adam Shortt and A. G. Doughty (eds.), *Documents Relating to the Constitutional History of Canada, 1759-1791* (2nd. ed.; Ottawa: Department of Public Printing and Stationery, 1918), pp. 572-573.

A MANDEMENT FOR LOYALTY

Both the Church and the people of New France were deeply appreciative of the religious freedoms they enjoyed under British rule. Such generous treatment of the conquered by the conqueror was indeed rare in a century when religious persecution was generally taken for granted. Even before the peace of 1763 Catholic church leaders showed their gratitude for this fair treatment. When George II died the clergy of Montreal wore mourning crepe in their hats. When young George III was married in 1762 the entire clergy of the occupied colony were ordered by the Church to sing Te Deums *for the happy event and to say special public prayers for the king, Queen Charlotte, and the whole royal family!*

This mutual respect of Catholic church and Protestant state was reinforced by the Quebec Act of 1774. One year later, when rebellion flared up in the Thirteen Colonies to

*the south, the church rallied at once to the British cause,
and the loyal Bishop Briand issued the following* mandement *or directive to his flock.*

To all the People of this Colony, Greetings and Blessing.
A body of subjects in rebellion against their lawful sovereign, who is also our sovereign, have just started an
invasion of this Province, less in expectation of being able
to maintain it than with a view to dragging you into their
rebellion, or at least of pledging you not to oppose their
wicked plan. The singular kindness and leniency with
which we have been ruled by His Very Gracious Majesty
King George III, since the time when, by the fate of war,
we were made part of his empire; the recent favours that
he has heaped upon us, by giving us back our laws, the free
exercise of our Religion, and by extending to us all the
privileges and advantages of British subjects, will be enough
to excite your gratitude and your zeal to maintain the
interests of the Crown of Great Britain. But even more
pressing motives ought to speak to your hearts at this time.
Your oaths and your religion impose on you a necessary
obligation to defend your country and your king with all
your might. So, dear Canadians, close your ears, and do
not listen to the seditious persons who are trying to make
you unhappy and to stifle those feelings of obedience to
your lawful rulers that training and religion have engraved
on your hearts. Perform with joy everything asked of you
by a benevolent Governor, who has no other objectives but
your interests and your happiness. You are not required to
carry the war into the distant provinces; you are only asked
to strike a blow to repel the enemy, and to stop the invasion
that threatens this Province. The voice of religion and of
your own interests are conjoined here, and assure us of
your zeal to defend our frontiers and our possessions.

Given at Quebec, under our sign, the seal of our arms
and the signature of our Secretary, 22 May 1775.

J. Ol., Bishop of Quebec

From H. Têtu and C. O. Gagnon, *Mandements, lettres pas-
torales et circulaires des Evêques de Québec* (Quebec, 1887),
Vol. II, pp. 264-265.

A TOKEN OF FRIENDSHIP

Except for a handful of merchants and government officials the population of Canada was still exclusively French fifteen years after the Conquest—virtually no English settlers had been attracted to the new colony. The American Revolution, however, brought more than five thousand Loyalists to the province, thereby adding two new ingredients—the English language and Protestantism.

A wide variety of Protestant denominations were represented among the Loyalist refugees, but in Canada they all faced the common problem of lack of church buildings. In frontier areas log chapels soon appeared. In the older and settled regions the practice of sharing Roman Catholic churches (begun by Eli Dawson's service in the Ursuline chapel) continued for several years.

In Montreal the Presbyterians were invited by the Récollets to use their chapel just as the Anglicans had been doing, with the Protestant services being held after the Sunday mass. In time the Presbyterians built their own place of worship, the famous St. Gabriel Street Church, but while guests of the Récollets they showed their appreciation to the fathers with a very practical if unusual token of friendship.

A great deal of interest gathers around the eleven years that Mr. Young spent in connection with the St. Gabriel Street Church. It was under his *régime* that the oft-mentioned display of religious hospitality on the part of the Récollet Fathers took place. Their church, of which we present an engraving, was put at the disposal of the Scotch Presbyterians in 1791, as it had been, for twenty years up to 1789, at the service of the English Church and on the 18th of September, 1791, the Sacrament of the Lord's Supper was administered in it, as has been already stated, according to the practice of the Church of Scotland. The "Society of Presbyterians," as they were then called, continued to occupy the old Récollet Church from the date mentioned until their own edifice in St. Gabriel Street was ready for divine worship. The Fathers politely refused any remuneration for the use of their church, but were induced to accept of a present from the congregation, in acknowledgment of their kindness, consisting of two hogsheads of Spanish wine, containing 60 odd gallons each, and a box of candles,— amounting in all to £ 14 2s. 4d. Mr. Hunter, in his manuscript, closes the narrative with the quaint remark—"they were quite thankful for the same." Again, in 1809, when the present roof was put upon the St. Gabriel Street Church, and the steeple and bell were erected, the Scots' congregation assembled for public worship, for two months or more, in the Récollet Church. This reads wonderful in these days when the lines are so strongly drawn betwixt Protestants and Roman Catholics.

From Robert Campbell, *A History of the Scotch Presbyterian Church, St. Gabriel Street, Montreal* (Montreal: Drysdale Publishers, 1887), Vol. II, p. 59.

A HOLE IN THE ICE

After the American Revolution the British government tried to discourage settlement in the Eastern Townships of Quebec because the area was so close to the United States. By the 1790's, however, settlers were crossing from the American side to join the handful of Loyalists already located in the region. Among the new wave of immigrants were a sizable number of Baptists who proceeded almost at once to form their own "gathered" churches. Beginning in 1793 these churches, which had no resident ministers, were visited occasionally by Baptist missionaries from the neighbouring states. One of these missionaries, Elisha Andrews, answered an invitation in January, 1794, from Caldwell's Manor on the Quebec shore of Lake Champlain. His description of the baptismal service there suggested that the pioneers were truly a hardy breed of men, women, and children!

As I was the only Baptist minister in the region, except Elder Call, and he was an aged man, and ten miles further off, there could be no doubt with respect to the path of duty. A friend of mine volunteered to take me down in his sleigh. We started Monday morning and proceeded to Highgate,

(Vt.); here we put up at the house of a German by the name of Wagoner. In the morning we followed his direction, crossed Missisque Bay and arrived at the Manor in season to appoint a meeting in the evening. We put up with Dr. Cune, a Baptist from Rhode Island. In the morning we crossed over to the west side of the Manor about eight miles, into the neighbourhood where the revival had been the most powerful. Soon after we arrived, the house was filled with people, and I preached to them; and again in the evening. The next day we met at 9 o'clock in the morning, and spent the whole day examining candidates for baptism; we heard and received thirty of all ages from 10 to 50 years. . . . The next day we repaired to the Lake, cut a hole in the ice, and fifteen of those happy and devoted disciples were, in the name of the Father, Son and Holy Ghost, immersed agreeably to the command of the divine Saviour. The baptism of the remaining fifteen was deferred until the next Monday, it being their choice to have it performed in the vicinity where they resided.

From Stuart Ivison and Fred Rosser, *The Baptists in Upper and Lower Canada before 1820* (Toronto: University of Toronto Press, 1956), p. 156.

DIVIDED LOYALTIES

The independent position of the Roman Catholic Church and its happy relationship with the government were endangered by an after-effect of the American Revolution. Britain's new policy of appointing Anglican bishops for the colonies brought to Canada in 1793 the proud and rather difficult Jacob Mountain, first Anglican bishop of Quebec. Mountain was distressed to discover that his Roman Catholic counterpart wielded more authority than any Anglican bishop had ever been allowed by Parliament. Vexed and jealous at his own inferior position, Mountain for years urged his political friends in Quebec and London to impose controls on the Roman Catholic bishop. In 1805 Quebec's attorney general, Jonathan Sewell, proposed to transfer some of the Catholic bishop's power to the Crown by putting the bishop on the government payroll and by making the curés into government appointees. Because the bishop, Denaut, was living near Montreal, Sewell nego-tiated with the coadjutor, Joseph-Octave Plessis, the most outstanding Catholic bishop in Canada's history.

Time after time Plessis managed to stall this plan for turning the Catholic clergy into civil servants, until the War of 1812-14 gave him another opportunity to prove that his church could be both loyal and independent. A grateful British government showered Plessis with honours and abandoned forever all attempts to interfere with the Catholic Church in Canada.

Plessis. I have lately spoken to the Governor respecting the present situation of our Church, and he has referred me to you on the subject.

Attorney General. The Governor has given me permission to explain my own private sentiments on the subject to you what I think you may ask, and I will answer candidly. But before I state what I have to say, let me observe that the object is of the last importance to your Church, and (I admit also) important to the Government. It is highly necessary for you to have the means of protecting your Church, to the Government to have a good understanding with the Ministers of a Church it has acknowledged by the Quebec Act, and at the same time to have them under its control. Let me also remark that the Government having permitted the free exercise of the Roman Catholic Religion ought, I think, to avow its officers, but not, however, at the expense of the King's Rights or of the Established Church. You cannot expect, nor ever obtain, anything that is inconsistent with the rights of the Crown, nor can the Government ever allow to you what it denies to the Church of England.

Plessis. Your position may be correct. The Governor thinks the Bishops should act under the King's Commission and I see no objection to it.

Attorney General. My principle is this, I would not interfere with you in concerns purely-spiritual, but in all that is temporal or mixed, I would subject you to the King's authority. There are difficulties, I know, on both sides; on the one hand, the Crown will never consent to your emancipation from its power, nor will it ever give you more than the rights of the Church of England, which has grown with the Constitution, and whose power, restrained as it is, is highly serviceable to the general interests of the state; on the other hand, your Bishop will be loth to abandon what he conceives to be his right, I mean particularly the nomination to Cures; yet that he must do so, for no such power is vested in the Bishops of England, and if permitted would be highly dangerous.

•   •   •

Plessis. How are Rectors (Curés) appointed in England?

Attorney General. Where the King is patron, and he is of all livings not in the possession of individuals, by title, he presents to the Bishop, who, if there be no legal cause of refusal inducts the Clerk presented. If there be cause, he certifies that cause to the King, and if the King is satisfied he presents another, but if not, a writ issues to the Bishop requiring him to certify his cause of refusal into the King's Courts, who try the merits of the refusal and declare it good or bad according to law; on this footing I would place your Church.

•   •   •

Plessis. Presentation by the Crown agrees with the tenets of the Church of England, but not with ours. It would be against our spiritual duty.

Attorney General. . . . I will tell you also frankly that Curés dependent upon the will of the Bishop, would be little subject to the controul of Government. If this was the case, the situation of the Curé would not be enviable, nor could you expect that the better class of people would educate their sons for the Church. Your Court of the Bishop would be perfectly unnecessary, and the presentation of the Crown an idle ceremony, if the Bishop could afterwards remove when he pleased.

Plessis. The situation of a Curé under such restriction would be better then, than the situation of the Bishops of Canada at present. For myself, I have enough, I am in a cure which gives me all I want, but Bishop Denaud is in poverty, holding a living and acting as a parish priest, in direct contradiction to the Canons.

Attorney General. My mind upon that subject is completely made up. The Government recognizes your religion and making its officers officers of the Crown, should provide for them as for all others. The Bishop should have enough to enable him to live in a splendour suited to his rank, and the coadjutor a salary in proportion.

Plessis. I do not want to see the Bishop in splendour, but I wish to see him above want. I do not wish to see him in the Legislative or Executive Council, but as an ecclesiastic only, entitled to the rank which is due to him in society.

Attorney General. When I said splendour, I qualified the expression, by calling it "a splendour suited to his rank." I mean by that, that his income should be that of a gentleman, and equal to a proper expenditure. There is in fact no such thing as splendour in Canada.

Plessis. We mean the same thing. But there is a great delicacy in this matter. If the Bishop was pensioned and relinquished the right of nominating the Curés, the public would not hesitate to say that he had sold his Church.

Attorney General. To stop the public clamour is a useless attempt. If matters of State were to be staid for fear of popular abuse, Government would be able to do but very little; the governed but seldom approve. In our instance, if the matter is viewed as it ought to be viewed, the world must be satisfied that, instead of relinquishing a right you have in fact never to relinquish, you abandon the shadow and receive the substance; surely, this is sufficient answer to any vulgar declamation against a Bishop who makes terms highly advantageous to his Church and must be satisfactory to himself.

Plessis. I don't know; it is his affair.

Attorney General. There is one idea which I wish to suggest. If you ever mean to fix the officers of your Church upon any footing, this is the moment. The present Lieut. Governor is a gentleman of most liberal principles, he has been long enough in the country to know all that relates to it, is well disposed to serve you, and is on the point of going to England where this matter must be settled.

Plessis. I am well aware of all this. Whatever is to be done must be done now.

Attorney General. If I say what I ought not to say, you will excuse me, but I feel convinced that if you forego this opportunity, it will never return. It is your interest to avail yourself of the present moment, and make the best terms you can.

Plessis. You cannot say anything which can hurt or offend me. I consider this a free conversation on both sides, for effecting a very important object, which, without an unreserved communication, can never be effected.

Attorney General. I will not take up any more of your time at this moment.

Plessis. I am much obliged by the time you have bestowed on me. Something must be done, and tho' we may differ in the detail, I think we shall not in the outline, and if we do differ we must be temperate, and in that case we shall ultimately agree. I am, however, a subordinate officer, I must first write to the Bishop, and when I know his sentiments I will wait upon you.

Attorney General. Do so, but pray keep in mind what I have said, that you never can obtain anything inconsistent with the prerogatives of the Crown, nor at all events any right that a Bishop of the Church of England does not possess.

From *Report, 1892* (Ottawa: Public Archives of Canada), Note C, pp. 23-24, 26-27.

THE CHURCHES IN THE MARITIMES

THE FIRST PROTESTANT ORDINATION

The "foreign Protestants" who settled around Lunenburg, Nova Scotia, beginning about 1750, came from several European countries but were mostly German-speaking. Wanting a Protestant minister who could speak German, and unable to get such a person from "home," a group of Dutch Calvinists prevailed upon two Presbyterian and two Congregationalist ministers to form a presbytery and ordain Bruin Romcas Comingo, a fisherman, upright in character and well versed in the Scriptures but lacking any formal training for the ministry. In the presence of the Nova Scotian governor, Lord William Campbell, and members of his council and of the Church of England, this irregular presbytery performed at Halifax in 1770 the first Protestant ordination to take place in Canada.

A Representation of the distressed State of the Dutch Calvinists of Lunenburgh having been made to us who are here on this Occasion Assembled or Convened together as the Ministers of Gods word, We accordingly took the same into our serious consideration. We have found upon due enquiry . . . (?) a number of the Inhabitants of the aforemention'd place being destitute of One who might break the bread of life amongst them, and perform the other duties of the Ministerial Function, agreable to the Scriptures and the Dictates of their own Consciences; in consequence of which they have made Application to the Ministers of their own Denomination in Philadelphia; the Answer to this Application was that no relief could be expected from that Quarter:

and moreover, that none could from Germany, as the Distance of the place and many other difficulties rendred it in a great Measure impracticable Their last resource then appears to have been the ch(oo)sing (one of their own number) Mr. Bruin Romkess Comingoe, known commonly by the name of Brown.

To the amount of Sixty families have petitioned us to set apart the Said Mr. Brown to the office of the Ministry amongst them. Lest the Vital Religion should be injur'd by Such a procedure, we have Used all that precaution which was possible for us in so important an affair.

An inquiry has been made into his moral Charecter; and we find from Gentlemen of Undoubted Veracity that it stands fair and Unblemished.

We have moreover proceeded to enquire into his qualifications for so Sacred an Employment; viz., his knowledge of Speculative religion and practical, his ability in rightly dividing the Word; the Articles of his faith, etc.—And we can Assure the Audience (or others) that he has given us ample Satisfaction in all these particulars; and that if we are Judges of these Matters, his knowledge of the Scriptures makes that commonly received Maxim amongst the Schools true concerning him, Bonus Textuarius est bonus Theologus: and consequently cannot be stigmatiz'd with the name of a Novice.

We have been aware of some Objections which have been made against the Candidate's Admission into this Sacred Office, viz.

1. That he has not had a Liberal Education and is Unacquainted with the Languages. To this we reply that we only follow the Example of the best reformed Churches.

The Assembly of Scotland in the year 1708 (the records of which we have had before us) appointed the Presbytery of Skey to ordain one in the Parish of St. Kilda on the Account of his particular Gifts, who had not a Liberal Education, or even the knowledge of the Latin tongue: And we find that both in former and later periods in Cases of necessity, (wh appears to be the State of Lunenburg) when the sd Church was not harrased with Divisions have practised accordingly.

We have moreover Instances on this Continent of persons who were not endowed with a Liberal Education who have been regularly admitted into holy Orders, and have in the judgment of Charity been Instrumental in turning many unto righteousness.

2. That this is only Supporting a faction—We have also enquir'd into this particular, and on due examination find this Charge groundless. They have in their Native Land been brought up in the Calvinistic Presbyterian Religion; and do still, as we are well informed continue in the same Sentiments.

As the Legislature then of this Colony has wisely enacted that such shall have free Liberty of Conscience; shall have liberty to Erect and build Meeting houses, or places of Worship, and Serve God in that manner which appears to them congruous to his Will. We, from this and the foregoing considerations together with the Information we have had that some of them who always have been Useful Inhabitants would leave the Province Unless this matter could be accomplished, have concluded to Set the Candidate apart to the office of the holy Ministry.

1. Having therefore Judged Mr. Brown qualified to be Pastor and Minister of the Congregation at Lunenburg who have petitioned us to set him apart to that office, we do hereby give notice to all present, That if they have any thing to Object why he should not be admitted Pastor of the aforesaid Congregation, that they now make a Declaration of the Same. If no Objection is offer'd we shall proceed without further delay.

2. Mr. Kaulback and Mr. Supley, do you, as Commissioners from the Congregation of Calvenists at Lunenburg, renew in their behalf, your Call to Mr. Brown?

Do you Mr. Brown Accept of the Said Call and Invitation to be their Pastor?

Ques. 1. Do you believe the Scriptures of the Old and New Testament and the Truths therein contained to be the Word of God?

2. Do you own, and will you adhere to the Confession of faith which you have made to us, The Heidelburgh and Assemblies Catchisms, and the Doctrines therein contained

as being founded on and consonant unto the holy Scriptures?

3. Will you by the Grace of God be faithful and Zealous in maintaining the truths of the Gospel, the Unity of the Church and peace thereof against all opposition you may meet with?

4. Do you likewise own and will you adhere to the Worship, Discipline and Government of the Protestant reformed Presbyterian Churches, as being founded on and agreable to the Scriptures?

5. Have you been led in your designing the Work of the Ministry by a Single and Sincere Love to God, and aim at his glory, and not by filthy Lucre and the motives of worldly gain?

6. Do you engage to be diligent and assiduous in praying, reading, meditating, preaching, administring the Sacraments, Catechising, Exercising Discipline, and in performing all other Ministerial Duties toward the people committed to your Charge?

7. Will you humbly and willingly Submit your Self to our Admonitions and the Discipline of the aforementioned reformed Churches?

Will you take care that you and your family walk Unblameably; by Examples to the flock, and adorn the profession of the Gospel by your Conversation?

8. Do you own and promise Allegiance to his Majesty King George the third in all things Civil and lawful?

We do hereby certify that the Revd Mr. Bruin Romkes Comingoe (alias Brown) after due Examination, and trial was this day Set apart by prayer and the Imposition of hands to the office of the holy Ministry over the Dutch Calvinistic Presbyterian Congregation of Lunenburg, by Us.

John Seccombe
Ja: Lyon
Benajah Phelps
James Murdoch

Halifax, July 3, 1770.

From *Bulletin, 1958* (Toronto: The United Church of Canada), pp. 23-25.

A GATHERED CHURCH

Encouraged by the government's promise of religious liberty New Englanders flocked to the new colony of Nova Scotia in the fifteen years before the American Revolution. Small settlements sprang up almost overnight along the coastline and especially along the shores of the Bay of Fundy. In many cases the settlers came together in a body from some New England town to a site in Nova Scotia where they at once established all the institutions they had known in their former home, including a Congregational or Independent church.

Congregationalism began in the England of Queen Elizabeth I. Each church was a "gathered" group, a self-starting body of believers who came together and professed their common faith by signing a Covenant. Every church formed this way was governed entirely by its own covenant and was independent of all other churches. The following contemporary account tells how the church at Yarmouth began through the initiative of local settlers.

Yarmouth in Nova Scotia Wednesday, August 12th, 1767. Met together at the house of Mr. Richd. Rose, a considerable number of persons, who had been members of churches in full Communion and had owned the Covenant where they had formerly lived, who have lately settled in this Town; and spent most of the Day in prayer with Fasting and in conference together, relating to their entering into the Church State. Their religious exercises and conferences were carried on with solemnity and regularity. And they were generally agreed to proceed into Chh. State as soon as could be conveniently. But their having no written credentials (tho' they had verbal ones), nor any Dismission from nor consent of the church they belonged to, for their Purpose was a Difficulty; which they would gladly have removed; but sending this summer and Fall to the many distant Towns in Massachusetts and Connecticut where they had lived was impracticable—and they were very loath to put off so good a work to another year if it might be done this, without too great impropriety—Whereupon, having considered of the matter, they concluded that their brethren in New England would be glad at their making all convenient Haste, rather than defer their Purpose for the Interests of Religion among them until they had opportunity to send. Whereupon, they appointed another meeting on Wednesday, the 19 instant, for conferring further about the Matter, on which Day they had a sermon preached suitable to the occasion—and apprehending themselves called of God, they concluded to proceed into a Church State, and appointed Wednesday the second of September following to be the date for the Purpose.

Accordingly, on the Lord's Day 23 of August publick notice was given of ye intended Proceeding into a Church State, the names of the Persons who had agreed thus to unite were read; and their Covenant was read; and the manner of their Proceeding was declared—and it was signified in the Assembly that if any had reasonable objections to make against either of the Persons, or any part of the Proceedings they might have opportunity and were desired to signifie it before the Day appointed for gathering the Church:

The same publick Notice was given in the assembly at Jebogue on a publick Lecture the Wednesday following the Sabbath.

On Wednesday the second of September 1767 the Brethren met in the forenoon and there having been no objection made against any part of their Proceeding, nor any Person, but was entirely removed; The Brethren signed their Covenant.

And at eleven o'clock all the People met, a sermon upon the Occasion was preached, the Brethren were solemnly charged and exhorted, the Church Covenant was read the Brethren all standing, and holding up the Hand while it was read—the Exercises of the Day were concluded, as they were begun, with solemn Prayer and Praise. "And all the People rejoiced and gave Praise unto God."

J. M. Lawson, *Yarmouth Past and Present* (Yarmouth, 1902), pp. 516-517.

ALLINE OF THE NEW LIGHTS

The North American religious revival of the eighteenth century known as "the Great Awakening" began in the 1730's among the English colonies along the Atlantic coast with the preaching of Jonathan Edwards in Massachusetts. A generation later the movement got a new impetus from George Whitefield who had been associated with John Wesley in England. The Great Awakening was not limited to any particular denomination; in fact the urge to holier living tended to break up old established congregations. The movement had its greatest and its most disruptive impact in the New England colonies where some two hundred Congregational or Independent churches broke up over the issue of which members were more godly than their neighbours.

Because Nova Scotia was originally settled by New Englanders the Great Awakening inevitably was carried into that colony too. The messenger of the "New Light" was Henry Alline, a mystical figure who became the "scourge of the churches." "Newlightism" combined with political pressures during the American Revolution to smash the early Congregational churches of Nova Scotia and virtually to obliterate Congregationalism in that colony for half a century.

Down in Nova Scotia, in the year 1776, word was passed among many of the settlements of a young man who had become a sensation as a preacher. This young man, Henry Alline, had been a leader in gaiety and the pursuit of worldly pleasures, but of a sudden, like Saul of Tarsus, he had been converted. His ambitions swung round in an opposite direction and he determined to give his entire life to the service of Christ. His thoughts turned to the ministry and as he had had no theological education he decided to go to New England to study. He set out from home and reached Cornwallis, where he was to board a schooner, only to learn that trouble had developed and that it would not sail till the next spring. Just then his parents were stricken with smallpox. This and other circumstances led him to conclude that God was closing the door to the classroom and that he must depend on the schooling of experience and especially on spiritual preparation for the preaching of the Gospel.

It should be explained that at that time, in New England, there were two contending groups of Church leaders, called Old Lights and New Lights. This was the result of great religious revivals which had been in progress for a number of years. Many felt that there was not enough intellect in the revival method, while others contended that Christian experience and zeal were of vastly more importance than scholarship. The former were called Old Lights, and the latter New Lights. Henry Alline, who had been born in Rhode Island, carried with him the influence of the New Lights when, as a boy, he had come with his family to live in Nova Scotia.

The year after his conversion found him preaching like a veteran. In that year he organized at Newport the first New Light Congregational Church in Nova Scotia. His fame spread rapidly. His whole heart was in his message and his one ambition was to bring men into a living contact with Jesus Christ. He was invited to preach in Cornwallis and made two or three visits to that place, where he was finally ordained as pastor of the New Light Church. The ordination ceremony took place in a barn.

But the young preacher did not confine his work to the church of which he was pastor. His soul aflame with the love of God, he went on evangelistic tours that had wonderful results. And no one better than Henry Alline himself knew that these results came not from his own abilities. He says, "one day in my meditation, I had such a discovery of Christ's having everything I needed, and that it was all mine, that I saw I needed nothing to qualify me but Christ, and that if I had all the wisdom that could be obtained by mortals without having the spirit of Christ with me, I should never have success in preaching; but if Christ went with me, I should have all in all."

None of his journeys was exactly a triumphal procession. Travel was difficult and tiring. He had to make his way on foot or on horseback over bad roads and in all weathers.

One day, for example, after riding thirty miles in a heavy rain, he was so exhausted that he could scarcely walk, but had to begin to preach almost at once. This was not an unusual experience. But neither fatigue nor the severe opposition which he met in many quarters could discourage him. From place to place he went, with no selfish thought of comfort or of fame, consumed with the one ambition of bringing the saving love of God into the life of men.

And hearts that were worn and weary with sin gave welcome to the message. Men and women whose religion was outward and formal found it replaced by something that was real and vital—a living, dynamic faith. Crowds came to his meetings and sometimes a number of people would ride with him along the road or through the woods, holding a service as they went, with prayers and singing. Once as he was leaving a place where he had preached for four or five days, quite a number of people accompanied him for several miles. Their hungry hearts were not yet satisfied. So the young evangelist halted his journey and stayed with them all night and preached to them the next morning, then bade them farewell. He tells again of being up many times till three o'clock in the morning talking with people over their spiritual problems and of one occasion when three young men came over forty miles to hear his message.

The sort of influence that he had on his journeys through all that region is well illustrated in the case of Liverpool, on the south coast. There had been a church there, but for some time it had been without a pastor, its light burned low and its power was almost gone. When Alline arrived he found "a kind people, but in midnight darkness and vastly given to frolicking, rioting and all manner of levity." But hearts opened to his message. His diary says that "the hearers were greatly taken hold of, and it seems they could not go away; some followed me to my lodgings and stayed till midnight." He reorganized the church in Liverpool, and it has had a continuous history down to this day.

Henry Alline was still a young man, thirty-six years of age, when he died. He had been preaching only eight years. But he had organized at least a dozen congregations, he had brought a spiritual glow into the life of a large section of Nova Scotia and in many places the fires that he lighted are burning yet, though a century and a half have passed since then. Down through all those years there come to us now as a benediction and a challenge the words that before his death he spoke to the minister with whom he was staying, "Tell my friends that the blessed Gospel which I have preached to them is *true*. Oh, Sir, preach that blessed Gospel."

From J. L. Murray, *Nation Builders* (Toronto: The United Church of Canada, 1925), pp. 26-29.

PREACHING IN TWO LANGUAGES

James MacGregor arrived in Nova Scotia in 1786, fresh from his ordination, in response to a plea from the Highland settlers of Pictou for a minister with the "twa tongues." Shocked by the immorality and poverty he saw, MacGregor would have returned at once to Scotland except that "I had not the money to pay my passage home." Instead he remained in Nova Scotia for the rest of his life, preaching, ministering, founding churches and travelling often under the most arduous conditions. A man of extraordinary stamina and mental acuteness, MacGregor left a vivid account of the social habits, economic conditions and religious practices of Nova Scotia in his day.

In his first fifteen months at Pictou James MacGregor did not receive one shilling of salary from his congregation, but as conditions improved in later years he was able to visit more Scots settlements in Nova Scotia, and even to journey as far as Cape Breton and Prince Edward Island. At this death in 1830 his many friends erected a tombstone to his memory. Its inscription reads in part: "When the early settlers of Pictou could afford to a minister of the Gospel little else than a participation of their hardships, he cast in his lot with the destitute, became to them a pattern of patient endurance, and cheered them with the tidings of salvation." In the following reminiscences James MacGregor has described some of the problems, both human

and physical, that he encountered during forty-four years of
service in Nova Scotia.

During summer the session had several conversations about
dispensing the sacrament of the Supper, but I got it delayed
for this year. I had dispensed the ordinance of baptism
often, sometimes indeed with fear and trembling, but I
could not prevail upon myself to dispense the Lord's Supper;
partly because I believed that not many of the people were
prepared, but chiefly because I thought it too heavy a
burden first to converse with the candidates one by one,
and then to go through all the customary services in both
languages; so it was put off.

Preaching in two languages, and in two places so far distant from one another, created me many difficulties, for
everything I wished the whole people to know needed to be
told them four different times, viz., in the two languages
and the two places. Though I preached two sermons every
Sabbath, yet the people heard but one sermon in two weeks,
except those who understood both languages. Even this
circumstance was sometimes productive of trouble; for
some who were backward to support the gospel, insisted
that they who understood both languages should pay a
double share of the stipend. Sometimes the Highlanders
complained that I did not give them their due of the public
services, but the rest complained that they got too much;
and it was impossible to carry always with such an even
hand as to please both parties. Sometimes they contended
for precedence. The Gaelic was most prevalent on the East
River, and the English on the West River and Harbour.
This decided that at the former public worship should begin
in the Gaelic, and in the English at the latter. At other
meetings, however, little bickerings continued for some time
but they learned to yield to one another, as they saw that no
partiality was intended. At examinations and marriages I
made it a rule to speak to those who knew both languages in
that which they preferred. In one instance only of marriage
had I to speak in both languages, telling the man his duties
and engagements in English, and the woman hers in Gaelic.
How they managed to court or to converse afterwards I

know not; but they declared to me, and the neighbours confirmed it, that they could hardly speak a single word of one another's language.

•   •   •

1791. This winter I had to break in upon my plan of winter visitation and examination, by a few missionary excursions. To have given a little supply of sermon to Onslow and Stewiacke in summer would have been a sacrifice quite out of the power of the congregation, as one Sabbath in summer was worth two, or even three, in winter. I therefore determined, with the consent of the session, to give each of them two or three Sabbaths in winter. This however, was no easy task when the snow was two or three feet deep. Here I had to travel forty miles on snow shoes, a journey almost three times as long as any which I had hitherto performed in that way. Travelling on snow shoes is eligible only when the snow is neither very soft nor very hard; for when it is very hard the snow shoes are apt to slide, and when it is very soft they sink deep, and become wet, and so heavy as to clog the feet greatly. It was soft then, and though I had three or four men before me making the road more solid, yet I was quite faint by the time we had travelled eleven miles. One of the company had with him a little rum and bread and cheese, of which we all partook, and by which I was recruited more than by any meal of victuals which I remember. But I became faint again before I reached a house, which was four miles distant. Then, having dined and rested, we travelled on to Truro, ten miles, where I had a sound sleep.

From George Patterson, *Memoir of the Rev. James MacGregor, D.D.* (Philadelphia, 1859), pp. 135-136, 246.

CHARLES INGLIS, LOYALIST

The American Revolution shocked the conscience of Great Britain. What caused this catastrophe? The answers offered by contemporaries may not satisfy today's historians, but those answers were nevertheless the foundation for imperial policies after the Revolution when politicians tried to ensure that the remaining colonies would never revolt. One of those answers blamed the Revolution on the lack of a proper state church establishment in the Thirteen Colonies —if only the mother country had supported the Church of England, if only there had been colonial bishops, republicanism would never have got a foothold in America. Such was the reasoning behind the appointment of the Loyalist, Charles Inglis, as bishop of Nova Scotia, the first colonial bishop in the history of the Empire.

Charles Inglis was born in America, the product of several generations of Anglo-Irish clergy. Inglis had been influenced by the Great Awakening before he became rector of Trinity Church in New York. That city was a bastion of loyalty during the Revolution, and Inglis was outspoken, even rash, in his defiance of the rebels even after they occupied the city in 1776. In his own words he reported his encounter with George Washington and the revolutionaries, before they burned his church during their retreat. The determination shown by Charles Inglis, as tory rector, was later balanced by the diplomacy of Charles Inglis, loyalist bishop.

About the Middle of April, Mr. Washington, Commander in Chief of the Rebel Forces, came to Town with a large Reinforcement. Animated by his Presence, & I suppose, encouraged by him, the Rebel Committees very much harrassed the loyal Inhabitants here & on Long Island. They were sumoned before those Committees, & upon refusing to give up their Arms, & take Oaths that were tendered, they were imprisoned, or sent into Banishment. An Army was sent to Long Island to disarm the Inhabitants, who were distinguished for their Loyalty, many had their Property destroyed, & more were carried off Prisoners. It should be observed that Members of the Church of England were the *only* Sufferers on this Occasion. The Members of the Dutch Church are very numerous there, & many of them joined in opposing the Rebellion; yet no Notice was taken of them, nor the least Injury done to them. About this Time, Mr. Bloomer administered the Sacrament at Newtown, where he had but 4 or 5 Male Communicants; the Rest being driven off, or carried away Prisoners. At this present Time there are many hundreds from this City & Province Prisoners in New England; & among these the Mayor of New York, several Judges & Members of his Majesty's Council, with other respectable Inhabitants.

Soon after Washington's Arrival, he attended our Church; but on the Sunday Morning, before Divine Service began, one of the Rebel Generals called at the Rector's House (supposing the latter was in Town), & not finding him, left Word that he "came to inform the Rector that General Washington would be at Church, & would be glad if the violent Prayers for the King & Royal Family were omitted." This Message was brought to me, & as You may suppose, I paid no Regard to it. On seeing that General not long after, I remonstrated against the Unreasonableness of his Request, which he must know the Clergy could not comply with; & told him further—"That it was in his Power to shut up our Churches; but by no means in his Power to make the Clergy depart from their Duty." This Declaration drew from him an awkward Apology for his Conduct, which I believe was not authorised by Washington. Such Incidents would not be worth mentioning unless to give those who are at a Distance a better idea of the Spirit of the Times.

May 17 was appointed by the Congress as a Day of public Fasting, Prayer & Humiliation throughout the Continent. At the Unanimous Request of the Members of our Church, who were then in Town, I consented to preach that Day, & indeed our Situation made it highly prudent; tho a Submission so far to an Authority that was usurped, was exceedingly grating & disagreeable. In giving Notice the preceding Sunday, I only mentioned that there would be a Sermon the ensuing Friday, which was the 17th; without saying any Thing of the Reason, or by what Authority. It was exceedingly difficult for a loyal Clergyman to preach on such an Occasion, & not incur Danger, on the one Hand, or not depart from his Duty on the other. I endeavoured to avoid both—making Peace & Repentance my Subject, & explicitly disclaimed having any Thing to do with Politics. This Sermon, in the Composition of which I took some

Pains, I intend to publish for various Reasons, should I be able to recover it from the Place, where it now is, with all my Books & Papers, in the Country. The several Churches in this Province, (except two, where the Clergymen thought they might without Danger, omit Service) & so far as I can learn, thro all thirteen united Colonies, as they are called, were opened on this Occasion.

Matters became now critical here, in the highest Degree. The Rebel Army amounted to near 30,000—all their Cannon & military Stores were drawn hither, & they boasted that the Place was impregnable. The Mortifications & Alarms which the Clergy met with, were innumerable. I have frequently heard myself called *a Tory & Traitor to my Country*, as I passed the Streets, & Epithets joined to each which Decency forbids me to set down. Violent threats were thrown out against us, in Case the King were any longer prayed for. One Sunday when I was Officiating, & had proceeded some Length in the Service, a Company of about one hundred armed Rebels marched into the Church, with Drums beating, & Fifes playing—their Guns loaded & Bayonets fixed, as if going to Battle. The Congregation was thrown into the utmost Terror, & several Women fainted, expecting a Massacre was intended. I took no Notice of this, & went on with the Service; only exerted my Voice, which was in some Measure drowned by the Noise & Tumult. The Rebels stood thus in the Aile for near fifteen Minutes; till being asked into Pews by the Sexton, they complied. Still however the People expected that when the Collects for the King & Royal Family were read, I should be fired at, as Menaces to that Purpose had been frequently flung out—the Matter however passed over without any Accident. Nothing of this Kind happened before or since, which made it more remarkable. I was afterwards assured that something hostile & violent was intended; but He that "stills the Raging of the Sea & Madness of the People," overruled their Purpose, whatever it was.

From J. W. Lydekker, *The Life and Letters of Charles Inglis* (London: The Society for Promoting Christian Knowledge, 1936), pp. 162-165.

ACADIE VIVANTE

Fear that the French residents of Nova Scotia might form a "fifth column" was the main reason for the forcible expulsion of more than five thousand Acadians from their homes during the Seven Years' War. After the return of peace in 1763 many Acadians found their way back to the Maritimes where they settled mainly on Prince Edward Island and in New Brunswick. Despite their tragic experience the Acadians bore no grudges and were soon accepted by the government as loyal and peaceable citizens. But the greatest problem confronting them was the lack of religious services. The bishop of Quebec had few missionaries to spare for this remote area, yet a handful of dedicated priests came to the Acadians and preserved both the faith and the culture of these distinct people. Among the priests who made possible the Acadian survival was the famous Abbé Sigogne who will always be remembered with gratitude as the first leader towards the revival of Acadian nationalism in the Maritimes.

Poor and isolated, the Acadians were thrown almost entirely on their own resources. Even with the French of the St. Lawrence Valley the Acadians had few contacts and got little help.

Affairs took a decided turn for the better with the arrival in 1799 of Jean-Mandé Sigogne, an exile from revolutionary France. Before coming to Nova Scotia Sigogne had lived for a time in England, where he had learned to admire English public institutions. This made him an admirable selection for the purpose of reconciling the Acadians to British rule. A fellow feeling of sympathy drew him to the returning exiles who had settled along St. Mary's Bay. Here he met a challenge of the first magnitude in the form of a seriously deteriorating social and religious situation. His first concern was to restore the spiritual life of the people, but he also applied himself vigorously to a revival of civic virtues by prescribing a code of communal conduct which he enforced with vigorous precision. He also gave leadership in the economic development of the community by persuading the inhabitants to combine agricultural pursuits with fishing and lumbering. Not the least of his contributions to the future welfare of the Acadians was his insistence that they should learn to speak English, so that they might be able to play an honourable part in the social and political development of the province. In furtherance of this object he himself began a school in his rectory at Church Point. It was this priest's pleasure before his death to see one of his pupils take a seat in the legislative assembly at Halifax.

On the site of this first Acadian school on St. Mary's Bay there now stands Ste. Anne's College, an institution which has trained a notable succession of Acadian priests, who in the great tradition of Abbé Sigogne have spread the gospel of *Acadie vivante* throughout the Maritime Provinces and even beyond.

From H. H. Walsh, *The Christian Church in Canada* (Toronto: The Ryerson Press, 1956), p. 92.

BISHOP PLESSIS VISITS HIS ISLANDS

During his important episcopate the remarkable Bishop Plessis made two tours of the Maritime colonies that formed part of his vast diocese. His first visitation in 1812 had barely started when the war with the United States began. Despite warnings that he would be in danger from American privateers cruising the Atlantic coast, the bishop insisted on fulfilling his mission to his numerous flock.

Since the return of the Acadians many Scotch Catholics had arrived in the region and had settled in large numbers around Antigonish and on Prince Edward and Cape Breton Islands. Over half the population of the two islands was now Roman Catholic. Coming from the sophisticated surroundings of Quebec City, with its impressive church buildings and formal religious services, Bishop Plessis was shocked by the poverty and casualness of his churches in the Maritimes. He was also taken aback by the deeply emotional piety shown by the Scotch Catholics whose behaviour during the mass must have reminded him of the fervour to be seen at Methodist services.

People in Canada have little idea of the extreme poverty of the Acadian chapels of St. John's [Prince Edward] Island, and still less of the Scottish churches wherever they are found. Only a priest brought up in Scotland would ever think of celebrating the Sacred Mysteries with the trash that is found therein. So the Bishop took care to bring his Mass-kit with him, and he was glad he took this precaution.

In one chapel there are neither altar breads nor the means for making any; in another no missal. Further on, there is a chalice with a cup of gold-plated copper, and in another place one entirely of tin. In most of the chapels there are neither cruets, nor albs, nor chalices, nor altar cloths, nor credence tables, nor surplices, nor ciboria, nor holy-water stoups, nor baptismal water. In the whole of St. John's Island, and in all the Scottish missions of Cape Breton and Nova Scotia, the people do not know what is meant by a censer or a monstrance, for such things have not been seen within the memory of man. Happy then is anyone visiting these missions who has taken care to provide himself with these articles, for there are many calls for them.

A Scottish priest, wearing lay attire, places around his neck a stole, which is often nothing more than a ribbon, and has been in use for 20 years. With this he preaches, hears confessions, and administers all the sacraments. When he has to carry Holy Viaticum to a sick person, he puts into one pocket the pyx containing the Blessed Sacrament and into the other his wrinkled stole, and thereupon, in lay attire, he sets out to visit his patient, shaking hands with some people, chatting with others, and sometimes stopping overnight on the way, without giving anyone a hint of the precious treasure he is carrying.

If the sick person lives very far away, the priest brings with him what he calls his chapel, a kit which often enough is poorly equipped. He sets it up near the bed of the sick person and there celebrates Mass and gives Communion. If there are children to be baptized, he administers the sacrament in whatever house he happens to be, since he always carries the holy oils and blesses for each occasion ordinary water which is not baptismal water.

This is one of the effects of the persecution of the poor Catholics in Scotland. Their pastors were obliged to administer the sacraments and preach the word of God to them in secret, and, fearing that they might be betrayed to the secular tribunals and condemned to death if they were discovered, they found it necessary to suppress all the exterior forms of worship which were not strictly essential and doubtlessly they were authorized to act in this way.

When the persecutions ended, they continued by force of habit to fulfill their functions with the same lack of ceremony. When they came to a strange land, they brought their customs with them; and it is almost impossible to make them understand that, in a diocese where entire freedom of worship prevails, the respect due to religion requires of them something more in the way of exterior propriety. Singing is as rare in their churches as are ceremonies and vestments. And yet, wonderful to relate, the faith of the people who are thus served is so strong that it surpasses all imagination. Examples of it will be found later in this diary. . . .

Before leaving St. Andrew's [P.E.I.], he thought it his duty to admonish the Scottish people on their lack of respect of the church, in that, before and after Mass, they were in the habit of talking freely, as if they were in a profane place. They also allowed their dogs to enter the church and run around, as if they were in their masters' houses, without anyone checking them; all of which, according to our way of doing things, is extraordinarily indecorous.

But his greatest cause for complaint was the immodesty of the women, who came to the Sacraments with their throats exposed to a degree that should not allow them even to enter the church. While it is impossible to reconcile this mode of dress with the practice of good morals, it can be attributed only to their simplicity, which, if it can be excused in the girls, is nevertheless dangerous for the boys. When the pastor spoke of it they all hastened to cover themselves. It remains to be seen how long they will remember the reprimand occasioned by their want of order.

Apart from this, the good Scottish people seem sincere in their religion, strongly attached to their pastors, and as demonstrative in their piety as are the Irish. During Mass you hear them sighing, and at the Elevation they burst forth into sobs. Many of them keep joining and separating their hands while they pray, and their arms are in continual motion during the Holy Sacrifice. Others strike their breast with great force. Still others remain prostrate, with their face to the floor all through the Mass. When they come to Communion, both men and women drag themselves forward on their knees, and, in their holy ardour, they would even mount the steps of the altar if they were not prevented.

From A. A. Johnston, *A History of the Catholic Church in Eastern Nova Scotia* (Antigonish: St. Francis Xavier University Press, 1960), Vol. I, pp. 230-233.

THE CHURCH ON THE FRONTIER

A PECULIAR CLERGYMAN

The challenge of serving Christ's churches in Canada has attracted many men of outstanding ability, but the churches have also had a fair share of "characters" among their clergy. One of the more famous eccentrics was John Langhorn, the pioneer Anglican missionary at the Bay of Quinte. Langhorn's manners were so formal and his dress so unusual that even his fellow missionaries wondered if he was the right sort of person for the informal and democratic life of a frontier community. Even during his lifetime semi-legendary stories about Langhorn's devoted service and his peculiarities circulated among the scattered settlers, so that now it is difficult to separate fact from fiction about this remarkable man who served the Anglicans of the Bay of Quinte for more than a quarter-century.

REV. MR. LANGHORN

According to the statement made to us by the late Bishop Strachan, Mr. Langhorn was sent to Canada as a missionary by a Society in London, called "The Bees," or some such name. He was a Welshman by birth, possessed of but little education or talent, yet a truthful, zealous, and useful man. Odd in his manner, he nevertheless worked faithfully among the settlers from Kingston to Hay Bay. Upon arriving he took up his abode in Ernesttown, living at Hoyts, the present site of Bath. Here he was instrumental in having, before long time, erected an English Church. Soon after coming he visited Adolphustown, and preached at Mr.

96

Hagerman's, where Mr. Stuart had previously occasionally held service. Steps were at once taken to build a church also at Adolphustown, and Mr. Langhorn came to hold service regularly every second Sabbath. Mr. Langhorn was a diligent pastor in his rounds among his flock, over an extensive tract with great regularity and once in a great while he went as far as the Carrying Place, where it is said he preached the first of all the pioneer ministers. He likewise occasionally visited Prince Edward, and preached at Smith's Bay, and at Congers, Picton Bay. He was very careful to have all the children christened before they were eight days old, and never failed to question the larger in the catechism. Marriage he would never perform but in the church, and always before eleven in the morning. If the parties to be joined failed to reach the church by the appointed time, he would leave; and would refuse to marry them, no matter how far they had come, generally on foot, or by canoe. Sometimes they were from the remote townships, yet were sent away unmarried. After performing the marriage ceremony, he would insist on receiving, it is said, three coppers for his clerk. For himself he would take nothing, unless it was to present it to the bride immediately. Seemingly he did not care for money; and he would go in all kinds of weather when wanted to officiate, or administer to the wants of the sick. One person tells us that he remembers his coming to his father's in winter, and that his feet were frozen. No wonder, as Mr. Langhorn never wore stockings nor gloves in the coldest weather. But his shoe buckles were broad and bright; and a broad rimmed hat turned up at the sides covered his head. Upon his back he generally carried in a bag some books for reading. We have referred to his peculiarities; many extraordinary eccentricities are related of him, both as a man and clergyman. He was very fond of the water, both in summer and winter. "In summer," (Playter says) "he would, at times swim from a cove on the main shore to a cove in the opposite island, three miles apart, and in winter, he would cut a hole in the ice, and another at some distance, and would dive down at one hole, and come up the other. He had some eccentricities, but he seemed to be a good and charitable man."

Mr. Langhorn, when the war of 1812 commenced, acquired the belief, it is said, that Canada would be conquered by the United States, and so determined to escape. The following somewhat singular "Notice" appeared in the Kingston *Gazette*:—"Notice—To all whom it may concern,—That the Rev. J. Langhorn, of Ernesttown, intends returning to Europe this summer, if he can find a convenient opportunity; and all who have any objections to make, are requested to acquaint him with them, and they will much oblige their humble servant,—J. Langhorn,—Ernesttown, March, 1813."

From W. Canniff, *The Settlement of Upper Canada* (Toronto, 1869), pp. 268-269.

TRIALS OF A CIRCUIT RIDER

The Methodist system of sending preachers out "on circuit" was ideally suited to the frontier conditions of the isolated settlers. With his meagre worldly possessions packed in his saddlebags the circuit rider threaded the lonely forest paths that linked the various knots of settlement, and wherever an audience could be gathered he preached and prayed in a humble log home or barn, or even from a tree stump. Usually self-educated, the circuit rider spoke of damnation and salvation in homey terms that his unschooled hearers could readily understand. To people who often had not heard the Word of God for years the circuit rider brought a message of hope to fill the deep longings of their hearts. By contrast the "parish-minded" churches waited for the faithful to come to the church—only slowly did they too take up the circuit or mission system as the only way of meeting the challenge of distance and separation on the frontier. It is small wonder then that in the earliest period of settlement the Methodists attracted the largest following, or that so many Methodist attitudes—on drinking, gambling, dancing, politics, etc.—became so deeply imbedded in the Canadian way of life.

MY FIRST CIRCUIT.—I had purchased the best young horse I could find in the township, got my saddle-bags, completed my travelling outfit, and was ready for my appointment. I had received no intimation from anyone to what circuit I would probably be sent; nor had I the slightest anxiety on the subject. Still, I had an impression that I would go to the Smith's Creek Circuit. And, sure enough, that was my place. When the Bishop had finished reading the appointments, the Presiding Elder came to me, on the Conference floor, and said, "You are appointed to the Smith's Creek Circuit." I thank you, said I; just where I expected to go. On the morning of September, the 7th, in company with a pleasant young preacher by the name of Griffis, I mounted my beautiful steed, with saddle-bags and valise well filled, and started on my mission as a TRAVELLING PREACHER.

● ● ●

Thursday, the 9th, I PREACHED MY FIRST SERMON in our Church at Cramahe, now called Colborne, from 1 Peter 4: 18. I did not venture into the pulpit, but spoke from the chancel. I had tolerable liberty, but was not greatly encouraged. On Sunday, preached at Haldimand, Four Corners, from "What will this babbler say?" I scarcely knew myself what he would say, but he tried to preach Jesus and the resurrection. In the evening, at the school-house, at what is now called Grafton, from Romans 10: 13. Had good liberty, and was comforted.

Sunday, 19th. At Hawkins' school-house, in Hope, from Matthew 11: 25; and in Cobourg, in the evening, from Romans 5: 2. Cobourg is the name of a small village of some 100 inhabitants. The Church of England has a young clergyman here by the name of McCaulay. He has a small Church, the only one in the village, while we preach in a school-house. There are two small stores here, several mechanics, and plenty of taverns. The court-house and its surroundings form a small villa, more than a mile distant. We have a good Church two miles north of the village, with a small log cabin near it, which they call the parsonage. Here my colleague is to live, and this is really the head of the circuit. The Church is respectable; but oh, the parsonage!

● ● ●

Monday, Sept. 27th, start for the bush, a distance of twenty-miles, over rough roads, with plenty of corduroy bridges. Stop at De Ells', and preach in a house just erected both for a church and a school-house. It had no windows, doors, nor floor, and yet we had plenty of light coming in through the doorway, and between the logs with which it was built. Our position was as novel as it was awkward. The people sat upon the sleepers, with their feet dangling below, while I took another sleeper for my pulpit. It being my birthday, I took a text in accordance with my feelings,— "The world passeth away, and the lust thereof, but he that doeth the will of God abideth forever." Much of my time has run to waste. It pains me to reflect upon the little good I have done. May I be of some service in the future, and that quickly, for

> "Our life is a dream; our time as a stream
>   Glides swiftly away,
> And the fugitive moment refuses to stay."

On the 28th September I started for the township of Smith, passing through where the town of Peterboro' now stands; but there was only one house there then, and that one down on the river's bank, quite out of my sight. My path was a winding Indian trail, where no wheel carriage had ever passed. I was obliged to jump my horse over logs, ride him through deep mud-holes and bridgeless streams, guided sometimes by marked trees. When I got a short distance beyond Peterboro', I entered a clearing with two or three log cabins in view. In one of these lived a godly old Yorkshire woman, who received me joyfully. Her house was covered with hollow logs, halved, and so arranged as to shelter its inmates from the rain and snow. The room was about fifteen by twenty feet in size, and it served for our kitchen, bed-room, parlour, dining-room, and church. Here I preached to a congregation of eight souls, and was happy. O how these people in the bush value the Gospel, and love the messengers who deliver it to them.

●   ●   ●

While riding back towards the front, over rough roads and through gloomy forests, I dismounted to relieve my horse a little and stretch my own limbs by walking, leaving my saddle-bags on the saddle. But the cunning beast proved treacherous—I had good cause to regret my kindness. I had left the bridle on his neck and was walking by his side, when he managed to get a few steps in advance. Having walked a couple of miles in this way, I began to feel weary, and asked my horse to stop; but he seemed to prefer walking alone, and resolved to keep out of my reach. When I walked fast, he increased his pace accordingly. When I ran, he ran—then off came my saddle-bags, which I had to carry. This appeared to amuse him much, and no intreaty could induce him to wait for me. Is it possible, thought I, that I am doomed to walk and carry this burden, through this solitary wilderness, all the way to Cobourg. In my dejection and weariness, a happy thought came into my mind. There is a long corduroy bridge about a mile ahead, and on that bridge I can outrun the cruel beast. The plan was laid and the conquest effected; but I learned that too much liberty was a bad thing for a horse, while there might be circumstances under which even these miserable log-bridges might be of service to a travelling preacher.

●　　●　　●

I received twenty-five cents travelling expenses, but no quarterage, as my colleague required all the money paid in to meet his moving expenses.

From Anson Green, *The Life and Times of the Rev. Anson Green, D.D.* (Toronto: Methodist Book Room, 1877), pp. 48-51, 53-55.

THE STATIONS OF A PRIEST

Until the "Great Migration" of the Irish in the late 1840's Roman Catholics in Upper Canada were very few in number, and this only aggravated the frontier problem of distance that faced all clergymen. The Roman Catholic Church quickly adopted the same circuit system that the Methodists were using so successfully to reach their own scattered flocks. Two essentials for both Methodist circuit rider and Catholic priest were a rugged physique and an indomitable will to serve His Kingdom despite every hard-

ship and discouragement. Such a devoted servant was Edward Gordon—let him stand as one example for the many of every denomination who faced and conquered on the frontier.

Father Gordon was a man endowed with all the gifts of mind and body necessary for a great and onerous duty; of strong physical powers, much austerity of life, indomitable will and shrewd mental qualities. No difficulties daunted him; no slight or rebuff discouraged him, and in the presence of danger he was a man. He put his hand to the plough, walked the furrow to the end, sowed the good seed, the harvest of which we are now reaping. On the 3rd of May, 1832, on block 24, of the town of Niagara, four acres were cut off from the military reserve and deeded to Bishop Macdonnell by the Crown. This extraordinary prelate, in recognition of his loyalty and patriotism, was granted blocks of land for church purposes in Toronto, Kingston, Hamilton, and, indeed, wherever there was a Catholic settlement. The young priest signalized the beginning of his pastorship by the erection of the first Catholic church on this peninsula. In three months, with the co-operation of his people, his ceaseless energy overcame all obstacles, and for the first time in the history of the Catholics of Niagara, they worshipped in a temple of their own—every stick of timber of which was paid for by their contributions.

After the completion of his church, Father Gordon entered upon a tour of his vast parish; he visited Niagara Falls, Dundas, Trafalgar, Toronto Gore and Adjala, saying mass, hearing confessions, and preaching in barns and log huts. In less than ten years he built the first Catholic churches in these places; and, indeed, was the only priest that many of the Catholic settlers had seen since they moved into the clearings. In those days these pastoral visits were known as "Stations," and when, during the Lenten and Advent seasons, the priest began his visitations, announcement was made on Sunday that on the following Wednesday he would say mass at a particular place. This notice was conveyed to the congregation in words to the following effect: "If there be anyone here living in the neighbourhood of Edward Keating, of the Twenty-mile Creek, send word to him that a 'Station' will be given at his house next Wednesday, and tell him to be sure to let all of his Catholic neighbors know it. I will be there on Tuesday night." The priest, after mass, took particular care to ascertain if there was any neighbor of Keating's present, and if not, he commissioned some one to bear a message to him. On the following Tuesday, carrying with him the vestments, altar stone, wine and altar breads, he left home on horse-back, and through the clearings and forest held his way till he reached Keating's house, where he was greeted warmly by the stalwart settler and his family. That night a few of the neighbors dropped in, and after desultory remarks about the weather and crops, the conversation flowed into the subjects of Ireland and the Catholic Church. The following morning the priest rose early, placed a table on four chairs, put the altar stone thereon, covering it with the three linen altar-cloths. He then nailed a crucifix to the wall, arranged the altar cards, opened the missal or mass-book, with the mass of the day marked, and after hearing the confessions of the people blessed the house, and offered up the Holy Sacrifice. In many of the settlers' log shanties the ground floor was but one room, forming the kitchen, dining and living apartment, and the ceiling was often so low that a tall priest was obliged to offer up the Holy Sacrifice in a bending position. After mass he instructed them in the teachings of the Catholic Church, encouraged them to lead good lives, to hold fast to the faith, and bring up their children in the fear and love of God. During this time the good woman of the house was preparing dinner, and from the blazing hearth, upon which the dinner was being cooked, there came forth a heat that made the room almost unbearable. Before finishing his exhortation, the priest announced another "Station," fourteen or fifteen miles farther west; and thus, from week to week, in the pelting rains, over swollen streams, across fallen timber, he pursued his journey for months, till the man of God had completed his biannual visitations.

From W. R. Harris, *The Catholic Church in the Niagara Peninsula, 1626-1895* (Toronto, 1895), pp. 188-191.

DOCTOR STRACHAN FACES THE GENERAL

John Strachan had arrived in Canada as a young man of twenty-one years, in the closing hours of 1799. In turn as teacher, clergyman, legislator and bishop, he left his mark on Canadian life in many ways until his death just a few weeks after Confederation. Before the War of 1812-1814 Strachan's main impact had been on the young men of prominent families who attended his famous school at Cornwall. But the American attack on "Muddy York," the modest ancestor of today's Toronto, proved to be a turning point in his life. The Reverend Doctor Strachan had recently moved to the tiny Upper Canadian capital and now he found greatness thrust upon him as the British troops and leading citizens evacuated the town in April, 1813. The events which he recounts in this letter to his old friend, Doctor Brown of Edinburgh, made John Strachan aware for the first time of his powers of leadership. After this encounter with the American General Dearborn, John Strachan followed his star of destiny to become a maker of Canadian opinion in church, state and school.

On hearing the tremendous explosion of the magazine, hurried home and found Mrs. Strachan greatly terrified, and off with the children to a neighbor's house. Sent her to a friend's, a little out of town. Go up towards the garrison, which we had by this time abandoned; find the General and his troops in a ravine, the militia scattering. The General (Sheaffe) determines to retreat to Kingston with the regulars, and leaves the command with Colonel Chewitt and Major Allan, two militia officers; and desires them to make the best conditions they can with the enemy for the protection of the town. Offer my services to assist them. Go to Mr. Crookshank's house, and meet Major King and Colonel Mitchell, on the part of the enemy. Our Attorney General, Mr. Robinson, also went with us, and assisted us to discuss the points of capitulation. A difficulty arose from a ship and naval store having been set on fire during our negotiation; this considered very dishonourable. At length a capitulation is agreed upon, subject to the ratification of the Commanding Officer. Soon broken through: Major Allan, though under the protection of a flag of truce, is made prisoner and deprived of his sword. I accompany him to town in the midst of the enemy's column. The militia on our side ground their arms. The enemy return to the garrison, with the exception of the rifle-corps, which is left under pretence of protecting the town.

●   ●   ●

Wednesday, April 28, met Major King at the Hon. Mr. Selby's; complain of the indignity offered Major Allan, and that the capitulation had not been ratified, nor a copy so ratified, returned in a few minutes according to promise; and declared that the whole appeared a deception. Major King was sorry; would do every thing that lay in his power, and desired us to go to the garrison, and every thing should be amicably adjusted. Went to the garrison, but the commanding-officer, Colonel Pierce, can do nothing. The militia had been detained in the blockhouse without victuals, and the wounded without nourishment or medicine. Complain to Colonel Pierce, who ordered rations for the prisoners. Meet a deputation from General Dearborn, to discuss the articles of capitulation; find that they cannot parole the militia officers and men.

Demand an officer to take me on board the principal ship, where Dearborn was. Meet him coming on shore, and present him with the articles of capitulation. He read them without deigning an answer. Request to know whether he will parole the officers and men, and demand leave to take away our sick and wounded. He treats me with great harshness; tells me that we had given a false return of officers; told me to keep off, and not to follow him, as he had business of much more importance to attend to. Complained of this treatment to Commodore Chauncey, the commander of flotilla, declare that, if the capitulation was not immediately signed, we should not receive it; and affirmed that the delay was a deception, calculated to give the rifle-men time to plunder, and after the town had been robbed they would then perhaps sign the capitulation, and tell us they respected private property. But we were determined that this should not be the case, and that they should not have it in their power to say that they respected private property, after it had been robbed. Upon saying this, I broke away. Soon after General Dearborn came to the room where his deputation were sitting; and having been told what I had said, settled the matter amicably. The officers and men were released on their parole, and we began to remove the sick and wounded.

Spent the whole of Thursday the 29th, in removing the sick and wounded, and getting comforts for them. On the following day, the Government building on fire, contrary to the articles of capitulation, and the church robbed. Call a meeting of the judges and magistrates; draw up a short note stating our grievances, and wait upon General Dearborn with it. He is greatly embarassed, and promises every thing.

From A. N. Bethune, *Memoir of the Right Reverend John Strachan, D.D., LL.D., First Bishop of Toronto* (Toronto: Rowsell, 1870), pp. 47-49.

FAIRFIELD'S DEATH BLOW

The Moravian missionaries to the Delaware Indians led their "children" westward from the Susquehanna Valley to escape the French-English wars, and on from Pennsylvania to Upper Canada to escape the effects of the American Revolution. Always seeking a refuge where they could build a Christian Indian community in peace, the Moravians believed they had found their promised land at Fairfield on the Thames River. But in the golden autumn days of 1813 American invaders met, fought and defeated the British and their Indian allies led by the famous Tecumseh on the very outskirts of the Moravians' village. The Delawares, though neutrals in the war, fled from the site of the battle, while the missionaries stayed to succour the men of both armies. Fairfield was, however, doomed. The missionaries were ordered to follow the Indians out of the village and then the buildings were put to the torch. Although a new village rose from the ashes in 1815, Fairfield never really recovered from the blow it received on that day when the victorious Americans burned the settlement.

The scarlet streak that flashed down Main Street, over the bridge and into the darkening woods—the British general "with about fifteen men" on their mad dash for freedom, with ten Kentuckians after them—was Fairfield's first inkling of the disastrous turn of events. The cannon, placed by Procter by the side of the roadway, well beyond the ravine, were being spiked by twenty dragoons when the horsemen galloped by.

With the arrival, shortly after, "of fugitives from the battlefield," the tale of humiliating defeat was unfolded. Women and children refugees spilled out of the houses and ran eastward up the road. Some climbed into wagons, others stood, stunned, as the Americans "one hour before dark, filled our town with several thousand so that one could only with difficulty get through." The Schnalls' escape was cut off. At the outset, Schnall wrote "our new guests were remarkably friendly and promised to do us not the least harm, and nothing was to be taken of our private possessions." For the moment the Schnalls and others who remained in Fairfield seemed safe. The Denckes and the Christian Indians, supposedly, were settled safely six miles up the Thames.

Sister Schnall was the unsung heroine of those trying hours. By the sheer force of her benevolence she had, for days, converted flour, raw meat and vegetables into nourishing food to warm and strengthen the crowds at her door. With administrative ability she had directed her helpers to do her bidding while she cut apples for *Schnitz* and dried them, a tray at a time, in her oven's embers. Now, triumphantly, she closed the trap door below twelve bushels hanging in the attic. She was tired and so was Elizabeth Dolson, John's wife, who with her family had assisted with the work since they had come to Fairfield, just ahead of the American advance up the Thames.

The American commissariat did not feed all the troops. But while the cold and famished British prisoners huddled over a campfire on the battlefield, roasting meat provided by their captors and eating it "without benefit of salt or bread," the American troops swarmed over Fairfield looking for food. Their search led them straight to Margaret Schnall's large fragrant kitchen.

She took her stand again before her kitchen table, issuing rapid orders to those who would help while she speedily and practically fed "as many as possible" of the hungry horde. When her bread was gone, the dough-tray scraped, she set more to rise in the straw baskets and turned her attention to pumpkin and fruit pies (or cakes, as she called them, as she could spare flour for only one crust.) While they baked, corn-meal mush could be prepared for those who had almost snatched the unbaked dough out of her hand. As long as the milk supply lasted, Margaret Schnall could make one of the traditional "poor soups,"—brown flour soup or rivvel soup (thickened with rubbed flakes of egg and flour). Meanwhile, ham stock, simmering on the fire with either potatoes, corn, or beans, flavored with potherbs or a pinch of saffron, was soon ready to serve and could be stretched with water, if need be. With a bowlful of this frugal goodness inside of him, a man could roll himself in his blanket and soon be lost in deep sleep.

When, at last, Sister Schnall dropped from exhaustion, heroic evidence of the Moravians' gift of hospitality had once more been shown to the strangers within their gates.

From Elma Gray, *Wilderness Christians* (Ithaca: Cornell University Press, 1956), pp. 237-238.

A SAD EVENT AT HAY BAY

The Bay of Quinte region was a veritable womb of Methodism in Upper Canada. On the shores of the Bay stand two of the oldest churches in the province of Ontario— Conger's or the White Chapel at Picton, built in 1809, and Hay Bay Chapel, constructed in 1792 and now preserved as a shrine by the United Church of Canada. At Picton also the first conference of the Methodist Church in Upper Canada was held in 1824. At that time about one of every five Methodists lived in the Bay of Quinte area. The following story of a tragedy at Hay Bay Chapel during the frontier period is still well known to local residents.

About five weeks after the Conference, and when the preachers from Canada had returned, and had entered on their work, a sad event occurred on the Bay Quinte circuit. Although forty years ago, the relation is even now sometimes accompanied with sighs and tears. The preachers, Isaac Puffer and James Wilson, who were re-appointed to the circuit, resolved on a special quarterly meeting at the Adolphustown chapel, on Sunday, August 20th. The meeting was looked forward to with much interest. The work of God was still prospering on the circuit. The morning was fine, and the sky with scarcely a cloud. While the pious members were coming to the chapel from Ernestown, Fredericksburgh, and the southern parts of Adolphustown, the members and their families in the northern part and along the Napanee river, were also on their way. Adolphustown and more than half of Fredericksburgh are cut in two parts by a narrow bay, called Hay Bay, running in from the Bay of Quinte waters. The land around the shore was early settled, and the bay is now surrounded with good farm houses and fertile farms. On the south shore is the chapel; and to get there all from the north must cross the bay. Some had already crossed this morning; and others were about venturing out in boats and canoes. Among the rest a company of eighteen young persons, most of them pious, and the fruit of the late revival, and belonging to the families living on the shore. They were all dressed in good and modest apparel, as befitted the day, and the house and worship of God. Buoyant with the cheerfulness of youth and the emotions of piety, they sang as they stepped into the boat, and as they made progress to the other shore. The boat being rather leaky, and so many pressing it too near the water's edge, the water came in, and increased fast, and they had no vessel to bale with. Unhappily, the young men did not think of baling with their clean hats, or did not like to do so, until it was too late. The boat filled and sunk, when near the other shore, and these eighteen young men and women, crying and shrieking, went down into the deep water. At the time of crossing, there was a prayer meeting begun in the chapel by those who came first. One was now engaged in prayer, and had just uttered the petition that "it might be a day long to be remembered," when a shriek was heard, another, and another. The prayer was stopped, and some ran up to the pulpit to look out, and saw the youths struggling in the water. All ran to the shore, and some plunged in to render assistance. Eight were taken to the shore. Ten bodies were yet in the water. A seine was prepared, and so the bodies of these unhappy youth, a few hours so blithe and cheerful, were brought dripping to the land. One was not recovered till the next morning. Two young men were drowned, and eight young women. Two were of the German family, two Detlors, one Bogart, one Roblin, one McCoy, one Clark, one Madden, and one Cole. The grief of the families, so suddenly bereaved, gathered together on the shore, gazing at the loved bodies, may be better imagined than described. The grief, too, was partook of by the large congregation assembled, and the minister. No public worship was attended to, but preparations for the solemn funeral.

Monday was a day of mourning. News of the disaster soon spread far, and a great congregation was assembled. Nine coffins were laid in order outside the chapel. One of the corpses was buried in another grave-yard. Mr. Puffer took for the text, Job xix, 25-27, *"I know that my Redeemer liveth,"* &c. He stood at the door, and tried to preach to those within and without, but was so affected by the catastrophe, the weeping congregation, and the coffined dead before him, that he confessed he could not do justice to the subject, or the occasion. But he offered consolation from the Gospel to the stricken families mourning. Next, the coffins of the youthful dead were opened, that friends and neighbours, and young acquaintances, might take a last look and farewell. Six of the graves were in rotation, and the coffins were placed in the same manner. The others were near departed friends in other parts of the ground. After the reading of the burial service, the graves, one after another received the dead, and then were closed up again, until the day when *"the trumpet shall sound, and the dead shall be raised incorruptible."*

From George F. Playter, *The History of Methodism in Canada* (Toronto: Wesleyan Printing Establishment, 1862), pp. 174-175.

MAN'S BEST FRIENDS

The rough surroundings of the frontier influenced every aspect of the pioneer's life. Visitors from Europe invariably noted with disapproval the coarseness of manners, dress and living habits that contrasted so sharply with the supposed sophistication of life "in the old country." Especially shocking to genteel souls was the easy North American habit of treating all classes, high or low, as social equals. Even church life was marred by a certain crudeness, and W. H. Elgee has cited some examples of how frontier life could damage the decorum of religious services.

And then the dogs! The dog of value on the frontier was of the rugged, heroic, and fighting type. It was no place for the cultivation of the lap dog or the Pomeranian. Since the pioneer's dog may have saved his owner from the wolves or from being lost in the bush, he was appreciated accordingly. And though his bark was loud he was accustomed to come indoors at his master's heels. What this meant to the church of the primitive community is easily seen. Thomas Shillitoe, the Quaker from England, found the dogs unbearable. To Bishop Medley in New Brunswick the dogs were "a profane and intolerable nuisance" even among the Anglican churches. Rev. Robert Cooney gave great credit to the chairman of an anniversary service who "would not suffer a single dog to remain." This was far toward the middle of the century, yet the phrase, "no matter who owned it," shows the danger of hurting the feelings of some leading member. The difficulty need not be emphasized which confronted the minister who was trying to achieve a devotional atmosphere with half a dozen mutually jealous dogs snarling at one another about the church stove.

Further, in the earliest days, many of the churches had no stoves. This illustrates the conservative nature of the religious instincts. Religion finds it most difficult to dissociate itself from the ancient forms in which it has been clothed, the mediaeval robe, the flint circumcision knife, music without instruments. So English people carried the custom of unheated churches into the sub-zero weather of Canada, and made no change in some cases for forty years.

Even the example of a heated church did not immediately change the point of view. The primitive building in which Trinity congregation of St. John worshipped for a few years had been equipped with stoves. Yet when the new church, so much nearer the desire of the true churchman's heart, was erected in 1791, it was left, according to English custom, unheated for thirteen years. Added to the strength of tradition were the ignorance of iron stoves and the difficulties of fireplaces. During the early decades the people of St. Paul's church, Halifax, carried with them either hot bricks or charcoal foot warmers. During some of the winter months the service was abbreviated because of the cold. Among other denominations many a small church was not used in the winter, services being held in the homes. Stoves were sometimes acquired which, through the ignorance of workmen, either were not used, or when installed, gave more smoke than heat.

From W. H. Elgee, *The Social Teachings of the Canadian Churches, Protestant:* The Early Period, before 1850 (Toronto: The Ryerson Press, 1964), pp. 100-101.

THE VARIETIES OF RELIGIOUS EXPRESSION

THE LONG COMMUNION

The Presbyterian communion service in North America was usually held out-of-doors, lasted several days, and whenever possible involved several ministers. Unlike the Methodist camp meeting that was open to all who sought salvation, the solemn long Presbyterian communion was "closed"—only members in full communion and in good standing could participate in the Lord's Supper.

When James MacGregor held such a long communion at the Middle River in Nova Scotia, local farmers opened their homes and barns to accommodate those who had come from a distance. They also provided such food as they could spare from their own meagre resources, and one host, Robert Marshall, was in the habit of explaining the small quantities offered to the visitors with these words: "Gin ye're Christians, ye'll be content wi' it, an' gin ye're no, it's mair than ye deserve."

The spot selected for the observance of the ordinance was on the Intervale, on the Middle River a little below the bridge at Archibalds, on what is now the farm of Mr. John Douglass, under the shade of a high bank on the west side of the river. But the stream has encroached so much upon the Intervale, that its waters now pass over the spot where the sacred Supper was observed. By midday the sun was so far round, that the bank shaded the worshippers from his rays. Here a tent was placed for the minister, the multitudes sat or reclined upon the green grass of the Intervale, or

113

under the leafy shade of the trees on the bank, facing the minister.

Early in the week people began to arrive, so that by the day the services were to commence they were assembled by hundreds, in after years by thousands. The ordinance was dispensed in the manner common at that time in Scotland, and as this is in many places now known only as matter of history, we may give a particular account of the services which were usually observed in connection with this solemn rite of Christian worship. Thursday was the first day of "holy convocation," it being called the day of humiliation or fasting.

●　　●　　●

Friday was what was called by the Highlanders, "the day of the men,"—a day for private religious meetings conducted by the elders, catechists, or more experienced Christians, similar to what is called in the United States and other places, conference meetings. Prayer, praise, mutual exhortation, remarks on the subject especially selected for consideration, or, as it was commonly called, "the question," (which, however, usually involved marks of grace,) formed the exercises of this day. Saturday was the preparation day, and again he preached a sermon in each language, generally of such a nature as was fitted to prepare the minds of Christians for the solemn services before them.

●　　●　　●

Then came the Sabbath, in which all the services had to be conducted by himself. After the opening Psalm and prayer, came what was called the Action Sermon, usually devoted to the great central truths of Redemption, specially exhibited in the ordinance of the Supper. This was followed by prayer and praise, and then by the service usually known in Scotland as "the fencing of the tables," which consists in a plain statement of the character of those who have and those who have not a right to observe the ordinance, and which was generally concluded by the reading of such passages of Scripture as Psalm xv.; Matt. v. 1-12; Gal. v. 19-24. Then followed part of an appropriate Psalm, during the singing of which the elders brought forward the elements and placed them upon the communion table, while the first company of communicants slowly and reverently took their places on the seats, provided for them. These consisted of two long benches on which they sat facing one another, with a narrow table covered with a pure white cloth between them. On the seats being filled, the minister took his place at the head of the table, and having first read as authority for observing the ordinance, one of the scriptural narratives of its institution, usually Paul's in 1 Cor. xi. 23-26, he offered up prayer, especially giving thanks for the blessings of salvation, and for this ordinance in which it is commemorated. Then followed what was called the "serving of the tables." A short address was delivered to those at the table, when the minister broke the bread and handed a portion of it and afterwards the wine to those nearest to him, repeating as he did so the words of institution. The elements were then passed along from one to another, to the foot of the table, the attending elders supplying deficiencies, while the minister continued his exhortation. When the address was concluded, he dismissed them from the table with such words as the following, "Go then from the table of the Lord singing his praise, and may the God of peace go with you." At the utterance of these words, the precentor gave out the first line of the verse immediately following what had been last sung of the Psalm of which the singing had commenced; and as the singing proceeded, those who had been at the table rose, and began, many with moistened eyes, slowly and reverently, as if treading on holy ground, to retire, while another band with the same measured tread advanced and took their places. Another table service followed and another singing, and so on till all those who spoke the one language were served, when those who spoke the other were served in a similar manner in their native tongue, until on the whole altogether there would commonly be seven table services. After the service of communicating was over, a Psalm or Hymn, in imitation of the Saviour, (Mark xiv. 26,) was sung, after which the minister delivered the concluding exhortation, usually called "the directions." This consisted commonly of advices to those who had communicated, as to their future conduct, and an earnest appeal to those who had been merely spectators, to embrace the Saviour and profess his name. Then came the evening sermon, the whole being concluded with prayer and praise. These services often occupied the most of the day. They commenced at ten or eleven o'clock, but the sun would be far down the western sky before the last sermon would be over. On Monday, which was commonly called the Thanksgiving day, there were again two sermons.

From George Patterson, *Memoir of the Rev. James MacGregor, D.D.* (Philadelphia, 1859), pp. 194-198.

THE FIRST CAMP MEETING

After the "Great Awakening" of North America in the eighteenth century a second tidal wave of religious revivalism swept the Protestant churches beginning about 1800. One of the most characteristic institutions of this "Great Revival" was the camp meeting—a gathering of the settlers at some outdoor spot where religious services went on for several days. The camp meeting was an outgrowth of the Presbyterians' long communion. It had a social aspect as well as religious, for it broke the lonely routine of frontier life, by bringing people together and giving them the chance to make new friends and the younger generation to find mates.

Camp meetings were usually marked by extreme displays of emotionalism that many people found distasteful. Perhaps the shouting and physical convulsions of the "saved" were genuine actions of grace—perhaps they were no more than the release of pent-up emotions from lonely souls. In either case camp meetings became an established feature of religious life during Canada's early days. Such meetings were held by various denominations but most commonly by the Methodists. The first camp meeting in Canada took place at Hay Bay in 1805 and its team of evangelistic Methodist preachers included the famous Nathan Bangs who left this report of the historic event. People had come on foot, in waggons and by boat from many miles around. Two hundred and fifty were at the camp ground, with all their equipment for living out for several days, when the

*meeting began, and many more streamed in during the first
day of hymns, prayers and exhortations that went on until
midnight.*

The night was clear and serene, and the scene being new
to us, a peculiar solemnity rested upon all our minds. The
lights glowing among the trees and above the tents, and the
voice of prayer and praise mingling and ascending into the
starlight night, altogether inspired the heart with emotions
better felt than described. During this meeting six persons
passed from death unto life. At five o'clock Saturday morning a prayer-meeting was held, and at ten o'clock a sermon
was preached on the text, 'My people are destroyed for lack
of knowledge.' At this time the congregation had increased
to perhaps twenty-five hundred, and the people of God were
seated together on logs near the stand, while a crowd were
standing in a semi-circle around them. During the sermon
I felt an unusual sense of the Divine presence, and thought
I could see a cloud of Divine glory rest upon the congregation. The circle of spectators unconsciously fell back step
by step, until quite a space was opened between them and
those who were seated. At length I sprang from my seat to
my feet. The preached stopped, and said, 'Take it up and
go on!' 'No,' I replied, 'I rise not to preach.' I immediately
descended from the stand among the hearers; the rest of the
preachers all spontaneously followed me, and we went
among the people, exhorting the impenitent and comforting
the distressed; for while Christians were filled with 'joy
unspeakable and full of glory,' many a sinner was praying
and weeping in the surrounding crowd. These we collected
in little groups, and exhorted God's people to join in prayer
with them, and not to leave them till he should save their
souls. O what a scene of tears and prayers was this! I
suppose that not less than a dozen little praying circles were
thus formed in the course of a few minutes. It was truly
affecting to see parents weeping over their children, neighbors exhorting their unconverted neighbors to repent, while
all, old and young, were awe-struck. The wicked looked on
with silent amazement, while they beheld some of their
companions struck down by the mighty power of God, and
heard his people pray for them. The mingled voices of

prayer and praise were heard afar off, and produced a solemn awe apparently upon all minds. Struck by the grandeur of the spectacle and the religious interests of the crowd, a preacher mounted the stand and proclaimed for his text, 'Behold he cometh with clouds, and every eye shall see him.' The meeting continued all night, and few, I think, slept that night. During this time some forty persons were converted or sanctified.

●   ●   ●

After breakfast, a host being on the ground, we held a love-feast. The interest and excitement were so great, and the congregation so large, that while some assembled around the stand, a preacher mounted a waggon at a distance and addressed a separate congregation. The impression of the word was universal, the power of the Spirit was manifested throughout the whole encampment, and almost every tent was a scene of prayer. At noon the Lord's Supper was administered to multitudes, while other multitudes looked on with astonishment; a young woman of fashionable and high position in society, was smitten, and with sobs entreated the prayers of the people. Her sister forced her away; a preacher went forth without the camp and led them both back, followed by quite a procession of their friends; a circle gathered around them and sang and prayed. The unawakened sister was soon upon her knees praying in agony, and was first converted; the other quickly after received the peace of God, and they wept and rejoiced together. A backslider, who had become a maniac, and was in despair, was brought to the camp. His symptoms were like those of the New Testament demoniacs. It required the strength of several men to hold him; especial prayer was offered for him. We first besought God, for Christ's sake, to restore him his faculties, which was done. He then earnestly prayed for himself, and before the meeting closed he was not only delivered from despair, but filled with joy and peace in believing.

The time was at hand at last for the conclusion of the meeting. The last night was the most awfully impressive and yet delightful scene my eyes ever beheld. There was not a cloud in the sky. The stars studded the firmament, and the glory of God filled the camp. All the neighboring forest seemed vocal with the echos of hymns. Turn our attention which ever way we would, we heard the voice of prayer and praise. As it was the last night, every moment seemed precious; parents were praying for their children, and children for their parents, brothers and sisters for one another, neighbors for neighbors, all anxious that before they left the consecrated ground they should be 'sealed as the heirs of salvation.' I will not attempt to describe the parting scene, for it was indescribable. The preachers, about to disperse to their distant fields of labor, hung upon each other's necks, weeping and yet rejoicing. Christians from remote settlements, who had here formed holy friendships which they expected would survive in heaven, parted probably to meet no more on earth, but in joyful hope of re-union above. They wept, prayed, sang, shouted aloud, and at last had to break away from each other as by force. As the hosts marched off in different directions the songs of victory rolled along the highways. Great was the good that followed.

From J. Carroll, *Case and His Cotemporaries* (Toronto: Wesleyan Printing Establishment, 1867), Vol. I, pp. 114-118.

THE CHILDREN OF PEACE

Some time around 1800 David Willson arrived in the Quaker settlement along Yonge Street, north of Toronto. Willson soon became a Quaker minister, but he always regretted the lack of music in Quaker worship so much that in 1812 he formed his own sect, the Children of Peace. An accomplished musician himself, Willson encouraged the use of vocal and instrumental music among his followers with great success. In 1825 the Children of Peace began to build their own temple at the village of Sharon. Although the Children of Peace gradually disappeared after Willson's death in 1866, their remarkable temple of wood and glass still stands and is preserved as a museum by a local historical society. This description of Sharon Temple was written by William Lyon Mackenzie, journalist, politician, and later rebel, just after the temple was completed.

The new church or chapel of the Children of Peace is certainly calculated to inspire the beholder with astonishment; its dimensions—its architecture—its situation—are all so extraordinary. On a level plain, inclosed first with a fence, and afterwards by a row of maple trees, on every side, stands the chapel or temple of Hope. It is a regular square, each of the four sides measuring sixty feet at the base. The main body of the chapel is twenty-four feet high, and is lighted by twenty-four windows, with seventy-two panes each; having also one door in each front. Surmounting a pavilion roof, so near a level as to permit me to walk upon it without danger, adding only six feet to the height of the main building, rises a square tower, hall, or gallery, measuring twenty-seven and a half feet on each side, and sixteen feet in height. Inside, this place is one blaze of light, containing twelve windows of sixty panes each: it is to be used as an orchestra or music room, being open within as a part of the chapel below. Here will be placed, as in a gallery, the musicians and organist, at least thirty feet above the congregation. And when the large full-toned and soft-set organ, built by Mr. Coates, of York, shall be set up in this room, together with the players on the flutes, violins, bass-viols, bassoons, clarionets, and flageolets, used by the society in their worship, the effect will remind a visiter of "the music of the spheres," about which bards of old have sung, and poets, in "lofty lays," recorded fancy's fictions. This tower or gallery is supported inside by sixteen pillars, and, like the former building, has a pavilion roof, rising so gently, however, as to permit us to walk on it with ease. Beautifully placed on the centre of this roof, and supported inside by four pillars, is a third tower, in exact accordance with the architectural taste displayed throughout the work. It is twelve feet high; square, each side being nine and a half feet, with four double windows of fifty-four lights each. At the corners of each roof, and also on the four corners of the highest tower, are placed large ornamented lanterns, which add to the beauty of the temple, and are lighted up at the annual grand festival, which commences on the morning of the first Saturday of September, and continues till the Monday following.

The highest tower is surmounted by a gilded ball, on each side of which is inscribed "Peace." The temple is painted white; and when finished inside, will be the most surprising and original fabric allotted for divine worship in the colony. Being seated on a rising ground, it has a fine effect when viewed from the surrounding country, towering above its mother earth, unequalled and alone, in all the sublimity and majesty of castellated grandeur. The elevation of the new chapel is from seventy to eighty feet, measuring from the grounds to the tops of the four highest lanterns.

The religious services of the society are performed as yet in the old chapel, a plain building outside, but finished within in very handsome style. The number of members and hearers is about 200, and the utmost regularity is said to prevail at their meetings. As I remarked before, the Children of Peace, like the Quakers, have no written creed; the church discipline being altered and amended, if need be, on motion, by a vote of the majority of the congregation. As yet, however, every alteration of church government has been carried without opposition.

On Saturday, at noon, there is a relaxation from labour— the children give over their work or tasks, amuse themselves, and take their recreation in the fields. In the evening there is a meeting in the chapel for religious exercises: besides, I was informed that the sabbath is strictly kept.

In the old chapel, I observed several paintings by Coates, —Peace, represented by an elegant female figure with an infant on each arm, and Eve trampling the serpent under foot; there is also a third painting of Peace by the same artist. On one side of the organ is a picture of King David's harp; on the other, his spear, bow, and shield. Four black flags, used at funerals, with a star in the centre, and gilt at the top of the staff, wave from the organ-loft.

Early on the morning after I arrived, I found some of the singers in the chapel practising their hymns and tunes. A number of young females sang a hymn, composed, as is all their poetry, by members of the society. Two young men had bass-viols, and the full-toned organ aided the music, which, I will venture to say, is unequalled in any part of the

Upper, and scarcely surpassed even by the Catholics in the Lower province.

From W. L. Mackenzie, "The Children of Peace," *The Colonial Advocate*, September 18, 1828.

WAKING THE DEAD

The custom of "waking the dead" or keeping a vigil around the body of a deceased person seems to have been universal in pre-Christian days. With the coming of Christianity, however, the wake was made an occasion for prayer, as the body was laid out on the death-bed with a plate of salt on its breast.

The wake is popularly but wrongly regarded as a Celtic custom—in fact it was practised in England until the Reformation. But it was from Ireland and Scotland that the wake came to Canada, and to this day waking the dead still occurs in some districts among residents who retain the culture of the "auld country."

In County Peel large attendance at a wake indicated respect for the deceased. Not to attend a local wake was looked on as a discourtesy to the bereaved family.

There were no "morticians" then and the necessary services were rendered by the family and neighbours. Copper coins were placed on the eyelids of the corpse to keep them closed, and damp cloths on its face and hands to prevent discoloration. The body of the deceased, dressed in its Sunday clothes and laid out in a lidless coffin, was carried into the best room feet foremost, the head to the west. This practice follows the Church rule that a dead layman is placed with his feet to the high altar; but a cleric, out of respect for his office, is placed with his head to the altar, and in liturgically correct churches the altar is in the east.

A lighted candle stood at the head of the coffin in a silver candlestick loaned by the priest, while on each side were three tallow dips in tin or copper holders.

A wake usually lasted two nights. At sunset folk began to arrive at the house of mourning. Catholics, as they entered, made the Sign of the Cross and said a short prayer for the repose of the soul of the deceased. Whisky was handed round; the guests could help themselves to tobacco.

The now obsolete profession of keening obtained for a time in Peel. A spectator of a wake at Silver Creek relates that the room was filled, men on one side and women on the other, each with a mug of whisky and a pipe. The women, after puffing their pipes in silence for a minute or two, would suddenly throw back their heads, singly or otherwise, and utter prolonged wails. After thus keening they would take a few more sips, then resume their pipes.

A century or so ago Mrs. Webb was hired to cry at Peel County wakes, but with the death of the old keeners the practice was gradually discontinued.

* * *

Perhaps exaggerated tradition has made the most famous of wakes that of Timmy O'Connor the cooper, still another of the emigrants from King's County who, in the 1830's, had made his way to Albion. In his later years he went about piping at dances, telling old tales and jokes, and fishing for trout in the west branch of the Humber. It was after a fishing trip that he took sick and died. Owing to his long life in the district, and his popularity too, Timmy's largely-attended wake lasted for three days.

The "o'er true" story has it that on this occasion shocking disrespect was shown to the dead. It is recorded that the chief offender met his death on the railway where it crosses the Humber between the fifth and sixth lines near Palgrave. The story spread that the bridge was haunted by the victim's ghost. His distracted widow appealed to Father McSpiritt, who advised her to thank God, for, quoth he, a spirit haunting the bridge is certainly not in hell.

* * *

The black frock-coats in which the men were usually married served throughout life for their Sunday best, and were oftentimes the garb in which they were buried. Similarly, the women had voluminous black silk dresses,

in which their bodies were customarily laid out. The backs
of the skirts were cut away, and used to make cravats for
their husbands and official male mourners.

From W. P. Bull, *From Macdonell to McGuigan* (Toronto:
Perkins Bull Foundation, 1939), pp. 328-340.

THE POWER OF THE PURSE

*The laity of the Canadian churches have not always been
generous in their support of religion. Because churches at
home in Britain were usually well endowed, laymen often
assumed religion was "free" in the colonies—or at least
ought to be free. Except in Quebec tithing could not be
enforced by law, and congregations sometimes used their
power of the purse to bring pressure on their ministers to
conform with what the laymen wanted in religion. Such an
incident is recounted by Canon Dyson Hague of Saint Paul's
Church, Halifax, where the laity had often shown very independent attitudes. The Reverend William Cogswell, a
native Haligonian, became curate of Saint Paul's in 1832
and almost at once annoyed some staid and important members of the congregation by his forthright denunciations of
sin. For his honesty he was threatened with the ultimate
weapon of the laity—the power of the purse.*

The new curate preached the Gospel with great earnestness,
and, as such preaching in those days was rare, so startled
the staid church-going people of the day that he was looked
upon almost in the light of a fanatic.

When the first Easter vestry meeting came around, a
prominent and somewhat pompous churchman got up and
spoke as follows: "Mr. Rector, I have a motion to make;
it is with regard to the new curate, your assistant. He is
no doubt a very estimable young man, and does his duty
according to his light, but the kind of sermon he preaches
is, in my opinion, altogether unsuited for this church. Why
he seems to look upon us all as if we were a lot of sinners
and had never been baptized. He says we need salvation
and personal conversion. In fact, I think he is not at all
fitted for a position such as that of the assistant minister of

St. Paul's church, and I beg to move, if anybody will second it, that the salary of the Rev. William Cogswell, be discontinued from this day three months."

As may be imagined, there was not a little commotion in the meeting when this bombshell-kind of a motion was made and seconded. The rector was visibly perplexed, and there was not a little whispering and talking amongst the parishioners, who seemed nonplussed and uncertain what to do or say next.

At last, however, a British officer of the blustery, autocratic type, not at all notorious for his religious convictions, and more familiar with claret and port wine than Church doctrine, stood up and said:

"Mr. Rector, I quite agree with the previous speaker with regard to Mr. Cogswell. I do not like the kind of sermons he preaches at all. I think he looks upon us all as a lot of heathen, and talks to us about conversion and the spiritual life as if we had never been to church in our lives. But–but–but—I must say I do not like this way of treating him. I like fair play, and I do not think this is fair play. We may say what we like, but he is a good man. He is a true Christian, and he preaches God's word. And, in fact," and here he blurted out the words with difficulty, "in fact, Mr. Rector, I am going to move an amendment that the salary of the Rev. William Cogswell be increased to $300 a year from this day forward."

A feeling that was almost electric swept over the meeting. The appeal to their better and more generous instincts touched them. The whole body rose to their feet. A seconder was immediately found, and that motion was carried unanimously.

From R. V. Harris, *The Church of Saint Paul in Halifax, Nova Scotia: 1749-1949* (Toronto: The Ryerson Press, 1949), pp. 194-195.

A ROMAN SPECTRE

Ignorance is the mother of fear, and only ignorance can explain the weird and wonderful stories about Roman Catholic practices and institutions that were so commonly believed by Protestants in years gone by. Perhaps there were similar stories about Protestantism that circulated among Catholics! The writer of this humorous anecdote suggested very charitably that such ignorance was at least based on "honesty and sincerity."

Many of the United Empire Loyalists who fled to Canada after the American Revolution, brought with them most exaggerated ideas about the Catholic Church and her priests. They were sturdy, honest people, loyal to the British Crown, and hating Pope and Popery with an honesty and sincerity that there was no disputing. The Catholic Church was to them the abomination of desolation seated on the high places, the Pope was anti-Christ, and the priests his obedient slaves. The repeated and time-worn calumnies of blood, poison and daggers associated with the priests, and woven into the fireside literature of the day, struck terror into the boldest hearts. The priest was a familiar and terrible figure—a dark, mysterious, unreliable spectre, with ten tricks at hand and ten times ten in a bag. The enlightened intelligence of our cities and towns has long ago banished this apparition, but the ghost still haunts some farming inland districts, where a priest is a curiosity if not an object of fear. Just before the stage drove out one morning on its way from Queenston to Niagara, a worthy, comely, well-fed and well-intentioned dame entered it, followed by a quiet, ministerial-looking, middle-aged gentleman, with a meek aspect and a benevolent smile. The two, as the stage progressed, entered into an animated conversation, and being each prepossessed with the other's appearance and sentiments, they formed what may be termed a stage acquaintance. The lady talked much, as ladies of that age are apt to do, of the wickedness of the times. "And then those Papists," said she; "those wicked, Popish Papists—they are worse than all put together. Whatever shall we come to if they settle amongst us?"

"Papists, ma'am?" said the gentleman. "What are they, and what wickedness do they commit?"

"Is it possible, sir," said the lady, "that you never heard of those Papists that are turning the world upside down?"

The meek gentleman admitted that he had heard of such people, but that he did not know a great deal about them, and as for turning the world upside down, the lady had just admitted that she did not see much good in the side which was now uppermost.

"Do you know," said she, speaking confidentially, in a low, solemn voice, and laying her hand upon his arm; "do you know that priest Campion himself sacrifices a lamb every Sunday?"

"Nonsense, my dear madam," said he, deprecatingly, "I am priest Campion, and I never sacrificed a lamb in my life; I have not the heart do it, and I don't know how to kill it, either!"

The air in the stage grew colder, and became so frosty that all conversation ceased in a short time.

From W. R. Harris, *The Catholic Church in the Niagara Peninsula, 1626-1895* (Toronto, 1895), pp. 183-185.

THE SECOND COMING

The early Christian church waited anxiously for the promised return of Christ but as years passed the idea of a literal "second coming" was abandoned. Still, millenialism —the belief that Christ will appear in person to claim His earthly kingdom at the end of a thousand years or some other period—has cropped up again many times. In the early nineteenth century three such millenialist or adventist groups were founded—one in England and two in the United States—and each attracted considerable attention and support in Canada. Irvingism arrived from England and Mormonism from the United States in the 1830's, but the prophecies of William Miller that the world would end in 1843 or 1844 had even more disturbing effects. Millerism drew many Canadians away from the Methodist churches and still held some of them even after Miller's date for Doomsday had passed without any catastrophe. Miller's critics were highly amused to learn that the prophet had spent his expected last week on this earth building a stone fence! Thomas Conant recalls some amusing incidents that happened in the Oshawa area where Millerites were very numerous.

During the winter of 1842-3 the Second Adventists, or Millerites, were preaching that the world would be all burnt up in February, 1843. Nightly meetings were held, generally in the school-houses. One E— H—, about Prince Albert, Ont., owned a farm of one hundred acres and upwards, stocked with cattle and farm produce, as well as having implements of agriculture. So strongly did he embrace the Second Advent doctrines of the Millerites that he had not a doubt of the fire to come in February and burn all up, and in confirmation of his faith gave away his stock, implements and farm. Sarah Terwilligar, who lived about a mile east of Oshawa "corners", on the Kingston Road, made for herself wings of silk, and, on the night of 14th of February, jumped off the porch of her home, expecting to fly heavenward. Falling to the ground some fifteen feet, she was shaken up severely and rendered wholly unfit to attend at all to the fires that were expected to follow the next day.

●   ●   ●

Mr. John Henry, on that 14th day of February, was riding alone and met a man on horseback coming at the top of his speed. Accosting Mr. Henry he said, "Say, stranger, do you see that sign in the sky?" Mr. Henry looked up and saw only a sun-dog, frequently seen then and now in the winter season, and replied, "Yes, what of it?" "Well, that's the Lord coming tomorrow to burn the world up," and Mr. H. replied, "Get out! that's only a sun-dog." "Oh! you are an unbeliever," was the retort, as the man dug spurs into his horse's sides as if to ride away from the fire he felt so near. My father told me that on the evening before the final great day, he took a sleigh-load of neighbours down to a meeting in a log school-house near where Ebenezer Church now is, in Darlington. So deep was the snow, he said, that they had no difficulty in driving over the fences. Arriving at the log school-house, they found it densely packed, and most of the auditors standing. Being late, they sought to push themselves in, when someone from the middle of the room called out, "Stand back, boys, you don't know breeding." But they pushed on heedless of breeding or the want of it, and got in a few feet from the door, where they stood and listened to some Millerite in the master's rostrum desk, as he told about the terrible fires to come on in a few hours. His words riveted the attention of all, cramped and uncomfortable as they were in the crowded room.

Tallow dips, fastened in tin reflectors, shed a mild light over all, and the heat from the crowded room became so great as to give a taste, an intense one, too, of the awful heat promised when the fires should appear. The old log school-house had been used before as a rude pioneer dwelling, and a cellar had been scooped out below the centre. Without an instant's warning the old floor-beams broke and the crowd, who all expected to go up, as the Millerite preacher assured them, were let *down* with unexpected precipitancy. The scene, my father said, was too ludicrous for description. Screaming, fainting, pulling, praying, squirming, the dense mass fought to get out. Fortunately the tallow dips were fastened to the walls and continued to light up the place. My father dryly said he made his way out, got his load and went home (at Port Oshawa) and to bed. The next morning he found the snow as usual upon the ground and no signs of fire.

● ● ●

A. S. Whiting . . . was peddling eight-day clocks from house to house—clocks which he had brought with him from Connecticut. For many weeks he had heard that the immense snow mantle in that part of Upper Canada around Port Hope would turn to blood and burn up. On the afternoon of the 14th February, 1843, he, with his horse and sleigh and a load of clocks, was driving north from Port Hope. It was a gloriously bright, sunny day of clear bracing cold, with not a cloud in the sky. Just at nightfall he arrived at a small village and drove direct to the tavern. Tying his horse to the hitching-post, he went into the bar-room to ask for lodging and food for himself and the steed. He found no one, so pushed on into the sitting-room usually provided for guests. No one was yet visible. Then he called out, but received no answer. Going on from room to room, he finally reached the kitchen. Here he found a woman crying and sobbing. Upon asking for the landlord, and also questioning the hostler where to find him, he was told they had "all gone to meeting."

"Well, I want to put my horse in the stable and then have some supper," the traveller exclaimed.

"There is no use of eating, for we shall all be burnt up before morning," the weeping woman managed to get out between her sobs.

"Well, never mind, I'll go and put up my horse, while you get me some supper."

On partaking of his supper he asked for his room; still there was no one else about, and on retiring he was told in faltering words that he would be burnt up while he slept.

The sun set that night in more than usual splendor; all nature seemed serene and peaceful, and he could discover nothing to betoken the awful deluge of fire so soon to rain upon them. He slept well, and did not waken at two o'clock in the morning to see the two feet of snow turn to blood and commence to burn. Next morning, at the usual hour, rising and feeding his horse, he called loudly for someone to get him breakfast. After a time the inmates appeared, looking haggard and worn, and very much surprised that they were still alive. After breakfast, when he was about setting out, he asked "if they wanted pay, since they were all going to die so soon." This broke the spell and brought them back to mundane things. They promptly enough asked for and received pay for the entertainment of man and beast.

From Thomas Conant, *Upper Canada Sketches* (Toronto: William Briggs, 1898), pp. 92-96.

THE HERO-TYRANT OF ST. ANN'S

By nature Norman McLeod was a restless, rebellious soul. Barred first from the Presbyterian ministry and later from teaching in his native Sutherland because of his attacks on the easy-going ways of his church, McLeod migrated to Pictou, Nova Scotia, in 1817. But in Pictou, that High- lander's haven in the new world, McLeod resumed his de- nunciations of the clergy. Soon he gathered a group of followers and formed them into a separate church. Seeking a godly Utopia several of these "Normanites" joined McLeod in building the Ark, a small sailing ship in which they intended to travel to Ohio via the Gulf of Mexico and the Mississippi River. The Ark never got beyond Cape Breton Island where McLeod and his group founded their own settlement at St. Ann's in 1819.

St. Ann's became a model of holy living, thanks to the reign of terror that McLeod as pastor and magistrate exer- cised over every member of the community. The extent of McLeod's spiritual tyranny is described in this passage from a recent biography. The settlers at St. Ann's suffered much from McLeod's attempts to play God; but it was famine, not rebellion, that caused McLeod to build another ship and depart with one hundred and forty Normanites for a new and more promising land in their epic voyage of 1851 to Australia.

"Normanism", the outsiders called the religious practice of the people of St. Ann's, and Normanism it presently became, to them and to their leader. Among hundreds of McLeods, McLeod-ism would have been meaningless. For Norman it would also have been unsatisfactory. He liked to refer to himself by his Christian name and by doing so to see him- self as a successor to Paul and the other apostles. Probably Paul was his ideal. He quoted him profusely and emulated him in his writing of admonitory epistles to his followers at Pictou and to his fellow clergymen, in his strong single- handed leadership and in his intense responsibility for all aspects of his people's lives.

To outsiders who heard Norman's abuse of their clergy and of the organized Church it seemed that Normanism was a negative thing which existed only in opposition. But the high ideal against which he battered other groups Norman also held for his own people, fighting down in their be- haviour every sort of human impulse that could conflict with a high spiritual purpose, and so convinced of the greatness of his cause that there was no limit to the meticulous ruthlessness of his warfare.

Every detail of the observance of the Sabbath he supervised with careful concern. Nothing but the work of necessity could be done on Sunday. The potatoes were peeled on Saturday, and the dishes left unwashed until Monday morning. To drink from the brook or pick an apple from a tree was forbidden. The children learned to evade the second restriction by leaving apples on the lowest bough at the right height so that they could stand below and sink their teeth in them with their hands clasped innocently behind their backs. The dangling cores were proof that the fruit had not been "picked". The settlers were not even allowed to profit by nature's Sunday work. Each Saturday evening in the maple sugar season they had to make the rounds of their trees, and upset the sap troughs so that they would not use the Sunday run of sap. If, on a Sunday walk, a boy discovered where a hen had hidden her nest, he must leave the eggs untouched but carefully remember their location till Monday morning.

Even necessity was not an acceptable excuse if there was undue pleasure in the deed. One Sunday after the bay was frozen over, two boys skated to church. They were ordered to cut a hole in the ice and throw in their skates. The cutting of the holes was apparently acceptable Sabbath labour. During the summer it was permissible to come to church by boat, and at any time, to ride a horse at a decorous speed.

In the strictest households only theological topics were suitable for Sunday conversation. The adults discussed the minister's sermon and the children studied the catechism. Norman recalled as an example of clerical degeneracy a visit to a Scottish manse where "after dinner, on a Lord's day, the samplers of his Reverence's daughters were brought forward around the table for inspection".

Since the church service was one of the few public events of the week, another offence associated with the Sabbath was extravagance in dress. "The greatest zeal and zest for the Lord's day among the run of our youth," wrote Norman, "is evidently in order to see and be seen to advantage." He even went back to Noah's time to demonstrate that immodest dressing was a provocation for the Flood. "The sons of God saw the daughters of men that they were fair" —that is, in Norman's terms, "immodestly dressed to tempt and tease the carnal and careless powers and passions of their fickle and foolish spectators." So he condemned as instruments of Satan the girls' gay bonnets and flowing sleeves. There is no better evidence of the spirit of the community than that the women continued to attend church but also continued to wear their bonnets, although more than one girl started bravely from home in her new bonnet and hid it in a bush by the roadside rather than face the minister's scorn.

Often Norman had assailed the Church of Scotland for the laxity of its discipline. Its punishments were usually confined to breaches of the seventh commandment, "Thou shalt not commit adultery", and the censure was often commuted for money. If the offenders were censured it was in the comparative privacy of the Session room, not before all.

Norman showed no such mercy, but so great was the fear of him that there was never an occasion for the public censure of adultery. The only family which was known to have a guilty member moved from the settlement before they had to face the public humiliation. For other offences there was opportunity for merciless public reproof. Before the whole community Norman forced the abasement of Donald McLeod. For vanity and conspicuous dress he indicted even his own wife.

From Flora McPherson, *Watchman Against the World:* The Story of Norman McLeod and His People (Toronto: The Ryerson Press, 1962), pp. 100-102.

CHURCH VERSUS SECT

The claim of the Anglican Church to be the state church of Canada was not seriously challenged until the 1820's. Then the attack on Anglican privileges came from two sides. The Church of Scotland started the row by insisting on equal rights and a share of the Clergy Reserves, because, like the Church of England, it was established in the mother country. From the other side came the protest of the voluntaryists—those believing in the separation of church and state—that there was no place in democratic North America for religious favouritism. The most outspoken voluntaryists were the Baptists and the Methodists. To publicize their convictions the Methodists of Upper Canada founded the Christian Guardian *in 1829, with Egerton Ryerson as editor. This most influential newspaper was the foremost defender of religious equality in the 1830's. Today the* Guardian's *successor, the* United Church Observer, *has the largest circulation of any Canadian religious journal, and Ryerson's tiny printing plant has grown into a publishing house,* The Ryerson Press.

In 1825 Bishop Mountain, head of the Church of England in Canada, passed away. In his sermon at the funeral, Strachan made an attack on the Methodists of Canada, charging that they were not only ignorant, uncouth, and idle teachers of religion, but also dominated by American connections and republican principles.

The following year Dr. Strachan set out for England to obtain a charter for a provincial university. This college was to have the Archdeacon of York, that is Strachan himself, as perpetual president, and all its professors were to accept the thirty-nine articles of the Anglican Church. Not only was the Church of England to be the state church, but education was also to be the special dispensation of the established church in Canada. While Strachan was absent in England his funeral oration was published, April, 1826. This ill-advised outburst singled out the Methodists for special oppression. Their ministers were declared to be of United States origin and sympathy, ignorant men who had forsaken their proper employment to preach what they did not understand, and which, owing to their pride, they disdained to learn. Moreover, they were eager in spreading disaffection and disloyalty. It gave great offence, as may be imagined, but to Ryerson, of Loyalist and fighting stock, it was intolerable. He was persuaded to prepare a reply. Riding about his circuit, covering over one hundred miles, and preaching as many as eight sermons a week, often making notes in farm kitchens by candlelight, he at last appeared with his manuscript at the monthly meeting, and his brother ministers were determined to see it published. After some polishing it appeared in William Lyon Mackenzie's paper, *The Colonial Advocate*. Anson Green says: "We read and we wept; and then kneeled upon the grass and prayed, and thanked God for the able and timely defence of truth against falsehoods that were being circulated amongst the people. Little did we think that the able reviewer was a youth who had been received on trial with myself at the previous Conference."

When the Methodist Conference met at Ancaster, in 1829, the following resolution was adopted: "That a weekly paper should be established under the direction of the Conference, of a religious and moral character, to be entitled *The Christian Guardian*. That the place of its location be the town of York. That the sum of $700 is sufficient to purchase all the apparatus for a printing establishment. That the sum of $2,050 will meet the annual expense of such a paper. That the stock to the amount of $2,000 be raised, by dividing it into 100 shares of $20 each, half of which is to be paid immediately, and the remainder subject

to the call of the persons who may be appointed to superin-
tend the publishing of the paper; and said stock to be paid
with interest as soon as the avails of the concern would
admit of it. That the members of the Conference do take
up the shares among themselves; but if all be not disposed
of in that way, that they use their influence with their friends
to have the remainder taken up immediately."

From Lorne Pierce, *The Chronicle of a Century* (Toronto: The
Ryerson Press, 1929), pp. 10-11.

THE CLERGY RESERVES

*The Clergy Reserves consisted of nearly four thousand
square miles of land, largely in Upper Canada, set aside by
the Constitutional Act of 1790 for the support of "the
Protestant clergy." As the established religion, the Church
of England claimed an exclusive right to these Reserves, a
claim that involved the Church of England in bitter quarrels
with the Church of Scotland and with voluntaryists. The
whole issue of the Clergy Reserves quickly turned into a
political question when the Reformers or liberals demanded
an end to the Reserves in the name of religious equality.*

*William Lyon MacKenzie, the most prominent member
of the Upper Canadian radical Reformers, commented on
the failure of one of many attempts in the Upper Canadian
parliament to use the Clergy Reserves for general education.
Just a year after writing this, Mackenzie led an armed
rebellion in the province to end, among other things, the
Clergy Reserves. The Rebellion of 1837 failed, and the
Reserves remained a political and religious bone of conten-
tion among Canadians until the lands were nationalized
in 1854.*

Up to Monday evening this really important measure has
slept its way upon the order of the day of the orange-tory
assembly—altho' rumour tells us that Lawyer Draper and
others, who know as well as we do that no such bill ever
will pass in this world, are about to angle for sectarian
popularity, by ministering to the gullibility and avarice of
the parsons, priests and preachers, and gravely proposing

to divide the reserves and their proceeds among the Church of England and Scots Kirk Clergy, the Catholic Priests and Prelates, and the Ryersonian Methodist Preachers. Of course the crafty crew at 14 Downing Street would never consent to build up three sets of paid priesthoods, made independent of them by law, to wit the Kirk, which owns the jurisdiction of an assembly in Scotland, the Catholics, whose spiritual head is at Rome, and the Wesleyans, who bow the knee to a Conference sitting in Leeds, Sheffield or Manchester. An old man in his dotage, a girl in her teens, a profligate George Guelph, or Charles Stuart, or a lustful and beastly Henry 8th, these, or either of them may be in turn the "one shepherd", who, according to the creed repeated from Archdeacon Strachan's soft cushioned rostrum every Sunday, the faithful call *The Head* of the Holy Catholic Church —that church, with that head, would have the reserves if the Assembly willed it—but the others—Never!

But why divide the reserves in this way? There can only be *One True Faith*, there cannot be two, three, or four. Are we to pay the three protestant churches for teaching, as we ourself were taught in infancy, that the head of the Roman Catholic Church, in which the whole christian world worshipped for 1500 years, is the "beast, the man of sin, and *the scarlet whore*," mentioned in the Revelations? Are we to pay the Episcopalians, Methodists and Presbyterian Parsons for preaching and teaching, as they do in their pulpits, homilies, associations, confessions of faith, and Christian Guardians, that the God of Heaven bestowed these names upon the Bishops of Rome, and that the Roman religion is damnable in its doctrines and idolatrous in its worship? Upon the other hand, would it be right, that the King, Governor, two Houses Parliament, Legislative Council, and the House of Assembly should consent to pay out of the public lands the ministers and prelates of the Roman Catholic Church, the ancient religion of Christendom, for denouncing the Protestant churches as the propagators of a damnable heresy, those in their communion as unbelievers and heretics, and on the broad way to hell and eternal destruction?

Again—how vehemently does the Presbyterian system assail English prelacy—as the eldest daughter of the scarlet whore—popery in disguise—an anti-christian hierarchy!

Once more—Are the five and twenty denominations left out in this calculation—the Quakers, Mormons, Tunkards, Independents, Irvingites, Congregationalists, Baptists, Unitarians, Seceders, Menonists, Children of Peace, Christians, etc. to have no share?

Of all these there can only be one true faith. Are we then to pay alike for truth and error—for religion and idolatry—and thus prove King and Parliament of no moral principle at all?

Better would it be for the Assembly to follow in the wake of past parliaments, and give the reserves for the education of the people of the country.

From W. L. Mackenzie, *The Constitution*, December 14, 1836.

THE REBELS AT GRANDE LIGNE

Although the Clergy Reserves were an important cause of conflict in Upper Canada, religion was not directly involved in Mackenzie's ill-starred rebellion of 1837. In Lower Canada, however, religion was connected with the rebellion in 1837, though for entirely different reasons.

Since the British conquest the Roman Catholic Church had loyally supported the government in every crisis, and for several years before 1837 the violent French-Canadian nationalists had been accusing their church of selling out to "les anglais." In the Montreal area the radicals were so anticlerical that Bishop Lartigue went into hiding when the fighting began. South of Montreal, in the Saint-Jean valley, the rebels threatened to take their revenge on the famous Grande Ligne mission, a French Protestant school operated by Henrietta Feller, a Swiss widow who was responsible for the conversion of several local Roman Catholics.

The movements of the rebels always took place at night. They met in companies of one hundred, two hundred, and sometimes more. They were all masked, and were furnished with instruments of every kind imaginable, to get up a *charivari*. They went from house to house, mingling with their infernal music shouts and imprecations still more infernal. Those who did not come out immediately and join them were pelted with stones and threatened with fire. Some houses were entirely destroyed, with their contents. No description of mine can give you an idea of those wretched men; you must have seen and heard them: for my part, when I had seen and heard them, I could hardly believe that they were men.

Almost all the inhabitants of the Grande Ligne being *patriots* (as the rebels called themselves), they became so violent that there were no bounds to their disorderliness. Some friends came to warn us that we were in danger, and that we ought to remove as quickly as possible, and absent ourselves for some time. But we could not think of seeking our own safety and leaving our Canadians in peril. We asked the Lord to show us our path. I was so sure that He had placed me here that I would not stir a step without his command or His permission, and He did not leave me long in uncertainty. On Saturday, Oct. 28th, a kind English friend, Mr. Richard McGinnis, came on horseback to warn us of the danger in which we were placed. Next day, Sunday, we held three meetings as usual. Our Canadians were in great distress. They saw clearly that it was our duty to leave, but they trembled at the thought of being forsaken at such a time. We were blessed and comforted by meditating on 2 Chron. xx. 4-29. Oh, how often did I exclaim, for ourselves and our friends, 'We know not what to do, but our eyes are upon Thee!' That night was terrible. The rebels were increasing in number, became more violent, and gave themselves up to every kind of outrage. The days were bearable, but every night brought fresh horror. On Monday morning Brother Roussy set off for Champlain, to ascertain whether accommodation could be obtained there, should God show us that it was our duty to leave. He had not been gone an hour when I learned that the patriots were determined to kill him: they spoke of it quite openly, and expressed themselves in the most violent manner. I passed a sad day. It appeared very evident that it was our duty to go away; but to give up my Canadians was to give up my life. I was warned that the patriots were preparing to come to my house that night, and that their intentions were of the worst kind. How I blessed God that Brother Roussy was absent! I spent the evening in reading and prayer, with some of my dear Canadians, encouraging myself in God, and expecting that He would guide me, for I knew not what I ought to do. Oh, how true it is that we must look to Jesus if we would not lose courage! I had full experience of it that night, for when the mob came to the house I felt no fear. Brave Brother Leveque went out of his house to ask them what they wanted. They told him, and in an imperious manner, that he must immediately discontinue the scandal of the new religion which he had permitted in his house. Leveque asked them who gave them the power to act in that way. They replied, that they assumed the power, and that they would show us that they were masters. I was obliged to go and speak to them at the door, and was able to do it calmly. They commanded Brother Roussy and me to go away, and said that if we did not go quickly they would return and force us; that we had come to trouble the country by bringing in a new religion; and that they would not suffer any persons to live in that place who did not profess their own excellent religion, and were not good patriots like themselves. They uttered many blasphemies and threats, and left me, to carry on their outrages at the houses of the members of our little church. They introduced themselves by the *charivari* and throwing stones at the windows. They ordered all who had renounced Popery to abandon their new religion, and return to the mass, and told them that if they would not do it they must quit the country, or expect to be burnt out. See how clearly the path was marked out for us; for all determined rather to give up everything than to go back. Then we prepared for our departure, trusting that the merciful God would find a refuge for His poor persecuted church. Brother Roussy returned on Tuesday afternoon. He was fired at from a house on the road, but the Lord preserved him from injury. He told us that there was hope of obtaining shelter for us all at Champlain. On Wednesday, Nov. 4th, we quitted Canada. Our company consisted of upwards of fifty persons, and we left behind thirteen others, who had not been able to complete their arrangements, but would follow us soon.

From J. M. Cramp, *A Memoir of Madame Feller* (Toronto, 1876), pp. 111-113.

THE FREE CHURCH IS COMING

Many of the most painful episodes in the history of the Canadian churches have had their beginnings outside of Canada itself. Such an episode was the Disruption of the Church of Scotland and the creation of the Free Church in 1843. The problems that smashed the Kirk in Scotland simply did not exist in Canada—but sympathy for the Free Church cause brought the same divisions to Canada in 1844.

The new Free Church in Scotland sent Dr. Robert Burns to the United States and Canada to enlist support for its cause, and wherever Burns travelled, the Disruption followed. When he spoke at Queen's University six of the seven students in theology decided to leave the Church of Scotland. The popular reception that Burns got everywhere simply proved that a Scot was a Scot even if he was thousands of miles from Scotland and the causes of the Disruption.

William Bell, the pioneer minister at Perth, recorded in his diary the heart-searching and discussion in the Canadian synod meeting at Kingston in 1844 on the course that the Church of Scotland in Canada should follow regarding the Great Disruption.

On Thursday it was evident that a strong party were desirous of cutting the connection with the Church of Scotland altogether. This subject was often and warmly discussed during the session, without either party convincing the other. All were willing to declare the Synod independent, but the majority were opposed to renouncing *all* connection with the Church of Scotland. Much time was spent in prayer for wisdom and direction from the Spirit of God, and more in conference on the subject in dispute, but without any satisfactory result. Friday and Saturday were spent in various attempts to preserve peace and unity, but without success. On Saturday night, just before we left the church, Mr. Chalmers of Dailly, a Free Church minister then in Kingston, very imprudently interferred, which led to a kind of tumult, painful to every lover of peace and order.

On Sabbath Mr. Gordon preached in Mr. Machar's church, in the forenoon, Mr. Barclay in the afternoon, and my son George in the evening. Many of the people, and even the ministers, had gone to hear Mr. Chalmers in the Methodist church. Mr. Alexander's conduct, in announcing this meeting in the Synod, the evening before, was bad.

The whole of Monday was spent in debating a series of resolutions, brought forward by each of the parties, favouring their own views. Tuesday was spent in like manner. At tea at night the vote was taken, when 56 voted for Dr. Cook's motion to retain connection with the Church of Scotland; and 40 for Mr. Bayne's, to cut all connection. All parts of the house were crowded with persons anxious to learn the result. The rain poured down in torrents all the evening, and all got well drenched going home, in a very dark night. The streets were overflowed ankle deep in some places, and I having only thin shoes, and more than a mile to walk, was in no pleasant plight. It was long past midnight when I got to bed.

On Wednesday, when the Synod met, the seceding party did not attend, but met by themselves in another place. This enabled us to conduct our business with facility, and in peace. At 8 in the evening, the other party marched into the church, in a body, and gave in their protest; then withdrew in the same manner. Our Synod closed soon after.

From "The Diary of William Bell" (MS), Vol. XIV, pp. 107-109, Douglas Library Archives, Queen's University.

TRAGEDY AT GROSSE ISLE

The failure of several potato crops in Ireland beginning in 1845 caused a tragedy that changed the course of Canadian and American history. Living in dire poverty, the bulk of

*the Irish population depended for their very existence on
the tiny potato patches that they rented at high rates from
rich absentee landlords. When blight destroyed their staple
food seven hundred thousand peasants died of starvation
and disease, and countless thousands more fled their native
land to seek a new life in the new world. The destitute
refugees on the crowded immigrant ships carried only one
thing—a typhus plague that carried off thousands more of
their numbers and killed many charitable persons who tried
to help them.*

*The Canadian government was quite incapable of caring
for this mass of sick humanity that descended on them in
1847. The best it could do was separate the dying from
the apparently healthy at the Grosse Isle quarantine station
near Quebec. The wretched survivors of the terrible migration had neither money nor skills, and they soon found
themselves crowded into ghettos in such cities as Boston,
New York, Montreal or Toronto, where the only jobs available to them were at menial and heavy labour. Yet they
survived, and added a new element to the population and
the traditions of both countries.*

The year [1847] was marked by a very large immigration
to Canada from Ireland. As a rule, it is to the interest of
colonies to promote immigration to their shores, but the
rule is subject to modification by circumstances. In 1847
the exodus from Ireland was chiefly due to the failure of the
potato crop, and the famine which ensued therefrom. The
immigrants to Canada were for the most part from the poor
and indigent classes. Many of them were enfeebled in
health by poverty, starvation, and suffering. Owing to their
unhealthy condition, and to the insufficient accommodation
provided for such immense numbers on the vessels which
conveyed them across the ocean, a malignant form of ship-
fever broke out among them. Many died on the way out,
and of those who reached our shores alive a large percentage
were fit only for the hospitals. Some idea of the extent of
the misery which prevailed may be formed when it is
known that nearly 100,000 immigrants were landed at
Quebec during the year, and that the number confined in

hospitals at one time was not far short of 10,000. The mortality was very great among persons of all ages, and though children suffered equally with adults, nearly 1,000 immigrant orphans were left destitute at Montreal alone. Other Canadian cities and towns underwent similar inflictions. Children and adults alike were compelled to depend upon public and private charity. "Army after army of sick and suffering people, fleeing from famine in their native land to be stricken down by death in the valley of the St. Lawrence, stopped in rapid succession at Grosse Isle, and then, leaving numbers of their dead behind, pushed upwards towards the lakes in overcrowded steamers, to burden the inhabitants of the western towns and villages." It is worthy of being recorded to the lasting honour of our people that, irrespective of politics, nationality or colour, they responded to the demands thus made upon their philanthropy, not only with readiness, but even with generous eagerness. Their grumblings at the burdens imposed upon them did not make themselves heard until the crisis was over, and until the gaunt wolf had been driven from the door. Relief committees were formed all over the Province, not merely on behalf of the sufferers who had arrived in Canada, but also on behalf of those who remained in Ireland. The wealthy gave from their abundance; the poor from such store as they could command. The Indians of Caughnawaga, of the Credit, of the Grand River, of Munceytown, and of the Bay of Quinté, contributed their respective mites to relieve the sufferings of their white brethren. The coloured inhabitants, not a few of whom were escaped slaves from the Southern States, and who, as was to be expected, were almost all in poor worldly circumstances, proved that they appreciated the blessings of manhood and of freedom, and that they could practise self-denial for a reason to relieve the pressing needs of their more indigent fellow-creatures.

The necessities of the time were indeed imperative. The official mind ceased, for the nonce, to concern itself with party questions. Government awoke to the urgency of the occasion. The duty of making public provision for the sick and destitute was apparent, and the task of doing so was practically withdrawn from the Civil Secretary's Department, and assumed by the Administration as a whole. Immigrant sheds and temporary hospitals were erected in the principal cities, and such professional assistance as could be obtained was pressed into the public service. In spite of all that could be done, thousands of the starved and fever-stricken victims died from disease and exposure. Many Canadians who volunteered as physicians or nurses fell victims to contagion, and died by the side of their suffering patients. The Roman Catholic priesthood and the Sisters of Charity, as is their wont in such emergencies, displayed a courage and self-sacrifice which awoke general admiration. Early in the season they repaired in considerable numbers to Grosse Isle, the quarantine station, about thirty miles below Quebec, in the middle of the St. Lawrence, where thousands of the sufferers were disembarked. A vast majority of the latter professed the Roman Catholic faith, and as such had special claims upon the Roman Catholic clergy. So numerous were the patients, and so foul was the disorder from which they suffered, that the island was for some time a mass of putrescent loathsomeness. The atmosphere was as deadly as that of the fabled valley of Java through which the upas was said to send forth its fatal exhalations. So malignant was the poison that in some instances healthy persons, landing on the island to minister to the wants of the sufferers, were struck down by the pestilence and lay dead within a few hours. It will hardly be denied that the courage which enables a human being to encounter such dangers as these is at least as worthy of emulation as that more demonstrative heroism which impels to such achievements as the charge of the Light Brigade. The priesthood and sisterhood of Rome descended upon Grosse Isle like angels of mercy. If it cannot be said that at their control "Despair and anguish fled the struggling soul," it is at least true that they did what in them lay to cool the parched tongue, to lighten the pangs of dissolution, and to prepare the mind of the sufferer for the great change before him. They ministered to the temporal comforts of the living, and held the crucifix before the fading eyes of the dying. They had indeed the courage begotten of that implicit faith which removes mountains. It mattered not to them that the air was laden with pestilence; that the next breath which they drew might be charged with germs as fatal to human life as was the death-dealing draught of the Borgias. They felt that in alleviating human suffering they were carrying out the injunctions of the Founder of all Christian faiths, and that neither pestilence, poison, nor any other deadly thing had power to harm them without their Master's leave.

From J. C. Dent, *The Last Forty Years* (Toronto, 1881), Vol. II, pp. 94-96.

ALESSANDRO GAVAZZI

Like the Disruption of the Church of Scotland, the so-called Papal Aggression—the return of Catholic bishops to England in 1850—had nothing to do with Canada. But the "Papal Aggression" controversy was taken up in Canada and was the cause of a generation of violent feelings between Catholics and Protestants in this country. Into this religiously tense atmosphere created by inflamatory newspaper articles came Father Gavazzi, Italian nationalist and "freedom fighter" of the 1848 revolutions, to lecture against the reactionary policies of the Roman Catholic Church that he had just quit. The visit of Gavazzi ended in unforeseen, unnecessary and still unexplained tragedy that fanned still higher the flames of religious hatred in Canada.

During the spring of 1853 the celebrated Italian patriot Alessandro Gavazzi, an ex-monk of the Order of St. Paul, visited America,. He had even at that time acquired a more than European fame by his exertions in the cause of Italian liberty. In England he had been hailed with the enthusiasm justly due to one who has fought and suffered in a righteous cause, and his reputation as an eloquent and impassioned orator had preceded him across the ocean. During a tour in the United States he delivered a succession of powerful lectures, chiefly devoted to what he regarded as the errors of

Romanism. Early in June, 1853, he reached Quebec, and on the evening of the 6th, pursuant to previous announcement, he proceeded to deliver a discourse in the Free Church, in St. Ursule Street, on the subject of the Inquisition. A large audience assembled to hear him. When he had been speaking for somewhat more than an hour he was interrupted by violent and abusive exclamations on the part of a gang of lawless ruffians who had distributed themselves here and there among the audience, and who had doubtless repaired to the lecture for the purpose of assailing the orator of the evening. The interruption was the signal for action on the part of other ruffians outside. A volley of stones came crashing through the windows of the church, and immediately afterwards a crowd of persons armed with bludgeons made a forcible entrance into the building. A scene of wild confusion ensued. The shrieks of terrified women and children sounded in all directions. The intruders pressed forward in spite of such resistance as decorous, law-abiding citizens, hampered by the presence of their wives and daughters, were able to offer, and a number of them reached the pulpit where Father Gavazzi awaited their assault. They had to deal with no craven, but with a brave and resolute enthusiast who had more than once been compelled to take his life in his hand, and to fight for it against overwhelming odds. The mob precipitated themselves up the pulpit stairs with intent to hurl him to the floor. He was a man of large and powerful build, with the courage of a Luther and the thews of a prize-fighter. He faced his assailants with dauntless front, and with eyes flashing like royal jewels. Armed with a stool, he struck right and left with lightning-like rapidity, and with such tremendous effect that sixteen of his assailants bit the dust before him. The contest, however, was too unequal, and after maintaining his position for some minutes he was thrown violently over the ledge of the pulpit on to the heads of those beneath. Regaining his feet, he fought his way to one of the doors. A division of the military providentially arrived on the scene, and soon all danger was over. Father Gavazzi escaped with a few contusions, but his secretary was so badly beaten that for several days fears were entertained for his life. After leaving the church the mob stationed themselves in front of the Parliament buildings, and roared in stentorian tones for Mr. George Brown, whose championship of Protestantism had made him an object of their hatred. That gentleman happened to be absent from his place in the House on that evening and did not fall into their clutches.

•   •   •

On Thursday, the 9th, a much more serious affray occurred at Montreal, in consequence of the delivery of a lecture there by Father Gavazzi. The place of delivery was Zion Church, Haymarket Square. In order to guard against a recurrence of a scene similar to that which had been enacted three nights before at Quebec, a strong body of police were stationed opposite the church. Another occupied the middle of the square; and a small body of troops was kept in readiness near by. While the lecture was in progress there was an attempt on the part of a band of Roman Catholic Irish to force their way into the church. In this attempt they would have succeeded in spite of the police but for a number of persons in the audience, who sallied forth and repelled the intruders. A few minutes afterwards the latter returned to the assault, and were again driven back. One of them fired a pistol in his retreat, and was immediately shot down by a Protestant. Several other shots followed, and in the confusion that ensued the lecture was hurriedly brought to a close, and the audience started for their respective homes. During their progress along the streets several shots were fired at them, and many of them were wounded by stones and other missiles. Two women were struck down and trampled almost to death. A child of nine years of age had its arm broken at the wrist. The streets resounded with the roars of murderous, half-drunken navvies, and the shrieks of terror-stricken women. Mr. Charles Wilson, the mayor of the city, for some unaccountable reasons, ordered the troops, who had issued from their place of concealment, to fire upon the crowd. The order was obeyed, and five men fell dead. For a moment it seemed as though though the massacre of St. Bartholomew was to be reënacted in the streets of Montreal; but the firing by the troops put an end to aggression on the part of the mob. The dead and wounded were conveyed to their homes. It is impossible even to approximate the number of the wounded, but among them were at least a score of respectable men, women and children, whose only offence was that they had sanctioned, by their presence, a lecture by Father Gavazzi.

From J. C. Dent, *The Last Forty Years* (Toronto, 1881), Vol. II, pp. 274-277.

THE VOLUNTARY PRINCIPLE

Voluntaryism has triumphed over church establishment in Canada, though the separation of church and state in this country is not nearly so rigid or so complete as in the United States. Probably the staunchest supporters of voluntaryism have been the Baptists who have steadfastly refused to accept one cent of government aid even for their educational projects. At great personal sacrifice the Baptists of Canada built the Canadian Literary Institute at Woodstock during the depression of the late 1850's. Six months almost to the day after the Institute opened, it was destroyed by fire. How the Baptists met this catastrophe and rebuilt their college on the voluntary principle of accepting no public money was recounted in the biography of Robert Fyfe, the founder and first principal of the Institute.

This morning, about half past three, a fire broke out in the wing of the Institute, and in a short time enveloped the whole building in flames. The labor of years is a mass of smouldering rubbish. Alas! alas! In less than an hour and a half that which had so long been a subject of prayer and interest to the Baptists of Canada was a mass of ruins. Little or nothing could be saved. One cause for devout gratitude is the fact that but few of the students had arrived. They will be pouring in to-day and to-morrow. God is trying us sorely; but I am persuaded that this is meant for good. The origin of the fire is a mystery.

●   ●   ●

So wrote Dr. Fyfe for the *Baptist*, on the eighth of January, 1861, the very day when the new pupils were coming up for examination and classification, preparatory to the opening of the term. The sequel cannot be better told than in his own words, in the "Historical Sketch," written seventeen years after:

"How the burning of the Institute still throws its lurid glare over the horizon of the past! Some thought it was a judgment upon us, which would quiet Baptist ambition for ever. Had the Baptists not failed twice, and this was the third and last time. But God meant for us good, and not evil. On the evening of the day on which the Institute edifice was burned, eighty students came in to join the School. They were billeted in Woodstock families (who showed much sympathy with us,) till the Committee should be able to decide what to do. Hamilton offered us the use of a building, and so did Brantford, if we would move. After long and earnest effort, 'Woodstock Hotel,' (rent free for two years) with all its furniture, was procured for us by citizens of Woodstock."

●　　●　　●

"The Institute building was burned on Tuesday, and classes were reciting on Friday in the old Hotel!

"Still there was not a ray of light showing us where we were to get another building. After paying out the whole insurance we had on the building, we were more than $6,000 in debt!"

●　　●　　●

The following extract from a "Financial Statement" prepared under direction of the Board of Trustees in 1862, by the late Rev. Hoyes Lloyd, M.A., may serve to supplement the foregoing:—

"Saddened with the intelligence he had received of the destruction of the building, a brother sought repose, but sleep fled from his eyes. He is one of the Lord's stewards, and his Master was giving him a commission that night. When the morning dawned he did not disobey the promptings of the Holy One, who had given him his life, his wealth, and his hopes of Heaven; but sitting down he penned a letter to Dr. Fyfe pledging $4000 towards the erection of a new building, provided that the balance of the sum required should be raised from other sources.

"This munificent offer from the Hon. William McMaster of Toronto, caused light to beam through the darkness. The campaign was opened, and there was a general girding on of armor, with a sanguine hope of success. Responses to the appeals that were made came in from all quarters with rapidity, and in the source of a very few months $21,186.04 were secured by notes and pledges.

"The inhabitants of Woodstock offered the Woodstock Hotel for the purposes of the Institute, for twelve months, and $1000 of the amount required for the rent of it were pledged. The balance of $600 not being obtained by private subscription, the Town Council passed a resolution to levy a special tax upon the inhabitants to that amount, which the Board declined to accept, preferring to advance that amount out of their own treasury, at the risk of having none refunded, to make any compromise of Baptist principles of voluntaryism."

From J. E. Wells, *Life and Labours of Robert Alex Fyfe, D.D.* (Toronto, 1879), pp. 319-322.

SHEPHERDS OF HIS FLOCK

CLANSMAN AND BISHOP

The life of Alexander Macdonell, D.D., first Roman Catholic bishop of Upper Canada, is an epic of devoted leadership to his Highland fellow-Catholics and of loyalty to his sovereign. Born by the shores of Loch Ness in 1762, just fifteen miles and sixteen years from the defeat of Bonnie Prince Charlie and the death of the clan system, Alexander Macdonell was trained to the priesthood in a Spanish seminary, but returned to Scotland to share the plight of his Glengarry kinsmen who were being driven from their crofts to make room for sheep. Distressed by such scenes of hardship Macdonell found work for the sufferers in Glasgow's factories and then got George III's permission to raise a regiment among them—the first Catholic unit in the British Army since the Reformation, with Macdonell as the first Catholic chaplain. The Glengarry Fencibles served their Hanoverian King against Roman Catholic rebels in Ireland, and when the unit was disbanded Macdonell obtained land for the veterans in Glengarry County, Upper Canada. Again in wartime—1812—Macdonell gathered the Fencibles to repel the American invaders. This time Macdonell's reward for loyalty and leadership was a government salary and official recognition as bishop of Upper Canada in 1826.

The bishop's efforts to help Upper Canadian Catholics included the founding of Catholic schools, the training of priests in his own home, and even experiments in cattle breeding. A friend of John Strachan and confidant of successive governors, Alexander Macdonell was made a Legis-

152

lative Councillor of Upper Canada. Always concerned about the depressed condition of the Highlanders he joined Dr. Thomas Rolph to promote further emigration to Canada and in 1839 travelled to Scotland to advertise their scheme. There, during an eighty-mile stagecoach ride to Dumfries the seventy-seven-year-old bishop had to take an outside seat in a freezing January rain storm. Despite his rugged six-foot-four frame the experience was too much for the aging prelate and he died of a chill three days later. Buried with great pomp at Edinburgh in 1840, the bishop's mortal remains were later reinterred in his Cathedral at Kingston in the heart of his adopted home. A farewell dinner in his honour on the eve of his sentimental and last journey to the Highlands gave the beloved clansman and bishop a chance to reminisce publicly about his full and faithful life of service.

FAREWELL DINNER

Given by the Celtic Society of Upper Canada, at Kingston, to Bishop Macdonell, on the occasion of his quitting the Province for Great Britain.

The *Celtic Society* of Upper Canada, gave a Dinner to this venerable Prelate, on Wednesday last, May 29th, in this town, previous to his departure for the United Kingdom. At seven o'clock, a very numerous and highly respectable party sat down to a table, groaning beneath every luxury which could be procured, and which was furnished in Carmino's best style. The truly respected Sheriff of this District presided on the occasion, supported on either side by Bishops Macdonell and Gaulin; and a goodly array of British Officers, dressed in their usual splendid uniforms, with the beautiful addition of the Gaelic garb. The vice chair was filled by Colonel Donald McDonell, M.P.P., of Glengarry. The admirable Band of the 83rd attended, and delighted the company by their exquisite and enlivening strains. After the cloth was removed, the chairman gave,

1. "Her Majesty the Queen, God bless her!" 4 times 4, (loud rapturous plaudits.) *Band*—"God save the Queen."

2. The Queen Dowager, and the rest of the Royal Family, 3 times 3.   *Band*—"Hail Star of Brunswick!"

The chairman said he requested a full and flowing bumper to the next toast. It was known that their worthy and venerable guest, who was President of this Society, was on the eve of his departure to his native land, and that, as he was endeared to the whole community by his dignified liberality, courteous demeanour, and unostentatious benevolence, they would join him in drinking,

3. Our worthy and venerable guest, the Rt. Rev. Dr. Macdonell, Bishop of Kingston.

The enthusiastic and rapturous cheering which followed this toast defies description, it was renewed again and again —the Band played in admirable taste and feeling,

"Auld Lang Syne."

After the Band had ceased, Dr. Rolph, of Ancaster, was prevailed upon by the chairman to address the company, which he did in a beautiful and feeling manner, eulogizing the merits of the Venerable Prelate, and affectingly alluded to the sacrifice he was about making, at his advanced period of life, for the temporal and spiritual benefit of the people committed to his charge.—Loud plaudits followed the conclusion of Dr. Rolph's address.

The venerable Bishop, evidently greatly affected, rose and addressed the Company, as follows:

I most sincerely thank you, gentlemen, for the very high honour you have done me, by assembling here this day, on my account, and drinking my health in the cordial and affectionate manner you have done. This is an honour, gentlemen, I certainly did not expect, nor think myself worthy of, but although I find myself greatly embarrassed, for want of words to express the feelings of my heart on this occasion, nevertheless it would be affectation and hypocrisy in me, to deny how vain and proud I am of the compliment.

I feel my heart swell within my breast, and transported with delight, at seeing this table surrounded with an assemblage of such loyal, brave, and respectable characters. I think I am warranted in saying, that no part of the British Empire can boast of inhabitants more loyal to their Sover-

eign, more devotedly attached to the parent country, and to
the British Constitution, than the people of Kingston; and
of this they have given the most substantial and unequivocal
proofs; to those virtues, you have added, gentlemen, the
more amiable and social qualities of the mind, benevolence,
kindness and goodness of heart; that so obscure an individual, as myself, walking in so humble a path of life, should
meet with so much continence and attention, proves this
truth to a demonstration. (Loud cheers.)

The only claim, or pretension, I would ever have to the
good will of my countrymen, was the warm interest I took,
at an early period of life, in the welfare of a great number of
poor Highlanders who were ejected by their landlords out of
their possessions, at the close of the last century, and they
and their families set adrift on the world.

Those poor people, to the number of several hundreds, I
conducted to Glasgow, and procured employment for them
in the manufacturies, where I remained with them myself,
till in consequence of the French Revolution, and the stag-
nation of trade on the Continent, the manufacturies were
ruined and the Highlanders thrown out of employment. It
was then, I represented their destitute situation to Government; got them embodied into a Fencible Corps, and accompanied them myself to the Island of Guernsey and to Ireland,
and attended them for the period of eight years, till they,
with all the other Scotch Fencibles, were disbanded in 1802.
Seeing them thus a third time set adrift, without home or
habitation, I applied to Government, and obtained lands for
them in Canada; came with them myself, and resided with
them in the county of Glengarry for 25 years. In the course
of the last American War, they raised a corps of Fencibles
and a Regiment of Militia, and during the late troubles in
these Provinces, the Glengarry men armed four Regiments
of Militia, and their services are too well known to the
present company to render it necessary for me to say a word
upon the subject. (Great cheers.)

I cannot sit down without observing with pleasure and
delight, that the descendants of our ancestors, the Celts,
have never yet tarnished the glory and renown of their fore-
fathers, of which we ought to be proud. Monuments of their

power, and of the extent of their Empire still exist in every part of Europe, in the Basque Provinces, in Biscay, Guipuscoa, Asturias, and Navare; in Britanny, Wales, Ireland, and the Highlands of Scotland, the Celtic language is still spoken, and there is not a mountain, a river, strait, or an arm of the sea, between the Mediterranean, the Black Sea, and the Atlantic, but is Celtic; this, with the certainty, that nineteen out of every twenty words in the Latin language, are pure Celtic, is sufficient proof that the Celtic Empire extended from the pillars of Hercules to Archangel. (Loud cheers.)

It being my intention shortly to visit Great Britain, probably for the last time, I must wish farewell, for a while, to my friends; but my hopes and my expectations are to return to Kingston, as soon as I can, and to spend my few remaining days among friends, whom I love and esteem, and in whose society I expect to receive whatever comfort this world can afford me, at my advanced period of life. The Venerable Prelate sat down perfectly overpowered by his feelings, and was greeted with the warmest applause.

From *A Retrospect: First Catholic Diocese of Upper Canada and the Evolution of the Catholic Separate School System* (Cornwall: The Standard Printing House), pp. 38-40.

TO HALIFAX—WITH DR. MCCULLOCH

The name of Thomas McCulloch is at least as well remembered in Nova Scotia as that of his friend, Dr. James MacGregor, but for different reasons. MacGregor's life was devoted to pastoral labours—McCulloch's fame was earned by his pioneer educational efforts in Nova Scotia. McCulloch came from Scotland to take up a post in Prince Edward Island in 1803 but arriving too late in the season for a safe passage to the Island he accepted a call from the Secession congregation of Pictou and remained there for most of his life.

Within months of settling at Pictou Thomas McCulloch decided to open an academy to rival the Anglican King's College. After many delays and disappointments he did begin a grammar school but his dream of a college was not realized until 1817 when the famous Pictou Academy opened its doors to twenty-three students. Money problems plagued the Academy for years and in 1838 McCulloch finally abandoned it to become principal of the provincially-supported Dalhousie College. Before reaching this fateful decision, however, he had used every imaginable means to raise money for his own institution, including giving public demonstrations of science (or natural philosophy as it was then called) before the leading lights of Halifax society. With physical experiments that today would be elementary to high school students Thomas McCulloch entertained and in a few cases enlightened his upper-class audience, but, as he related, he had found the journey to Halifax a distressing venture into an unknown world and he was only too happy to get back to the security and seclusion of Pictou.

After much foreboding, conjecture, and hesitation, I arrived at the conclusion that necessity has no law, and that nothing else would relieve me from incumbrances, and enable me to carry on. I saw that to Halifax I must go, and to Halifax I went. It was not so bad as going to be hanged, but I found it by no means comfortable. I was going to the very focus of power, and enmity, and my unsubdued spirit felt that I was going because I could not stay at home. In Halifax there had never been any public exhibitions but of players and showmen and I really felt as if I belonged to the vagabond race. A bear and a few dancing dogs would have been suitable companions to the mood in which I entered into our gay and dissipated metropolis. To mend the matter, when my apparatus on two carriages was moving along the street, some wag gave notice to our Collector of Customs, who is one of our enemies in the Council, that a great cargo of smuggled tea had just come into town, and instantly I had a Custom-house officer at my heels. But learning that the packages were mine, instead of thinking of inspection, he returned to his master, who by the jokes of his acquaintances about catching me for a smuggler, was sufficiently mortified.

Before my arrival curiosity had been excited by an expectation held out in some of our papers that I might lecture in town in the course of the winter. Some wished information, and others amusement, and not a few were curious to see and hear a man whom our Bishop and his friends had laboured to put down. Others again determined to attend me in the hope of obtaining the means of running down both the Academy and myself. With all this I had laid my account, and before leaving home I resolved that if success was attainable, it should not be impeded by want of either labour, or sacrifice of interest. The magistrates placed the County Court House and jury rooms at my disposal for containing my apparatus, and also lecturing if I pleased. But for the latter purpose I found it necessary to hire a much larger hall in the same building.

At the solicitation of Councillors, the Admiral, Commissary-General, and other grandees who dine after six, I lectured three days a week at three o'clock. On the alternate days I lectured to another class at eight in the evening. In the compass of twenty-one lectures I managed to squeeze together a mass of the finest experiments in philosophy, and left my audience as eager as at the commencement of the course. I had with me my two sons, Michael and David, who could operate as well as myself. We had those attending us who had studied at Oxford, London, and Edinburgh, and they all agreed that they had never seen experiments more dexterously performed. In the evenings we were crowded to excess, and were obliged to refuse admittance. At the same time it was generally understood that eagerness for money had not kept pace with my wish to gratify friends, and such a kindly feeling pervaded both my classes that my lectures were supposed to have done more good to the Academy than anything which had previously happened. They brought me into contact with numbers in the higher circles to whom I had been sadly misrepresented, and who did not find me that arrogant and violent man that they had heard me reported to be .... I must therefore tell you that without being puffed up in Halifax I was thankful to get away from it, and now, after paying a few pressing encumbrances, I am again facing Presbyterian hardship.

I however received one proof of friendly feeling which I must not omit. One gentleman high in rank told me that though not rich, he could afford me twenty-five pounds a year till the Academy question should be settled, and he pressed me to receive it. I assured him that my trip to town, by relieving me from immediate embarrassment, made me as rich as Croesus, and I begged leave, with grateful acknowledgments, to decline his offer. He is one of the Bishop's flock, and in an official situation, and I pledged myself never to mention his name. This, therefore, is inter nos............................If you had seen me leading into her dining room the daughter of the heir apparent you would have laughed as I did, and as she did, when I told her that I was as awkward among the ladies as she would be among my apparatus. I am now in Pictou, and grappling with difficulty. *Sic transit gloria.*

From William McCulloch, *Life of Thomas McCulloch, D.D., Pictou* (1920), pp. 118-120.

HOLY DYING

The attitudes of Canadians towards crime, punishment, poverty and social evils have changed radically over the past century. No one reading the following text can doubt that the change has been for the better. The complaint of this editorial in the Anglican newspaper may sound slightly humorous in this day, but its self-righteous author wrote in deadly earnest. His god exacts an eye for an eye and offers no forgiving love, even to a youth about to pay the supreme penalty. Since public executions have long been abandoned criminals can have no public "triumphs" and pastors have less cause to complain about the choice of improper hymns!

EXECUTION

The wretched boy-murderer, Grant—aged only 15 years— suffered the extreme sentence of the law in Niagara, on Saturday the 6th inst. A detailed account of the melancholy event has appeared in the Niagara *Mail*. Two hymns were sung by the persons who visited the offender in his last moments,—one in the cell; the other upon the scaffold. The verses, selected by the prisoner himself, were suitable to his fearful situation; although had his own education, and the religious habits and feelings of his friends been different, he might have chosen, or there might have been recommended to him, one of the Penitential Psalms of David. The selection, however, made by the unhappy lad, betokened a right state of mind; the other hymn—chosen by the persons who accompanied him to the scaffold—evinced, we must say, a very wrong state of mind. To introduce upon the gallows verses appropriate only to the quiet death-bed of the sincere Christian is, to our mind, an act of shocking profaneness. It confounds the distinction between righteousness and sin; and gives an ill-judged and debasing view of the Redeemer's merciful atonement. And besides this, the practical effect of such a proceeding must be, to diminish the sense of degradation in the criminal's mind; to take away the humiliation and ignominy of a public execution, by making it an occasion of triumph rather than disgrace; and to encourage of course, in that degree, the commission of murder.

From *The Church*, May 12, 1848.

THE APOSTLE TO THE MICMACS

One of the most remarkable chapters in Canadian church history is the lifelong mission of Silas Tertius Rand to the Micmac Indians of the Maritimes. A stonemason by trade, with very little formal education, Rand discovered he had an amazing gift for languages. Four weeks spent at grammar school opened his mind to the beauties of the Latin language and of literature generally. Thereafter, by dint of unremitting labour, he taught himself ancient and modern Greek, Hebrew, French, German, Italian, Spanish, Micmac, Maliseet and Mohawk. Of all these languages Rand claimed that Micmac was the most wonderful and the one he loved best.

Rand was ordained when he was twenty-four, and became pastor of the Baptist church at Parrsboro. Two years later he returned to the Academy at Horton for a brief period of study. Then followed pastorates at Liverpool, Windsor, and Charlottetown. By the time he entered on his duties at Charlottetown, in the summer of 1846, it had become his fixed purpose to devote himself completely to the evangelization of the Indians of the Maritime provinces. The suggestion that this would be an excellent way of putting his ability to master languages to good use came first from Professor Isaac Chipman.

The years at Charlottetown were divided between the regular duties of his pastorates and the study of Micmac. Somewhere in the city he was fortunate enough to find an old file of the Royal Gazette containing an outline Micmac Grammar. Aided by Joe Brooks, a Frenchman who spoke English, French and Micmac, Dr. Rand made rapid progress in his study of the language. The money to pay his tutor was contributed by several English naval officers (Anglicans) of the brig *Gulnare,* then employed in surveying the coast east of Charlottetown. In all this Dr. Rand saw something more than a fortuitous combination of circumstances. Surely God was working to His own ends when Anglican seamen provided the means to pay a French Roman Catholic to teach Micmac to a Baptist minister that he might convert the Indians to Protestantism! During his stay at Charlottetown Dr. Rand had an opportunity to converse with the Micmacs in their native tongue as he visited their few settlements on the island. It was during these years he actually began his missionary labours among the aborigines of the provinces.

Since Dr. Rand was a Baptist minister, it was only to be expected that his denomination would sponsor his work among the Micmacs. This it set out to do, and the Nova Scotia Baptist Association at its meeting in 1849 appointed him a missionary for the ensuing year. However, this was not entirely according to Dr. Rand's wishes, for, as a result of his travels and correspondence, he had discovered that many from other Protestant bodies were interested in the evangelization of the native Indians. He felt a much greater work could be done if he had a wider support than his own denomination could give him. Furthermore, he was not concerned primarily with leading the Indians into the Baptist fellowship, but with presenting them with the Gospel and allowing them to choose their own branch of Protestant faith. In pursuance of these convictions, Rand was instrumental in having a Micmac Missionary Society organized October 23, 1850. The officials came from the clergy and the laity of different denominations, and an effort was made to enlist the sympathies of "pious individuals of any of the evangelical Protestant denominations."

Contributions were soon offered toward the support of the mission, but usually Rand had to make the collections himself. This added another duty to an already lengthy list, and soon became more of a burden than a delight. In 1864, fifteen years after his appointment, Rand discontinued all appeals for funds and went on with his work in the confidence that God, knowing his every need, would not leave him in want. Twenty-two years later he reported, "During the whole of this time I have never had a demand I could not meet." The changed method of finding support for his mission did not alter Dr. Rand's relation to the Micmac Missionary Society. In the course of the year 1853 he settled at Hantsport, Nova Scotia, where he continued to make his home until his death, October 4, 1889. There he did much of the translation of the scriptures into the Indian dialects for which he became justly famous, and with Hantsport as a base of operations he travelled far and wide over the Maritime Provinces in the discharge of his ministry.

Anyone attempting to assess the results of Dr. Rand's ministry among the native Indian tribes in terms of conversions to Protestantism is certain to be disappointed. Twenty-five years after he commenced his work among them he wrote, "But a small number have openly renounced their connection with the Romish church; but I have reason to know that a widespread enquiry has been awakened among them." Dr. Rand regretted that so many white people held such "abominable and unreasonable ideas of caste" that they would not treat the Indians as equals, and he became so affected by this attitude of superiority that later in his ministry he gave little emphasis to conversions to Protestantism. "I have been so dissatisfied with the Protestant church generally," he remarked, "that I have had no heart to urge the Indians, even if I believed them converted, to leave their church and join ours."

This feeling in no wise decreased the apostolic zeal and passion of this tireless worker. He had the welfare of the Red Man on his heart, and never overlooked a service that would improve his physical lot or better his conditions, morally, spiritually, or intellectually. He approached the Indians entirely without fear; at times one might flourish a knife and "talk big" but that did not deter Dr. Rand. The service he was rendering made fearful demands on him; it led him into the rude wigwams of an almost primitive people, whose roving ways and poverty-stricken conditions made possible scarcely a minimum of comfort. Yet for forty years he gave the best effort of his days to help the Micmacs, Mohawks, and Maliseets of these provinces. Although he had not the satisfaction of seeing towns of praying Indians spring up here as they had in New England following the work of Eliot, Brainerd, Roger Williams, and the Moravians, he did feel his was a duty well done.

By no means the least important phase of Dr. Rand's missionary service was the translation of the scriptures into Micmac and the compilation of a dictionary in the same tongue. The former were published by the British and Foreign Bible Society. In the translations he employed a phonetic system which was an improvement over the characters used by the Roman Catholics in the translations of the Prayer Book and literature made many years previously, but not printed until the first of Dr. Rand's translations had come from the press. There is no finer tribute to the solid character of his scholarship than a few sentences taken from a report in connection with the printing of the Psalms. The British and Foreign Bible Society had asked for information that was indispensable in the publication of his manuscript. In compliance with the request—

Mr Rand accordingly drew up a document in which he pointed out nearly a hundred passages in which his version varied sometimes slightly, often essentially, from the authorized version. Arranged one under the other were in each case to be seen at a glance, the English, the Micmac, with a translation into English, the Hebrew, the Septuagint, the Latin Vulgate, and the Latin versions of Junius and Tremellius, and Castillo,—the German of Luther, and of De Wette, with an English translation of Hengstenburg's German version, the French versions of Martin and Ostervald, the Spanish of Sico, and the Italian of Diodati, with a brief remark following, giving the translator's reasons for adopting the translation given in the Micmac.

It was a source of deep satisfaction to Dr. Rand that on one of the last tours he made, he found Indians all the way from the Tobique to Cape Breton able to read the scriptures he distributed, and eager to "obtain learning and to learn the English language."

Dr. Rand's literary work was not confined to that of the translator and lexicographer. He kept a kind of polyglot diary, often going for long periods without making an entry, but using generally any one of the various languages with which he was acquainted. His poems would fill a fair-sized volume; he also rendered many English hymns into passable Latin. Among the best known of his poems is "The Dying Indian's Dream," which bespeaks the wealth of pathos and Christian fervour Dr. Rand always manifested toward the Indian and his spiritual needs. Honours came slowly—and late—to the "Apostle to the Micmacs." Acadia University conferred on him the honorary degree of Doctor of Divinity and King's College and Queen's University each gave him the degree of Doctor of Laws.

From George E. Levy, *The Baptists of the Maritime Provinces* (Saint John: Barnes-Hopkins Ltd., 1946), pp. 166-170.

A SAILOR-BISHOP

Edward Field was appointed second bishop of Newfoundland in 1843. His diocese contained not only the Island but also Bermuda and the coast of Labrador. The only practicable way to visit such a scattered flock was by ship. On his first trip to the distant points of Labrador in 1848 this sailor-bishop discovered settlements where no clergyman

*had ever been seen before. He also discovered the depths of
ignorance that perpetual isolation could produce.*

Tuesday, August 15.—The wind came round again to the
westward this morning, but was very light. We got under
way at ten o'clock, and did not reach the Seal Islands till
five. Mr. Howe kindly furnished a pilot. Here, as in every
other harbour, are several vessels from Newfoundland.
Messrs. Hunt also keep a small "crew" here; that is, a few
men dwelling together to prosecute the fishery in the summer and kill seals in the winter. Five Englishmen remained
together here last winter, who killed 500 seals. In the first
three months of the year they are in the woods, to cut
timber and fire-wood. Besides this crew, the only residents
are Indians (Esquimaux) and half Indians, who live together, crowded into two huts, with an Englishman who has
taken one of the half Indian women as his wife. Guided by
the skipper of Mr. Hunt's crew, we visited these Indians.
Nearly all (twenty out of twenty-three) crowded together in
one small hut, with our two guides, Messrs. Harvey and
Hoyles, and myself. A strange group, or crowd, we were.
Indians will compress into the smallest possible compass;
but still we were brought into painfully close proximity.
Most of them could speak English, and some of them spoke
and answered as correctly and intelligently as any poor persons I have ever conversed with. It would have been difficult,
if not impossible, to detect, either in their appearance or
speech, any trace of Esquimaux. The men confessed that
they had only taken the women to live with them as wives,
without any form of marriage; but they well knew, they
said, the propriety and necessity of the religious service and
sanction, and were anxious to avail themselves of this opportunity. They knew no prayers, and had no creed; but had
been baptized, they said, and procured their children to be
baptized, "in the name of the Father, and of the Son, and of
the Holy Ghost." This service had, of course, been performed by some lay hand, as no Clergyman had ever been
among them or in the neighbourhood. The Englishman who
had taken one of these women as his wife, professed to be
able to read, but he had taught them nothing, or nothing

good, either by precept or practice. It was very affecting to see such a number of fine intelligent human beings, young and old, absolutely without any form of godliness or instruction in religion. Some belief they profess of God and a future state, but of the most vague and imperfect kind. They seem to have cast aside or forgotten their old superstitions, and to have received nothing in their place. It is surprising that they are so civil and humane. They expressed a desire to be properly baptized and married; and I appointed them to attend at the "room" tomorrow, at nine o'clock, for that purpose. The full moon had risen before we left, but neither party seemed anxious to shorten the conference.

Wednesday, August 16.—Messrs. Harvey and Hoyles met the Indians at the "room" at nine o'clock, according to appointment. They first of all baptized an Indian woman, a widow, and then married her to the man, a half Indian, with whom she now lives as wife. Another couple under similar circumstances were married.

I had intended to proceed after these services, but the wind was contrary. I called on one of the small traders from Newfoundland, who brought goods in his vessel, which he intends to load with fish, and is now selling them at about 300 per cent. profit.

In the evening we rowed four miles to visit an Englishman, with whom lives a step-daughter, a young woman, and the mother of two children, by, as there is too much reason to fear, her step-father. The man, I presume, suspected that the evil report had reached us, for he was earnest in denying the fact, before he was charged with the crime, or any allusion to it had been made. The poor girl seemed of a violent temper, and could hardly be brought in to speak with us. I gave him warnings suited to his case, which he received with careless acquiescence, but civilly; and I exhorted him to send the girl home to her mother's friends at Brigus, and directed her, when she arrived, to call on the Clergyman, promising that he would advise and assist her. In returning I took an oar, as I have done on former occasions, hoping that it is as lawful an exercise for a sailor-

Bishop on the Labrador, as a ride in the parks for my brethren in England.

From *Journal of the Bishop of Newfoundland's Voyage of Visitation and Discovery on the South and West Coasts of Newfoundland and on the Labrador, in the Church Ship "Hawk", in the year 1848* (London: The Society for Promoting Christian Knowledge, 1849), pp. 63-66.

DEATH IN THE OUTPORT

Residents of Canada's Atlantic provinces have always been famous for the unstinting and warm-hearted hospitality they offer to any stranger. In bygone days a visitor in Newfoundland's outports was doubly welcome for the news he might bring from "outside." Today it is hard to imagine the sense of isolation of living without radio, television or newspapers. Perhaps an inkling of such loneliness can be gathered from this account of the death of a humble priest whose whole world was encompassed within the tiny Newfoundland outport to which the call of the cross had led him.

In 1850, Bishop Mullock of St. John's had sent Révérend Père Alexis Bélanger (of Quebec) to the West Coast. He made his headquarters in a little house at Sandy Point on St. George's Bay. "From there he (sic) carried on such stupendous missionary activities in Saint George's Bay, Codroy Valley and Bay of Islands that had we not authentic proof for them we should class them amongst either the mythical or the impossible."

It is the summer of 1868—eighteen years later. The people of Sandy Point gathered in the little house that was the priest's residence and gazed at the body of the late missionary. Then they whispered among themselves in consternation:

"The priest is dead? The priest is *dead*."

"No. It cannot be."

"Yes, the good Père Bélanger who has lived here among us for so many years. *It is true*."

"What shall we do?" the voices ask one to the other.

"He was fainting at the Baptisms," a woman puts in.

"And often in the middle of other exercises he was going

aside to lie down for a few minutes. So many marriages to be blest! So many coming to take instructions! And all the time long journeys up and down the coast."

"There was no fit place for him to live—or even rest. And the food! Now he is dead."

"See here my friends, have you thought of this: How can Père Bélanger be buried?"

"Buried?" The little group repeated the word in awe. "Why? Why do you ask?"

"We are just laymen. How would we know what to do with the mortal remains of a priest? If it was just one of ourselves we could say the Rosary, or something. But a priest, it is too much."

"We cannot bury it . . . The body . . . and this hot weather! What will we do!"

"Cannot we get another priest to come here for the funeral?"

"Impossible. Over four hundred miles to St. John's by land. No, there is no way."

Horror-stricken they gathered around, gazing fearfully at the face of the dead missionary. Perhaps they remembered now more than ever all the things that he had told them, and his sermons he had clinched in death.

The elders of the village and the wise men consulted. Rather than have anything to do with burying a priest they chartered a vessel and sent four of their number as a guard and took the remains up the St. Lawrence to Quebec. Though six hundred miles, it was clear sailing, safe and placid, compared to the rough seas around the Newfoundland Coast.

And so Père Bélanger was buried under the Church of St. Roch des Aulnaies in his native parish, below Quebec.

From George Boyle, *Pioneer in Purple:* The Life and Work of Archbishop Neil McNeil (Montreal: Palm Publishers, 1951), pp. 57-59.

EGERTON RYERSON VISITS THE POPE

After ten busy and constructive years as superintendent of education for Upper Canada, the Reverend Doctor Eger-

*ton Ryerson took a leave of absence in 1855-6 to visit
Europe. The trip was partly for reasons of health but Ryerson also used the opportunity to renew old friendships, to
examine the latest European developments in education, and
to buy copies of famous works of art for the provincial
museum he was establishing at the Toronto Normal School.
In the course of his travel through Italy he was invited to
meet Pius IX, the most famous and the most formidable
successor to St. Peter in several centuries. Accompanied by
his twenty-year-old daughter and one of her friends, Egerton
Ryerson, the former circuit rider, was introduced to the head
of the Roman Catholic Church. It was a meeting of deep
significance, for relations of Protestants and Catholics in
Canada were at that moment strained to the point of open
violence. Considering the temper of those times, Ryerson
was careful that no word of his meeting ever reached his
political enemies at home.*

On my arrival at Rome I duly delivered my letter of introduction, and the King of Bavaria's medal to Cardinal
Antonelli who received me with the utmost courtesy, offered
me every facility to get pictures copied by my own selection
at Rome, and proposed, if acceptable to me, to present me
to His Holiness the Pope. I readily accepted the attentions
and honours offered me; but told the Cardinal that I had a
young daughter, and young lady companion of hers, whom
I should wish to accompany me; His Excellency said, "By
all means".

On the day appointed we went to the Vatican. Several
foreign dignitaries were waiting in an ante-room for an
audience with the Pope, but the Methodist preacher received precedence of them all. "Are you a clergyman?"
asked the Chancellor, who conducted me to the Pope's
presence; "I am a Wesleyan minister", I replied. "Ah! John
Wesley. I've heard of him", said the Chancellor, as he
shrugged his shoulders in surprise that a heretic should be
so honoured above orthodox sons of the Church. We were
then in due form introduced to the Pope, who received us
most courteously, and stood up and shook hands with me
and with whom I conversed (in French) for nearly a

quarter of an hour; during the conversation His Holiness thanked me for the fairness and kindness with which he understood I had treated his Catholic children in Canada. Before the close of the interview, His Holiness turned to the young ladies (each of whom had a little sheet of note paper in their hands) and said, "My children, what is that you have in your hands?" The girls curtsied respectfully, and told His Holiness that they brought these sheets of paper in hopes His Holiness would have the condescension and kindness to give them his autograph. He smiled, and wrote in Latin the benediction: "Grace, mercy, and peace from God our Father, and Jesus Christ our Lord," and then kindly gave them also the pen with which it was written.

Thus ended our interview with Pope Pius IX, of whose unaffected sincerity, candor, kindness, and good sense, we formed the most favourable opinion, notwithstanding the system of which he is the head.

From Egerton A. Ryerson, *The Story of My Life* (Toronto: William Briggs, 1883), pp. 366-367.

A PLEA FOR CONFEDERATION

The Christian churches were unanimously in favour of Confederation, even though few of them felt it was necessary or desirable to make any public declaration of their support for the movement. Confederation offered the churches the same challenge that the politicians saw—uniting the separate colonies of British North America into a strong nation would also lead to union between the separate branches of each Christian communion. Yet in the Province of Canada (soon to become Quebec and Ontario) twenty-one of the forty-eight French members of Parliament voted against Confederation, and this was no doubt the reason why the five Roman Catholic bishops of Quebec publicly urged their flocks to support Confederation. Four of the bishops were strong Confederationists, while Bourget, the ultramontane bishop of Montreal, advised accepting Confederation as a necessity.

The bishops' pastoral letters were read from every pulpit on two successive Sundays in June 1867. This letter, issued by Bishop Thomas Cook of Trois-Rivières, shows clearly the ideas that moved the bishops to speak out for Confederation of British North America.

You are not unaware, Our Very Dear Brethren, of the liveliness of the debates on this [Confederation] project in the House of Commons. The great majority of the Members considered it the only solid hope that Providence offered our [French] nationality, while the minority rejected it with all their energy, without however having any better plan to put in its place as a way out of the deadlock in which the country finds itself. . . . It is painful to us to see the violence with which some of our fellow-citizens have opposed and risen up against the Confederation project; not that it was punishable to discuss it formerly, but the absence of moderaion is always reprehensible. . . .

Oh! how happy we would be, Our Very Dear Brethren, if, on this auspicious occasion, we saw men of all parties unite sincerely and march forward as one under the same flag to work with the same enthusiasm to promote the prosperity and assure the happiness of our common country.

From *Le Journal de Trois-Rivières*, June 11, 1867.

THE CROSS MOVES WEST

BIRCH BARK TALK

In every century the greatest problem facing the Christian missionaries had been communicating with the native North Americans. The Indians and Eskimos of North America were living in their own Stone Age when they first encountered the Europeans. Their languages were many and difficult, and they were also unwritten except for a crude and limited sign language. The name of James Evans will be forever associated with the syllabic alphabet that he developed and which has been adapted for use by virtually all the native inhabitants of northern Canada.

Evans began experimenting with a syllabic alphabet during the 1830's while teaching at the Methodists' Indian Mission on Rice Lake. After a year spent among the natives around Lake Superior he was chosen by the English Methodist Conference of England to lead a mission to the far West. Evans' own work at Norway House on Lake Winnipeg ended too soon in personal tragedy but he did perfect his syllabic writing and, using the rough materials to be found at hand in a fur-trading post, he made birch bark "talk" to the Indians in their own language.

For years his inventive genius had busied itself with syllables as a basis for a literature and a medium of instruction. He soon discovered that the Indian languages lent themselves admirably to the adoption of such a programme. His first attempt in this direction with the Mississauga dialect met with a rather discouraging reception by the Board of the British and Foreign Bible Society in Toronto, Ontario. . . . But now he was in a clear field in contact with a form of speech definitely susceptible to syllabic cultivation. The time was ripe, the occasion favourable, and so he set to work. He first had already invented a number of simple symbols, representing the various syllables prominent in the picturesque speech of the Red Man. He then cut in small blocks of wood pictures of these; and from the lead salvaged from old tea chests he was able to mould the type for the printing process. For ink he used the black soot, scraped from the old stone chimney, made liquid by the oil taken from the sturgeon, and for paper the yellow pliant bark of the birch tree, and for printing press the instrument used by the Hudson's Bay Company in baling furs to be shipped overseas for use in the London market. And so James Evans saw in the block of wood, the waste lead, the grimy soot, the unwanted oil, the pliant birch bark, and the clumsy jack press, the shining gateway opening out into the promising possession of a great literature. The story is told that his first attempt to present it was to paint the symbols on the face of a great granite rock and get the Indians to repeat the sounds after him. After practising them for a time on the sounds he took the symbol that represented the sound "ma," then the symbol that stood for "ni," and the next the one for "to," and put them side by side. The Indian read, saw in characters the name of his God and burst out in lofty expressions of deep satisfaction. These characters are so simple that an Indian of ordinary intelligence can learn to read the printed page by a few days' application and practice.

The news of this discovery spread far and wide over the plains and became the usual subject of conversation around the evening camp-fire of the busy trader. In a short time portions of hymn selections from the ritual and verses of scripture were brought to the Indian by means of the Cree syllabic. In the work of translating and printing much assistance was given to William Mason recently transferred to Norway House by Mrs. Evans and Mrs. Ross. With these, co-operated intelligently and helpfully H. B. Steinhauer, Thomas Hassell and John Sinclair. As a result of the co-operation of these workers in and for the Kingdom of God, the whole Bible was translated into Cree Syllabic and published in 1861 by the British and Foreign Bible Society of London, England. Later, the Rev. Archdeacon McKay became very proficient in the use of the Cree Syllabic, and went to London, England, where he spent much time in perfecting this remarkable invention and revising the Cree Bible of 1861.

The story is told that Chief Berens, from a point on Lake Winnipeg, some distance to the south, journeyed to Norway House to learn the new language, at that time widely known as the "Birch Bark Talk," that he might transfer its enlightening influence to the members of his tribe. After remaining at Norway House long enough to learn to read the language he undertook to interpret it to his own people at Berens River. Chief Berens was later baptized by Rev. George McDougall and admitted as a professing Christian to membership in the Christian Church. Many other incidents might be mentioned, but these will appear in the developing story. One need not wonder that Lord Dufferin, the Governor-General of Canada, when he saw the invention and witnessed its transforming power, remarked that the man who invented the Cree Syllabic was worthy of a resting place in Westminster Abbey. This system of phonetic teaching, based on syllabic characters, has been employed as a useful medium of instruction in some of the dialects of China. So the invention has found avenues of useful expression far beyond its native haunts.

From J. H. Riddell, *Methodism in the Middle West* (Toronto: The Ryerson Press, 1946), pp. 16-17.

DIVERSIONS OF THE GOLD-SEEKERS

Matthew MacFie arrived in Victoria from England in 1859, at the height of the first gold rush. He had been sent from England as a Congregational minister to establish a mission in the boom-town capital of Vancouver Island. Very soon, however, MacFie was embroiled in controversy because he separated the Negroes of his congregation and made them sit apart from the whites. Under pressure from his church superiors at home MacFie relented and abandoned racial segregation. He remained in the colony only a few years, and his account of life in the Pacific Coast colonies of Vancouver Island and British Columbia during the gold rush days was written after his return to England. He paints a vivid picture of the rough-and-tumble life on the western frontier and especially of the place—or lack of place—that religion held in those rude surroundings.

Society in the interior is very depraved. In Yale, Douglas, Lytton, Lillooet, Forks of Quesnelle, and the mining towns, little trace of Sunday is at present visible, except in the resort of miners on that day to market for provisions, washing of dirty clothes, repairing machinery, gambling, and dissipation. Out of the 5,000 souls in Victoria, a few may be found who respect the ordinances of religion. But at the mines, adherents of religious bodies have hitherto been numbered by scores and units.

Up to the present there have been but two places of worship in Cariboo—one connected with the Church of England, and the other with the Wesleyan Methodists. Till the fall of 1863, when these were built, the services of public worship were conducted in a bar-room and billiard-saloon. At one end of the apartment was the clergyman, with his small congregation, and at the other were desperadoes, collected unblushingly around the *faro* or *pokah* table, staking the earnings of the preceding week.

Profane language is almost universal, and is employed with diabolical ingenuity. The names of "Jesus Christ" and the "Almighty" are introduced in most blasphemous connections. Going to church is known among many as "the religious dodge," which is said to be "played out," or, in other words, a superstition which has ceased to have any interest for enlightened members of society.

From Matthew MacFie, *Vancouver Island and British Columbia* (London, 1865), pp. 414-415.

THE BLACK FLAG AT METLAKAHTLA

When a young Englishman, William Duncan, heard the call to service from the Church Missionary Society in 1853, he resolved to devote his life to work in India as a lay missionary. Fate instead brought him to Fort Simpson and the Tsimshean tribe on the northern coast of British Columbia. At Fort Simpson, Duncan soon convinced himself that associating with white men was demoralizing the natives, and so he founded a separate village for Christian Indians at Metlakahtla as an experiment in holy living.

Duncan drew up a set of rules to govern the new settlement, including regulations that required the natives to give up such ancient tribal customs as gambling, devil worship, magical practices and potlaches. Other obligations were to attend church, keep clean, keep busy, keep the peace—and pay taxes! Duncan's "black flag" system of ridding his village of undesirables was recounted by one of his several biographers.

In later years Duncan's disagreements with the newly appointed bishop of Caledonia over ritualism and proper missionary practices caused him to lead a second exodus of his Indians to Alaska in 1887.

Sometimes, it might, of course, be desirable to get some evil-minded, or evil-doing, man out of town. Mr. Duncan had a way of accomplishing this without violence, which occasionally might prove dangerous, and cause bloodshed.

In the centre of the village, close to the Mission House, was, after the first five years at Metlakahtla, located a bastion, an octagonal building, the lower part whereof was used for a jail. The upper part formed a balustrade, and was provided with a tall flagstaff, on which, on festive occasions, the English colours were hoisted.

When a bad man was desired to leave town, Mr. Duncan hoisted on this flagstaff a black flag, showing that there was a public enemy in camp. The man who was offensive knew well enough who was meant. Usually, the people knew it too. If they did not, Mr. Duncan let a few trusted ones know who it was. That was enough. In a few moments public opinion was aroused. As soon as they saw the flag, the tongues commence to wag. If any one met the man, he would look at him askance. Some one might say right to him:

"You better get out of here. We don't want you."

This was sufficient. No one could resist the public and general scorn and abhorrence which the black flag indicated.

In one instance only was the black flag not sufficient to drive a "devil" out of town.

He was a chief, who had just succeeded to his rank, upon the death of his old uncle, Neyahshlackahnoosh, the old head chief of the Kitlahns, and now was anxious to show what he could do, perhaps in order to do justice to the old adage, that new brooms sweep clean.

There were forty or fifty of his tribe at Metlakahtla. He was a surly, disgruntled fellow. One Saturday night he called a secret meeting of the members of his tribe, at which he railed about how their old, time-honoured customs were being abolished, their old, proud memories disgraced, and their warlike and brave family traits eradicated, and then exhorted them to go back to the old feasts, joys, and pleasures.

No one said anything. Not a single man expressed disapproval of what he had said.

Mr. Duncan learned of the meeting Sunday morning. This looked very much like mutiny. Heroic measures were evidently required, and that at once. He made up his mind that he must have that chief out of town before service, or no one could tell where it might end.

So he hoisted the black flag at once.

Oh, what a talk it started! "Who can it be?"

He called two constables, and told them to go at once, and tell the chief to take his canoe and get out of there before eleven o'clock.

The black flag was not sufficient in this case. It meant: "There is no one with you. You are our enemy. We are all down on you."

This man had an idea that so long as no disapproval was voiced at the meeting, he was backed by a certain element in the town—that public opinion was *not* against him. The black flag did not tell the truth as to him. He, therefore, refused to go.

Mr. Duncan now stepped out in front of his cottage with his revolver in his hand. He stood where the man could plainly see him, and told the constables:

"Go over and tell him from me that in ten minutes, by the watch, his canoe is to be hauled down, and he on his way out. If not, I will meet him face to face. And one of us, perhaps both, will die."

Inside of five minutes, the chief's belongings were

brought down to the beach, his canoe pushed off, and he went his way.

The black flag came down.

From J. W. Arctander, *The Apostle of Alaska* (2nd. ed.; Westwood, N.J.,: Fleming H. Revell Company, 1909), pp. 193-195.

AT THE END OF STEEL

The name of Albert Lacombe has become a legend in western Canada. Born in Quebec in 1826 he was one of the first Roman Catholic missionaries of the Oblate Order to enter the vast prairies. Travelling widely he became the trusted adviser of both the Blackfoot tribe and their mortal enemies the Crees. His influence among the natives was so great that he was called on by the CPR to mediate with Chief Crowfoot when Blackfeet threatened an uprising to prevent the building of the railroad across their reservation. The following acount describes Lacombe's efforts and their reward. Crowfoot too got a reward for his co-operation—a lifetime pass on the CPR which he wore ever after on a chain around his neck. After founding schools, churches and welfare institutions for his beloved Indians, Albert Lacombe died near Calgary, the site of so many of his labours, in his ninetieth year.

The times of long and tedious voyages in ox-carts were gone. The Canadian Pacific Railway had just entered upon its successful career, and as one of [Bishop] Taché's missionaries had been of very material assistance in its construction, the latter had received from the company privileges which he felt honoured to share with his ecclesiastical superior.

The difficulties which attended the laying of the steel rails from Winnipeg to the Pacific were not all of a physical order. Puzzled at first at the labours of the gangs of workmen who unceremoniously tore the bosom of their native prairies, the proud children of the plains had soon become incensed at the hardihood of the pale-faced strangers. Their irritation reached a climax when they were told of the wave of immigration of which the iron horse was but the fore-runner and instrument. The Blackfeet especially made themselves conspicuous by their opposition to the enterprise, and formally notified the workmen that they must stop meddling with land that was not theirs and return to their country, wherever that might be.

Fortunately, the foremen had made the acquaintance of Father Lacombe, and were aware of his immense influence over the redskins. In their distress they appealed to him. The missionary lost no time in repairing to the scene of the trouble; but, perfectly familiar with aborigine usage, he did not go empty-handed. Having bought a quantity of tobacco and some victuals, he gave to his indignant children one of those feasts without which no serious business can be transacted among the braves of the west.

When they had smoked and eaten to their hearts' content, he reminded them of all he had done for them in the past.

"Did I ever give you an ill-advised counsel?" he asked.

"Never," they confessed.

"Have I not always shown myself your best friend on earth?"

"Always."

Then in impassioned language he cautioned the young men, who are everywhere empty-headed, against the presumptuous use of violence towards the whites who, in their own country, are numerous as the mosquitoes on a sultry day, and would never leave unavenged any wrong done their fellows. He expatiated on the advantages of a railway, and gave assurances that the tribe's lands would ever be respected.

As a result, work was resumed, and now Archbishop Taché had a special car at his disposal when he first visited Regina and, later on (September 21, 1884), Calgary.

From A. G. Morice, *The Catholic Church in Western Canada* (Toronto: The Musson Book Company, 1910), Vol. II, pp. 156-158.

THE NEW ROME OF LOUIS RIEL

Louis Riel was hanged at Regina in 1885 for high treason because, in the eyes of the law, he was sane—he could dis-

tinguish between right and wrong. His prosecutors admitted that Riel suffered serious delusions about religion yet those delusions did not affect his other actions. Such at least was the argument that sent Louis Riel to the gallows instead of returning him to a mental hospital. If Louis Riel were on trial today the treatment and the verdict would certainly be different.

What were those religious delusions of Louis Riel? His early training for the priesthood had been stopped by his instability and had been followed by several periods in asylums. With the passing years Riel began to join his fervent love for his fellow half-breeds to a vision of a new papacy in Canada, with Louis Riel—or "David" as he now called himself—in the role of prophet and protector of the New Rome.

The following letter from Louis Riel to Bishop Taché, written from the jail in Regina, explained Riel's religious aims and suggested the depth of his mental instability.

On one side Rome is defiled, she is held captive, in the service of the Revolution as far as possible. By the simple lights even of common sense, it is reasonable to suppose that the jealous spirit of God has been unable to remain in Rome, after it had been finally doomed to the prostitution of the anti-religious ideas which unfortunately rule Italy and France today. Rome is to Jesus Christ like unto a ravished bride. On another side how could the fullness of the gifts of the Papacy be satisfied to remain in a bishop tied to Rome? Even if the pope were, quite apart from that, personally an entirely holy man, the mere fact of his staying in the midst of the abominations of desolation naturally seems contrary to the good pleasure of God. But just as a person in good health cannot remain in an unhealthy or infected place without becoming weak or sick, thus in the present condition of things which surround him, the bishop of Rome cannot prevent his moral state from being gravely affected and damaged.

As much because of Europe and Rome as because of Him, the Holy Spirit has left him.

Monseigneur, forgive me the assurance with which I speak to you. For this assurance is not mine. I humble myself before you and before your clergy to please God who, I am most firmly convinced, is aiding and directing me.

The comforting Holy Spirit of Jesus Christ has chosen another vicar for himself. He dwelt in Bishop Ignace Bourget since 8 December, 1875. It is pleasing to God that we should consider the holy Archbishop as the first successor of St. Peter in spirit and in truth, in the New World. This is what Divine Providence mercifully helped me to proclaim with the Métis in Saskatchewan.

But since the death of the good Archbishop Bourget, God has cast the eyes of his unutterable goodness upon you. He wants to reward you before the whole world and to render unto you an hundredfold the worldly goods which you have sacrificed for him these forty years, to serve and to please him. You are by divine election the true successor of Archbishop Bourget. And yet while you were paying the last honours to the mortal remains of this great servant of God, you became yourself for the happiness of many and the unhappiness of none, the vicar of Jesus Christ on earth. God has wished that, captured in a terrible war of defence, and in the midst of the greatest dangers, I should proclaim, assisted by His loving help and by the good faith of the Métis, the Pontificate of Ignace Bourget. In its mercy Providence has spared me, my wife, and my children from death, wounds, and misfortunes of all kinds. It has miraculously saved Gabriel Dumont and the existence of the Métis as a people. Let us thank God for innumerable blessings.

Now that I am imprisoned, accused of High Treason, with no means to defend myself, with no chance of having my witnesses and in such a situation that my best witnesses are angry with me, I entrust myself to this paternal Providence of God who cares for everything and everyone: *and this day the 24 July, 1885,* I humbly proclaim from the depths of this padlocked prison of Regina that you are the Pontiff elected by God, to instruct, console, comfort, lead, bless and save through the grace of Jesus Christ, the New World.

The day that the Holy Pontifical Spirit adopted Archbishop Bourget, He deigned to choose at the same time Ville-Marie as the religious capital of this continent and the French-Canadian people for His priestly people. Today when this divine Spirit of consolation dwells in you, the

Holy Spirit deigns to choose in advance the French-Canadian Métis for His priestly people and St. Boniface for his present city. After you, the Papacy will be returned to Ville-Marie, to remain there fifteen months and a week of years, that is, 457 years, beginning 8 December, 1875. Then it will come back to continue the thread of our succession in Manitoba and will be there one thousand eight hundred and seventy-six years.

Carte Blanche is granted to every Catholic to leave Rome. Having to proclaim this truth, it was fitting that I should have the courage of my faith and set the example. This is why I have separated from Rome and have begged the Métis to do as I, if they wanted to. It is also to march onward, in deed as well as word, that I have incited my brethren, the Métis of Saskatchewan, to recognize Archbishop Ignace Bourget as pontiff of the New World.

● ● ●

My present position is a position which can be counted among the most desperate that history can offer. To emerge triumphant is a blessing which can come to me only from God and His Church. I beg you and your clergy to come to my help. And the proof that I am doing the will of Our Lord is that everything will succeed for you wondrously. You will save me with ease. My earthly safety will then be the manifest proof that my difficult task is authorized by Heaven and will mark with a divine seal the sublime calling which I announce to you with all the joy of a tested recognition.

From *No. 422, Riel Collection* (Winnipeg: Manitoba Provincial Archives), pp. 147-154.

THE VOICE OF GOD

It may seem a far cry from Indian missions to the Doukhobor problem but there is a connecting link—the famous Methodist missionary John McDougall, "Pathfinder of the Plains," "Prophet of the Prairies." McDougall went west as a youth in 1860 when his father, George, was posted to

James Evans' old mission. The lives of these two men, father and son, were identified with the West and Indian missions for over half a century.

George McDougall died in a prairie snow storm in 1876 but John continued his father's work with the western Indians. As their friend John pleaded their cause with the Canadian government, and also as their friend he succeeded in keeping most of his tribes loyal during Riel's rebellion of 1885. A decade after that rebellion the West began to fill up with settlers, among them more than seven thousand Russian Doukhobors who found a refuge in Canada in 1899. The later arrival of their spiritual leader, Peter Veregin, however, created so many problems that the government sought the help of John McDougall whose arts of diplomacy had been proven so often with the Indians.

When it became known that Peter Veregin had been liberated in Siberia and was on his way to Canada, great expectations were awakened. Many of the people became so agitated that a pilgrimage comprising more than one thousand men, women and children wended its way in October, 1902, to meet Christ as incarnated in Veregin, without any provisions, with no money and little clothing. A sudden change in the weather brought much suffering until at last, on November 8th, at Minnedosa in Manitoba, a special train was sent by the authorities and the remnant of four hundred and fifty men compelled to return to their homes.

Peter Veregin arrived in December, 1902, and at once his influence was felt. After his liberation, he had an interview with Tolstoi, imbibing his teachings on love and non-resistance, and this explains to a certain extent the attitude of the people in general. They accepted him as a divine leader whose word was the voice of God.

Three years after Peter Veregin had arrived in Canada, John McDougall was appointed Commissioner for the Doukhobors for the purpose of investigating the causes of their internal troubles, settling difficulties and encouraging them in their work and in loyalty to the empire. Because of his eminent service to the country, his long and wide experience in dealing with the native tribes in the West, and his wisdom and tact, he was at that time the best man for the position that was available. Still he laboured under several disadvantages. He could not speak their language; he knew little of their peculiar religious tenets; he was a minister of the Gospel of Christ, and at the same time a representative of the Dominion. They were suspicious of anyone in this double capacity. There were some problems over land in Saskatchewan pending settlement in the courts of justice. McDougall was called upon to help solve them and ensure peace. He visited all the colonies in Saskatchewan and British Columbia, and that he was unable to bring their troubles to an end is not to be wondered at, when Veregin himself failed. The British and American Quakers, who had helped them so liberally, were disappointed with them.

After John McDougall had visited the colonies for three years, he reported that great progress had been made by the Doukhobors in Saskatchewan. For two years there had been splendid crops and they were becoming wealthy. The Doukhobors were specially adapted for an agricultural or fruit-growing country. Physically they presented a fine type of settler, while morally their conduct was equal to any class of people on the continent. When John McDougall visited their homes he found them clean and wholesome. The women were modest in demeanour, neat and comely in dress, and always hard at work, while the children were tidy, respectful and happy. The national costume, the preservation of their language, and their spiritual and social ideals have prevented these people from becoming Canadians. Still there is hope that by gentle compulsion and patience their suspicion and distrust, due to ignorance and years of suffering in Russia, will pass away, and with their greater freedom and comfort, they will become assimilated. They represent several great moral principles which lie at the foundation of the progress of the human race, and we are compelled to recognize these truths.

From John Maclean, *McDougall of Alberta* (Toronto: The Ryerson Press, 1927), pp. 238-240.

THE OUTCAST SIOUX

It was not only men that responded to the missionary call of the West. Women of several Christian churches also served there as nurses and teachers. Their problems were the same as those facing a Lacombe or a McDougall—hardship, loneliness and sometimes hostility were the missionary's lot regardless of sex. Lucy Baker was but one of that legion of unsung heroines. She had turned her back on a life of comfort, security and travel to work for the Presbyterian Church among the Sioux in northern Saskatchewan. Her perseverance in the face of difficulties such as those described below won her the Indians' respect and the title "Winoocha Waken"—"Holy Woman."

These Indians [the Sioux] were "of all men most miserable." They had come from across the border, where their presence was not desired save for punishment. Their tribe had thought themselves defrauded of their lands by the United States government, and they had sought redress by the terrible expedient of massacre. Some of them had fled into Canada for safety. Outlaws they were, with a price on their heads, and the Canadian government was unwilling to grant them a reserve in which they might find a home. And so it came about that near Prince Albert a number of these Sioux Indians had settled down in an encampment. Miss Baker's heart went out to them, so helpless and hopeless and friendless they were. She wanted to do something for them. And since the Nisbet Academy had been burned and the Government had established a high school in Prince Albert she felt that she was now free to devote herself to the service of the Sioux.

But, for several reasons, that was no easy task. In the first place, she had to learn their language. In doing this, she had the advantage of her experience in mastering French and the incitement of the noble use to which she would put the Sioux language when she had acquired it. Then there was the difficulty of getting the confidence of the Indians. If you have ever tried to make friends with some timid and badly frightened birds, you can realize something of the patience and skill and love that were needed on Miss Baker's part in order to overcome the fear and suspicion of these wild, unwanted outcasts, who had never known the meaning of friendship and who believed that every one's hand was against them. And yet with perseverance and incomparable tact this missionary of Christ disarmed their suspicions and won her way into their confidence and affection. The little children who at first would dart away from her in wild terror finally came completely under the spell of her charm and friendship. "By and by they became her abject slaves, and in the course of time would flee from the cruelties and hardships of their own homes to place themselves under her protection."

But there was a third difficulty, namely, the perils in getting to the encampment where these Indians lived. Her colleagues tried to persuade her to give up the idea as being too dangerous. "You will certainly be killed," said some of the Sioux whom she had managed to know, "if you visit the encampment."

And there were perils by the way. To get to Makoce Waste, where the Indians lived, it was necessary to cross the Saskatchewan River. She could not find a man who would dare to row her over, facing the dangers of the swift current on the way across and of the Indians at the end of the trip.

"Very well, then," said Miss Baker, "I must paddle my own canoe."

And she did. For that matter, ever since as a little girl she lost her mother, she had "paddled her own canoe." And now she did it in stern reality. Every day she went over alone to the north shore of the river. Once when she was nearly across, her paddle broke and she was drifted helplessly by the current towards the rapids below. She struggled frantically to edge the canoe towards the bank, and at the very head of the rapids managed to get hold of some bushes and hang on till an Indian, who had been watching her, rushed down and rescued her. Experiences like that she used to laugh at and call "a little turnover" in the "rut of monotony" or an "interesting adventure."

At last, one day, she was actually rowed over by an Indian. She was on the bank when this man, whom she had once cared for when he had a sore foot, was putting out from shore. Miss Baker stepped nimbly into the boat and told the Indian that he must take her over even if it meant death. He recalled his indebtedness to her and rowed her across. After that she did not find it so hard to persuade Indians to go over with her.

From J. L. Murray, *Nation Builders* (Toronto: The United Church Publishing House, 1925), pp. 52-54.

THE VOLUNTEER FOR HORSEFLY

Scottish-born James Robertson became superintendent of Presbyterian missions in Western Canada in 1881. His energy and the great authority he exercised won for him the nickname, "the Presbyterian bishop." For over twenty years, until his death in 1902, Robertson worked tirelessly to develop Presbyterianism in the West, and so successfully that he is credited with founding no less than one hundred and thirty-seven congregations and over twenty missions. His contagious enthusiasm for his work and for the West was not always shared by his fellow clergy. The great challenge of Canada's new frontier was apparently not felt by Robertson's young recruit for Horsefly as he explained in the following reminiscence.

The Superintendent was especially critical of those who would pick and choose their spheres of labour. One year he was sorely put out by the attitude of a number of men who, finding it impossible to secure appointments to the Foreign Mission field for which they had volunteered, declined service in his beloved West.

"I pleaded the case with them," he writes, "and finally a number of them promised to lay the matter before the Lord. I told them that they need not take the trouble, for I could tell them now what the answer would be, for I had found that whenever a man proposed to ask the Lord about Western work, the Lord as a rule indicated a less laborious sphere. Indeed, if I were to judge by the experience of these men, I would be forced to believe that the Lord had a kind of grudge against the West."

He discovered a peculiarly fine vein of sarcasm in dealing with men who shrunk from the hardships of missionary life and were fertile in excuse. In the following manner he writes a British Columbia Convener:—

"A number of men were approached with a view to going to Horsefly, but all complained of some ailment or physical defect that seemed to incapacitate them for this field. One had something the matter with his spine, another had his back wrenched by a chair being pulled from under him at college, a third could not ride without becoming seasick, the mother of a fourth was old, the father of another delicate and he could not go away so far, while the sixth was engaged to be married and Horsefly was not a place to which to take a wife. I hope that next spring so many of the men will not offer excuses of that kind when approached."

The Superintendent used to relate with grim relish an experience with a college graduate, a young man of fine ability and of genuine missionary spirit, who, under the inspiration of one of those great addresses of the Superintendent's, offered for Western work. Greatly delighted with his spirit and with his appearance, the Superintendent selected a field in British Columbia remote from civilization and calling for very considerable self-denial.

"But to my surprise, sir," said the Superintendent, relating the incident, "the very next morning I received a letter declining the appointment. I afterward learned the cause. This sudden change of mind was due to his young lady and her family. For on hearing the news of the appointment, it appears that the mother burst into tears, the sister went into hysterics, and the young lady herself lapsed into a succession of swoons from which nothing would recall her but a promise that her lover would abandon for ever so desperate a venture as a British Columbia mission field. I was hardly surprised to learn," he added with evident relish, "that within a year that engagement was broken. And for his sake, sir, I was glad of it."

From C. W. Gordon, *The Life of James Robertson, D.D.* (Westwood, N.J.: Fleming H. Revell Company, 1908), pp. 268-269.

IN CHANGING TIMES

THE BLACK BISHOP

Several of the Christian churches in Canada carried on special missions to the American Negro slaves who reached Canada and freedom on the famous "underground railway." Most of these former slaves were already members of some church and much of the mission work consisted of helping them to find employment and homes, sometimes in special Negro group settlements. Although the Negro refugees were devout church-goers, very few rose to important positions in their own churches. One outstanding exception was Bishop Walter Hawkins of the British Methodist Episcopal Church.

Born a slave in Maryland in 1809, Walter Hawkins' freedom was purchased by his father with $365 earned in overtime work for his master. Fearing he might be seized by slave traders the young Hawkins headed for Canada but actually settled in Buffalo about 1837. There Hawkins, a pious Christian, built his own small church and got married. The passing of the infamous Fugitive Slave law in 1850 made him afraid again of losing his freedom and so he moved on to Canada and soon became a Methodist preacher. After serving Negro congregations in several Canadian cities Hawkins was elected a bishop of his church in 1886 and re-elected to that high office in 1890. As a fraternal delegate to the Conference of the Methodist Church of Canada in 1890 he was invited to address that all-white body. The presence of this former slave, the black bishop, proved to be a moving and Christian experience for all who heard him.

"Mr. President," said Bishop Hawkins, with an accent and a pronunciation instantly recalling dear old Uncle Tom— "Mr. President and"—here he paused a moment, his lips trembling— "will you suffer me to call you brothers?" The pathos of this would have melted a heart of stone. "Yes, yes," burst from the conference, like the voice of one man. "Thank God," said the black Bishop, simply. It was a grand moment. Many of the ladies in the gallery put their handkerchiefs to their eyes. "You let me call you brothers in Christ. It seems like a dream. Here I am in this beautiful church" (looking slowly round the building), "and in the the presence of the best intellects in the country. You were born in all the advantages and refinements of Christian civilization. I was born a slave." (Many found it hard to retain their composure.) "I have heard that heaven is a beautiful place; I can well believe it; I must be near heaven now. (Applause and laughter) Yes, it seems just like a dream to be standing here. You are indeed in the midst of every elevating influence; I come from the auction block, an' dunno most how I got here. I am a little blacker than you are, but"—here he paused, and placed his hand on his heart; his eyes grew moist—"but my soul is whiter than snow, washed in the blood of the Lamb sixty years ago. (Prolonged applause) We are on a level, as far as Christianity is concerned, and I am looking forward to a time when complexion will be done away with. (Applause and laughter) I am a little darker; but we're one in Christ Jesus. (Applause) I remember when I first heard that a Negro might have a soul, and that, if he were good to his master and mistress, he might get into the kitchen of heaven; but I propose to go into the parlour of heaven with the president and the brethren." (Loud applause and laughter)

●　　●　　●

"Brethren, it is almost like a dream. I never saw such a beautiful church as this. I never saw such a wonderful conference as this. I feel so lifted up that I almost forget that I am black—feels like as if I dunno whether I'm black or not. I have been insulted in this city on account of my

colour, though you have received me like Christian gentlemen. (Applause) But I don't think my colour makes any
difference to God. (Applause) Well, brethren, I come to
you as a child of God, having got the blessing of salvation
sixty-eight years ago, 'way down thar in the South. Ah, it
was dark then! No privileges then. It was ten o'clock at
night. It was over the fence, away to the woods, one mile,
two mile, five mile, ten mile, to hear about Jesus. I became
His child. And it has been better all the time since. Better
as I grow older. This is the happiest day of my life. The
way has often been rough and dark. I have had a circuit of
100 miles to travel with my legs for a horse—(laughter)—
getting 100 dollars a year, with a large family to keep, often
without food for a whole day at a time; but I loved my dark
brethren, and I went amongst them, and did what you cannot do—I unlocked the door of their hearts with a key
which you could never get, and I sowed the seed there.
(Loud applause) It was hard work; but I had the marching
orders from the Master. (Applause) Now, my mind travels
back to the time when there was not a spot in North
America where the black man was free, and I think of my
own early days; but if I once begin I'd keep you too long.
(Cries of 'No, no,' 'Tell us about your slavery days,' etc.)
Well, then, everything was dark, and we heard that in
Canada there was freedom for the slave. I thought Canada
was behind the sun. (Laughter) I didn't know the east
from the west, the north from the south. But I got there,
and I was free. (Loud applause) I put myself under the
paw of the British lion—(prolonged applause)—and when
you're under the paw of the lion, and he gives a growl at
your enemies, you're safe. The Queen of England—God
bless her!—('Amen')—the best woman that ever wore a
crown or swayed a sceptre—(loud applause)—the Queen
of England meets the Negro the moment he touches British
soil—(prolonged applause and great enthusiasm)—and
that's why I am here today. (Applause) They wanted to
transfer us to the American Church, but this country and
this government are good enough for me" (Applause)

● ● ●

The Bishop's companion followed, and when he sat down Dr. Douglas rose and said: "We want to hear Bishop Hawkins sing". ("Yes, yes," "Sing," etc.)

"Will Bishop Hawkins sing 'I'm Redeemed'?" said Dr. Douglas.

"If I can get the key," said the Bishop, amidst laughter, "I'll sing 'Nearer my home'." He got the key, and his soft, rich voice put a crooning lilt into the music, and he closed his eyes, and gently swayed his body, and waved his arms, and abandoned himself to an ecstatic motion, which reached every heart in the conference.

"Sing the chorus," said the Bishop. "We can all sing it, for aren't we all going to the same heavenly home? We may never meet on earth again:

> "I'm nearer my home,
>   I'm nearer my home,
>   I'm nearer my home, to-day,
> I'm nearer my home, where Jesus has gone,
>   I'm nearer my home to-day."

●　　●　　●

About five hundred voices, above and below, sang that chorus with a volume of energy and feeling that swept every tittle of the conventional clean out into the street.

"Now, I'll sing," said the Bishop, " 'On my way to Canada'. This is the earthly home. But it was heaven to me in the old days, and many a time this song cheered my heart, for it seemed to anticipate heaven."

"On my way to Canada" represents the slave flying from the bloodhounds. He flees through wood and marsh until, on the other side of the lake, he sees the Queen of England standing with outstretched arms to receive him. The Bishop put his whole soul into this piece. A tide of emotion swept over him which glorified his poor old black, wrinkled face; his eyes became lustrous, his lips trembled; he raised himself, held his hands over his head, and sang with extraordinary energy:

> "I'm on my way to Canada,
> Where the coloured man is free."

The contagion spread over the house. Roar after roar of applause burst from the conference. 'Twas a thrilling scene.

"I move that we take up a collection for Brother Hawkins," said Dr. Douglas.

"A collection," "a collection," was the cry. "Well, get the hat going," said the Chairman, wiping his eyes. "A collection," he continued, "is a wonderfully cooling process." (Laughter)

But that collection amounted to ninety-two dollars, and every man and woman in the house put something into the hat.

From S. J. Celestine Edwards, *From Slavery to a Bishopric, or The Life of Bishop Walter Hawkins of the British Methodist Episcopal Church, Canada* (London, 1891), pp. 156-163.

SONGS OF PRAISE

The place of music in the worship service varies widely among the Christian churches. From the majestic anthems and Gregorian chant of the mass one can travel to the silent witness of the Quakers at the other end of the spectrum. Yet each church is attached to its own musical forms and reluctant to change practices that are fondly regarded as both essential and everlasting. In this age of folk masses set to a jazz beat it is interesting to look back to a day not so long ago when worship through music took other forms. Presbyterians, for instance, viewed the introduction of organs with the same misgivings and even resentment with which many people today regard the use of "pop" music in church services. They were sure that songs of praise should be sung without the aid of instrumental music, for church organs or even pianos were instruments of the Devil.

In the earlier days the leader in the service of praise was called the precentor, and his task was by no means easy. He had not the help of organ or of choir, and even the tuning-fork was regarded with suspicion. Only the psalms were sung, and after announcing the number of the psalm the minister read over the verses to be sung then repeated the first two lines, and the precentor led the congregation in the singing of them. Before singing the next two he must "line" them, repeating or chanting them over before singing them. And so with the following lines. The custom of "lining" the psalms originated, apparently, in the days when the people were poor and Bibles were few, and many who could speak the Gaelic were not able to read it. The difficulty for the precentor lay in the fact that he had to keep in mind the note with which the third line should begin, and begin and end his chant in the lining accordingly. That this simple service of song had a mighty influence we know from the manner in which the warm-hearted Highlanders became attached to it. They were loth to give it up and to adopt any new features.

●　　●　　●

A remit on Psalmody sent down to sessions was considered at a session meeting in February, 1867, when it was "unanimously agreed that the Psalms of David only shall be used in the public worship of God in this congregation, these being inspired by the Holy Ghost and pre-eminently suited to the experience of the children of God in all ages and nations."

Strange how these matters that we deal with and "settle" in our church courts have a way of coming up again. Only three years went by till the question of the use of hymns came up once more in a slightly different form. At a meeting held on March 28, 1870:

The Session held a long conversation with each other in regard to hymns being sung in the church. Afterwards the trustees by invitation (one being absent), joined the session in discussing whether hymns should be allowed to be sung in the church (with a special reference to a Hymn Book published by Russell and Needham); the session unanimously and the trustees present six in number (with the exception of one who appeared doubtful), expressed their disapprobation of using Hymns in the church in the service of praise to God.

For twenty-three years more the congregation goes on singing the "Psalms of David."

• • •

Just when the church choir came into being is not very clear. It was apparently taking shape in the seventies and early eighties when Mr. Wm. Abernetly was precentor. . . . In 1890 a platform or loft was erected for the choir.

There is evidence that in the following year the choir has been venturing to bring in some innovations, for at a session meeting held Jan. 26, 1891, it was moved by Jas. Mann, seconded by Far. Noble:

That whereas the singing of the "voluntary" at the morning service is not agreeable to many in the congregation, Resolved that the same be discontinued.

Moved in amendment by Hugh S. MacKay seconded by Jas. Smith; That the discussion of the matter of the "voluntary" singing by the choir be deferred at present, until brought upon the session by aggrieved persons in the congregation. . . .

We need not be surprised on hearing that several were wont to leave their pews when the choir would start the singing of the "voluntary," returning to their places when it was over—this to register their protest. They were not unreasonable as the man in a town in Huron county was, who, when the organ was brought into his church, left the church and went across the street to the Methodist church where the organ was already.

From W. D. McIntosh, *One Hundred Years in the Zorra Church* (Toronto: The United Church Publishing House, 1930), pp. 77, 79-81.

THE ROMAN CATHOLIC PROGRAMME

In mid-nineteenth century Europe the Roman Catholic Church equated liberalism with anticlericalism. Within the Canadian Church one party adopted the same position of opposing political liberalism on religious grounds, even though nothing like European anticlericalism ever existed in Canada. This party, known as the ultramontanes because they insisted that final authority in all matters rested with the pope in Rome "beyond the mountains," grew in strength after Confederation and exerted considerable political influence in Quebec. The ultramontane philosophy of papal supremacy was clearly stated in a pastoral letter of Bishop Laflèche of Trois-Rivières, leader of the ultramontanist party in the church, issued on the eve of a Quebec provincial election in 1875.

We belong in principle to the Conservative Party, that is, to that party which is defender of the social order. . . . In the political situation of our country, the Conservative Party being the only one which offers serious guarantees to religious interests, we consider it a duty to support the men at its head loyally.

But this loyal support must be subordinated to religious interests that we must never lose sight of. If then there exists in our laws some gaps, some ambiguities, or some arrangements which imperil interests of Catholics, we must require of our candidates a formal promise to work to eliminate these flaws in our legislation.

Thus the religious press complains with good reason that our laws concerning marriage, education, the establishment of parishes, and the registration of vital statistics are defective in that they injure the rights of the Church, constrict its liberty, shackle its administration, or lead to hostile interpretations. This state of affairs imposes on Catholic legislators the duty of changing and modifying the laws according to the wishes of Our Lords, Bishops of the Province, in order to put the laws in harmony with the doctrines of the Roman Catholic Church. But, in order that the deputies fulfil this duty more diligently, the electors must make it a condition of their support. It is the duty of the electors to give their votes only to those who are willing to comply entirely with the teachings of the Church on these matters.

Let us conclude then by adopting the following general rules in certain given instances:

1. If the contest occurs between two Conservatives, it goes without saying that we shall support the one who will accept the programme that we have just set forth.

2. If on the other hand it occurs between any shade of Conservative and a follower of the Liberal school, our active sympathies are for the former.

3. If the only candidates who offer themselves in a constituency are all Liberals or oppositionists, we must choose the one who will agree to our conditions.

4. Finally, in the case where the contest is between a Conservative rejecting our programme and an oppositionist who accepts it, the situation would be more delicate. To vote for the first would be putting us in contradiction with the doctrine that we have just expounded. To vote for the second man would be to imperil the Conservative Party which we wish to see powerful. Which decision should we take between the two dangers? We would advise the abstention of Catholic electors. . . .

From Robert Rumilly, *Histoire de la Province de Québec* (Montreal: Editions Bernard Valiquette, 1940), pp. 155-156.

IN DEFENCE OF LIBERALISM

So many French-Canadian Catholic voters heeded the Catholic Programme of the Church's ultramontane party that for many years Quebec was solidly and securely Conservative in its politics. Protests from the Liberal party that it was not anticlerical were received with disbelief until a young French Canadian whose loyalty to the Church was unquestionable spoke out clearly in defence of political liberalism and the supremacy of the state in civil matters. That young man was Wilfrid Laurier, the silver-tongued orator, and the place and date were Quebec City and 1877, just after several priests had threatened voters with hell if they voted Liberal at elections.

It is true that there is in Europe, in France, in Italy and in Germany, a class of men, who give themselves the title of Liberals, but who have nothing of the Liberal about them but the name and who are the most dangerous of men. These are not Liberals; they are revolutionaries: in their principles they are so extravagant that they aim at nothing less than the destruction of modern society. With these men, we have nothing in common; but it is the tactic of our adversaries to always assimilate us to them. Such accusations are beneath our notice and the only answer we can with dignity give them is to proclaim our real principles and to so conduct ourselves that our acts will conform with our principles.

*   *   *

I have too much respect for the opinion of my adversaries to ever insult them; but I reproach them with understanding neither their time nor their country. I accuse them of judging the political situation of the country, not according to what is happening in it, but according to what is happening in France. I accuse them of wanting to introduce here ideas, which are impossible of application in our state of society. I accuse them of laboriously and, by misfortune, too efficaciously working to degrade religion to the simple proportions of a political party.

*   *   *

You wish to organize a Catholic party. But have you not considered that, if you have the misfortune to succeed, you will draw down upon your country calamities of which it is impossible to foresee the consequences?

You wish to organize all the Catholics into one party, without other bond, without other basis, than a common religion; but have you not reflected that, by the very fact, you will organize the Protestant population as a single party and that then, instead of the peace and harmony now prevailing between the different elements of the Canadian population, you throw open the door to war, a religious war, the most terrible of all wars?

Once more, Conservatives, I accuse you in the face of Canada of not understanding either your country or your time.

*   *   *

But, while reproaching us with being friends of liberty our adversaries further reproach us, with an inconsistency which would be serious, if the charge were well founded, with denying to the Church the freedom to which it is entitled. They reproach us with seeking to silence the administrative body of the Church and to prevent it from teaching the people their duties as citizens and electors. They reproach us with wanting to hinder the clergy from meddling in politics and to relegate them to the sacristy.

In the name of the Liberal party and of Liberal principles, I repel this assertion.

I maintain that there is not one Canadian Liberal who wants to prevent the clergy from taking part in political affairs, if they wish to do so.

In the name of what principle, should the friends of liberty seek to deny to the priest the right to take part in political affairs? In the name of what principle should the friends of liberty seek to deny to the priest the right to have and express political opinions, the right to approve or disapprove public men and their acts and to instruct the people in what he believes to be their duty? In the name of what principle, should he not have the right to say that, if I am elected, religion will be endangered, when I have the right to say that if my adversary is elected, the State will be endangered? Why should the priest not have the right to say that, if I am elected, religion will be inevitably destroyed, when I have the right to say that, if my adversary is elected, the State will go into bankruptcy? No, let the priest speak and preach, as he thinks best; such is his right and no Canadian Liberal will dispute that right.

From U. Barthe, *Wilfrid Laurier on the Platform* (Quebec, 1890), pp. 67, 71-72, 75.

MOODY IN THE PULPIT

As more and more Canadians left the farms and moved to the cities the churches were faced with new conditions that demanded new techniques. The camp meeting, so well established by the evangelical churches in rural Canada, could not operate in the city. But the spirit and purpose of the camp meeting carried on in a new form—the protracted revival meeting in the big city church. These revivals still employed emotion-charged hymn singing, fervent preaching and extemporaneous prayers. The differences between the camp meeting and the city revival were the more sophisticated audience and the trend to greater interdenominational participation.

Dwight L. Moody, one of the most famous of the "hot gospellers" in the later Victorian years was, like so many of his clerical breed, an American. Both before and after Moody most touring evangelists who preached in Canada came from the United States because they had already established reputations there and because revivalist movements ignore national boundaries. In this account of Moody's leadership in a "Christian Convention" at Metropolitan Church, the "Cathedral of Methodism," readers will recognize many features found today in the evangelism of Billy Graham.

The recent Christian Convention in this city, under the management of the distinguished evangelist, Dwight L. Moody, was an occasion of very great interest. We have never seen the whole city and surrounding country so stirred as by this great religious gathering. At every one of the nine services the spacious Metropolitan Church was crowded to its utmost capacity. As early as half-past seven in the morning people began to gather at the gates, though the meeting did not begin till ten o'clock. At least twenty-five thousand persons, or half of the adult population of the city, must have heard him, and over-flow meetings were held besides. Nearly three hundred ministers were present at the Ministerial Conference on Thursday afternoon. Mr. Moody said that he never knew the people so eager, so hungry for the Gospel as now, and as right through the excitement of the Presidential election in the States. He summoned the Churches and the ministers to aggressive Christian work, to lead on the hosts of God in a glorious campaign of conquest. Twenty years ago he said such a Convention of ministers of the different Churches would have been impossible. It was a significant spectacle to see Baptist and Presbyterian, Methodist and Episcopalian taking part in these services side by side; and at the after meetings directing inquirers to the common Saviour and Lord. It was a grand demonstration to the world that notwithstanding the outward differences there is a grand unity of the faith binding the Churches in Christain brotherhood. Mr. Moody recommended that in small towns and villages union revival meetings should be held, the ministers uniting like a band of brothers in the common work.

The Convention was a triumphant refutation of the baseless sneer that Christianity is decadent or that the interest in the old-fashioned Gospel is dying out. The secular papers gave special prominence to the meetings, the *Globe* especially giving nine or ten columns a day of report of the meetings.

The grand congregational singing was a potent attraction and an inspiring influence. The melodies were simple and easily caught and the effect of the three or four thousand voices was sublime. Especially was this the case at the evening meetings when the only female voices were those of the ladies in the choir. A favourite hymn was the following:

> Oh, word of words the sweetest,
>   Oh, word in which there lie
> All promise, all fulfilment,
>   And end of mystery;
> Lamenting or rejoicing,
>   With doubt or terror nigh,
> I hear the "Come" of Jesus
>   And to His cross I fly.
>
>   Come! oh, come to Me!
>   Come! oh, come to Me!
>   Weary, and heavy laden,
>   Come! oh, come to Me!

"Now," Mr. Moody would say, "let the ladies of the choir sing the next verse and we will all join in the chorus."

After this was done, "Let all in the gallery sing that chorus all the way around," (swinging his arm so as to indicate the whole gallery in its sweep). The gallery sang with overwhelming effect.

Mr. Moody's theme was the old, old story of Jesus and His love—nothing sensational, nothing dramatic no straining after effect, but the old story told with an intense moral earnestness that burned the truth into the hearts and consciences of his hearers. The most striking characteristic of the man was his sanctified common-sense, his business-like shrewdness and tact in managing a vast audience; his vein of pathos whereby the simple narration of incidents in his personal experience touched almost every heart to tears, his sense of humour, and even of satire and sarcasm as he hit off popular faults and follies; his vivid imagination whereby he described Old Testament scenes in the realistic language of everyday life; above all, his yearning love for souls, and his living ever near to God and in constant access to the throne of grace. His well-marked Bible is as familiar to him as his A B C, and he brings out of this rich storehouse, illustration, argument, proof texts, and the strong confirmations of Holy Writ.

The broad human sympathies, the yearning love of souls of Mr. Moody gave him great power with the masses. He is not specially gifted by nature. He is unheroic in form and feature. He owes nothing to the arts of eloquence. He is unlettered in all lore save that of the oracles of God. Yet both preachers and people hear him gladly and hail his visits as those of an apostle, as he goes through the land arousing, inspiring, inciting the Churches to increased energy and zeal.

Another strong hold he has on the people is his absolute disinterestedness. He accepts nothing for his services. He stops the mouth of the caviller who would say, "Moody makes a pretty good thing of it." Now, while it is right that those who preach the Gospel should live by the Gospel, it is a great advantage to be able to say with Paul: "I seek not yours but you." We have not the slightest sympathy with the mousing critics who carp at the payment—even the liberal payment—of Christian workers. A popular actor comes along and receives more for a single night than many a faithful preacher receives for a whole year's toil for his fellowmen, and he is complimented on his genius and his fame;

but if a successful minister receives a tithe as much there are those who find fault. When a man therefore is able like Mr. Moody or like "California Taylor" to be independent of all payment for his services it is an added power.

From *Canadian Methodist Magazine* (1885), Vol. XXI, pp. 75-77.

A VISION OF UNION

The political union of the British North American colonies in 1867 was the inspiration for several church unions in Canada. All Presbyterian bodies in the new dominion united in a single church in 1875, and the Methodists achieved a Canadian-wide unity by 1884. The nationalism of Confederation was being echoed by the Christian churches, and beyond these denominational unions there was the growing co-operation of the churches in a wide range of interdenominational projects.

Nova-Scotia-born Principal George M. Grant of Queen's University was a leading nationalist both politically and religiously. As a teacher, writer and public speaker, Grant was a persuasive promoter of Canadianism. As a churchman he was one of the earliest advocates of Christian reunion in Canada. His address to the Evangelical Alliance in 1874 may yet prove to have been the voice of prophecy.

God will give us the church of the future. It shall arise in the midst of us, with no sound of hammer heard upon it, comprehensive of all the good and beauty that He has ever evolved in history. To this church, Episcopacy shall contribute her comely order, her faithful and loving conservatism; and Methodism impart her enthusiasm, her zeal for missions, and her ready adaptiveness to the necessities of the country; the Baptist shall give his full testimony to the sacred rights of the individual; the Congregationalist his to the freedom and independency of the congregation; and Presbytery shall come in her massive, well-knit strength, holding high the Word of God; and when, or even before, all this comes to pass, that is, when we have proved our Christian charity, as well as our faithfulness, proved it by deeds, not words, who shall say that our Roman Catholic brethren, also, shall not see eye to eye with us, and seal with their consent that true unity, the image of which they so fondly love? Why not? God can do greater things even than this. And who of us shall say, God forbid!

From W. L. Grant and F. Hamilton, *Principal Grant* (Toronto, 1904), pp. 155-156.

REMEMBER THE SABBATH

The Canada that celebrates its one hundredth birthday in 1967 is a Canada changed beyond recognition to our Victorian grandparents. Luxuries unimagined by former generations have become virtual necessities to many present-day Canadians. For better or worse we enjoy a standard of living that is the envy of most of the world. Gone, or going, are many of the Victorian customs that seem irrelevant in an urban, industrial, automated twentieth-century society. Gone is the notorious and puritanical "blue Sunday" that was originally intended to protect the working man from unscrupulous employers by ensuring that everyone had one day's rest in seven.

In today's Canada, where Sunday afternoon entertainment is accepted as the natural sequel to Sunday morning church services, the Victorian sabbath is a nostalgic memory to some and almost a fairy tale to the younger generation.

Some of us who were not born in Zorra and still have a considerable distance to go before reaching the half-century mark well remember interesting features about the Sabbath of childhood days. On Saturday evening the shoes were to be polished in readiness for Sunday, water must be taken in from the pump, a pile of wood must be in readiness in the wood-box, potatoes and other vegetables must be all ready for the Sunday meal, that there may be a minimum of labour on the Lord's Day. On Sunday the stock at the barn would be fed and watered, but the cleaning of the stables was left over until Monday. Whatever defects there might be in the observance of the day were more than counterbalanced by sincerity of purpose and by diligence in practice, and young lives received the impression that life is real and life is earnest. Much of the enterprise and achievement of the sons and daughters of Zorra may be attributed to the hallowing influence of that one day in seven as it was observed in the homes and community of their childhood.

Not that the day was in all cases respected, for human nature is ever the same. The case of the man who was brought before the Session for bringing home a load of lumber on the Lord's Day was not the only case of Sabbath desecration that came before the session. And these are but an indication of many other happenings of which no record has been made. An amusing story is told of a farmer, living in the southern part of the township, who had a pond on his farm and who had also among his flock a ram that was "cross" and good on the "bunt." On Sunday afternoons the boys would occasionally have sport in teasing this pugnacious animal. A youth would take his place on the bank close up to the pond and would start bowing his head as if daring the ram to a fight. True to his nature, the ram, gathering up all his strength and lowering his head would rush forward to battle; but when he came near enough, the lad would jump aside, allowing the ram to plunge into the water, much to the amusement of the boys. One Sunday afternoon the farmer caught the boys at their fun. He proceeded to lecture them on the sin of Sabbath desecration, and ordered them home to study the catechism. The boys took their departure; the farmer now began reflecting on the sport and the more he reflected, the more he felt constrained to experiment a little himself. Nothing daunted by his former "ducking" the brave animal, head down, came rushing once more to the encounter, but the farmer, lacking in agility, failed to get out of the way in time!

From W. D. McIntosh, *One Hundred Years in the Zorra Church* (Toronto: The United Church Publishing House, 1930), pp. 66-68.

THE WHIRLWIND CAMPAIGN IN MARIPOSA

Stephen Leacock's sly humour of understatement was directed at Canadians in every walk of life. His caricature of the Canadian clergyman is the well-meaning but ineffective Dean Drone of Mariposa. The fact that the Reverend Mr. Drone was an Anglican was merely incidental to Leacock. Dean Drone stood for all the clergy at whom Leacock delighted in poking gentle fun. Similarly everyone who has taken part in a church fund-raising drive will feel at home when he joins the Anglican Whirlwind Campaign in Mariposa.

It was all organized so that every team had its headquarters, two of them in each of the three hotels—one upstairs and one down. And it was arranged that there would be a big lunch every day, to be held in Smith's caff, round the corner of Smith's Northern Health Resort and Home of the Wissanotti Angler—you know the place. The lunch was divided up into tables, with a captain for each table to see about things to drink, and of course all the tables were in competition with one another. In fact the competition was the very life of the whole thing.

It's just wonderful how these things run when they're organized. Take the first luncheon, for example. There they all were, every man in his place, every captain at his post at the top of the table. It was hard, perhaps, for some of them to get there. They had very likely to be in their stores and banks and offices till the last minute and then make a dash for it. It was the cleanest piece of team work you ever saw.

You have noticed already, I am sure, that a good many of the captains and committee men didn't belong to the Church of England Church. Glover, for instance, was a Presbyterian, till they ran the picket fence of the manse two feet onto his property, and after that he became a freethinker. But in Mariposa, as I have said, everybody likes to be in everything and naturally a Whirlwind Campaign was a novelty. Anyway, it would have been a poor business to keep a man out of the lunches merely on account of his religion. I trust that the day for that kind of religious bigotry is past.

Of course, the excitement was when Henry Mullins at the head of the table began reading out the telegrams and letters and messages. First of all there was a telegram of good wishes from the Anglican Lord Bishop of the Diocese to Henry Mullins and calling him Dear Brother in Grace— the Mariposa telegraph office is a little unreliable and it read: "Dear Brother in grease," but that was good enough. The Bishop said that his most earnest wishes were with them.

Then Mullins read a letter from the Mayor of Mariposa —Pete Glover was mayor that year—stating that his keenest desires were with them: and then one from the Carriage Company saying that its heartiest good will was all theirs; and then one from the Meat Works saying that its nearest thoughts were next to them. Then he read one from himself, as head of the Exchange Bank, you understand, informing him that he had heard of his project and assuring him of his liveliest interest in what he proposed.

At each of these telegrams and messages there was round after round of applause, so that you could hardly hear yourself speak or give an order. But that was nothing to when Mullins got up again, and beat on the table for silence and made one of those cracking, concise speeches—just the way business men speak—the kind of speech that a college man simply can't make. I wish I could repeat it all. I remember that it began: "Now boys, you know what we're here for, gentlemen," and it went on just as good as that all through.

When Mullins had done he took out a fountain pen and wrote out a cheque for a hundred dollars, conditional on the fund reaching fifty thousand. And there was a burst of cheers all over the room.

Just the moment he had done it, up sprang George Duff —you know the keen competition there is, as a straight matter of business, between the banks in Mariposa—up sprang George Duff, I say, and wrote out a cheque for another hundred conditional on the fund reaching seventy thousand. You never heard such cheering in your life.

And then when Netley walked up to the head of the table and laid down a cheque for a hundred dollars conditional on the fund reaching one hundred thousand the room was in an uproar. A hundred thousand dollars! Just think of it! The figures fairly stagger one. To think of a hundred thousand dollars raised in five minutes in a little place like Mariposa!

And even that was nothing! In less than no time there was such a crowd round Mullins trying to borrow his pen all at once that his waistcoat was all stained with ink. Finally when they got order at last, and Mullins stood up and announced that the conditional fund had reached a quarter of a million, the whole place was a perfect babel of cheering. Oh, these Whirlwind Campaigns are wonderful things!

From Stephen Leacock, *Sunshine Sketches of a Little Town* (Toronto: McClelland and Stewart, 1944), pp. 96-98.

THE PERILS OF A PADRE

Six hundred thousand of Canada's sons went to war between 1914 and 1918. With them went the clergy of the Christian churches to offer the consolations of religion in the trenches and in No-Man's-Land, amid the clouds of poison gas at Ypres and in the muddy hell of Passchendaele. "In this sign" the padres served in the face of mortal danger throughout a war that mocked the ideals of Christianity. But even in wartime life had its lighter moments, and G. O. Fallis has related two humorous incidents that befell him as a padre.

When Sir Julian Byng was Commander of the Canadian Corps he issued an order, "No officer should pick up other ranks." When I read this order I felt that it should not apply to a chaplain, as troops carrying fifty-six pound packs would not look with favour on a chaplain passing them up with a big Cadillac car. The next morning at 5 a.m. I left for the front, parking the car at the west gates of Arras. I spent the day visiting troops in the front line. About 4 p.m. I was back at the car and with my driver turned west. It began to rain, then it poured. Suddenly we came upon five Tommies slogging along in the mud with their heavy packs. What should I do, pass them up and obey orders? Out of my subconscious self there came the recollection of a lecture given in the very earliest days of war by General Alderson, the first Commander of the Canadians, to his chaplains. He ended a very sage address by saying, "Ninety-nine per cent of the time a chaplain can be a good soldier.

But once in a while a situation arises when you cannot be a good soldier and a good chaplain at the same time. When the time arises my advice is to forget soldiering and be a good chaplain." I decided there was only one thing to do if I were to be a good chaplain and that was to pick up those Tommies. I ordered my driver to stop and we picked them up much to their relief and joy. The downpour was just a shower and in fifteen minutes the sun was shining.

Looking to the west we saw someone coming over a hill-top half a mile away on horseback with two horsemen riding behind. It looked for all the world like General Byng with his two A.D.C.'s. My courage almost failed me. My first impulse was to turn around and run away. I concluded that would be acting the part of neither a good soldier nor a good chaplain. There was nothing for it but to face the music. My heart sank to my boots as the three horsemen drew near. It was General Byng!

When one practically loves a man, one feels a bit of a rotter to hurt him. I had, as all other Canadians, a tremendous admiration for General Byng. To disappoint him as I knew I surely would, made me feel almost panicky.

At last we drew abreast. I asked the driver to stop the car. I stepped out and saluted. I could see he was greatly disturbed and possibly angry. He looked down from his horse and said:

"Fallis, did you read my order yesterday?"

"Yes, sir, I did."

After an appallingly awkward silence he continued:

"Fallis, I'm bitterly disappointed in you. I thought you were a soldier. What have you to say for yourself?"

It was then I played my trump card relying on his insight and sense of fitness. I looked up into his fine face and answered:

"Sir, I'm a rotten soldier but I'm a good padre."

A droll smile broke over his stern face. My heart bounded with relief when he replied, "You are perfectly right. Those lads would think you were a H—— of a padre had you passed them up in that cloudburst. I'll have the order amended not to include padres."

In 1918 I had an appointment with General Sir Arthur Currie, our Corps Commander. It was for two o'clock just after lunch. When I arrived at his headquarters there stood on the steps a young captain covered with decorations. He clicked his heels and gave me the most punctilious of salutes. We had a saying in the Canadian army that a good sergeant-major was often spoiled when he was given a commission. He could never completely throw off his rigid discipline of himself and take on the ease of a so-called "gentleman officer." I passed up the steps and Willis O'Connor, the A.D.C. to General Currie, ushered me into the presence of the Corps Commander. He was exceptionally genial and I took the liberty of asking him who the young officer was who had saluted so punctiliously. I told him he had spoiled a good sergeant-major when he gave him a commission.

General Currie rose and opening the door looked curiously down the corridor, then laughingly exclaimed, "You damn fool, Padre, that's the Prince of Wales!"

From G. O. Fallis, *A Padre's Pilgrimage* (Toronto: The Ryerson Press, 1953), pp. 87-89.

THY KINGDOM COME

James Shaver Woodsworth first encountered the social problems of the industrial age in the east end of London, England, before the First World War. With the return of peace Woodsworth became deeply disturbed by the hardship and poverty which he saw on every side. During the Winnipeg General Strike he supported the strikers unreservedly and was arrested on a charge of sedition for printing passages from Isaiah to emphasize his belief in social justice. To put his ideas into practice he ran for Parliament in 1921 and was elected in Winnipeg North Centre, a seat he held until his death in 1942. A little more than a decade after entering political life, Woodsworth provided leadership and vision for the founding of the Co-operative Commonwealth Federation. His life was devoted to championing the cause of a new social order based on the humanitarian principles of the Social Gospel movement. In

*a sermon entitled "Thy Kingdom Come" Woodsworth pro-
claimed the Church's responsibility to share in the shaping
of a new society.*

Otherworldly religion is rapidly becoming a thing of the
past. Our hymns still tell us that "there is a happy land,
far, far away," but most of us are really not so much concerned with that "beautiful isle of somewhere" as we are
in making Canada a country in which our children can live
happy and noble and useful lives. Nowadays it would be
a very abnormal child indeed who could say, "I want
to be an angel and with the angels stand, a crown upon my
forehead, a harp within my hand." Most healthy children
would much prefer to skip and play ball with a happy group
of school fellows. Some weary pilgrims may sigh for the rest
of "the sweet bye and bye." Most sturdy Christians are
happiest when they are up and doing "with a heart for any
fate." Let me in this connection quote a totally different
kind of song which occurs to me. It is included in the
collection used by the Industrial Workers of the World.
While doggerel of the worst kind, it hits off the situation
very well. Undoubtedly the needy no longer want the consolation of a "sweet bye and bye":

> Long-haired preachers come out every night;
> Try to tell us what's wrong and what's right;
> But when asked how about something to eat
> They will answer with voices so sweet:

> *Chorus:*
> You will eat bye and bye
> In that glorious land above the sky;
> Work and pray, live on hay,
> You'll get pie in the sky, when you die.

Of course that is shocking—that is why we quote it! Too
long the church has emphasized the future and neglected
the present.

How we have managed so long to make otherworldly the
plain and simple and homely teachings of Jesus is a mystery.
The petition "give us each day our daily bread" has been
interpreted as a prayer for spiritual strength or mystical

communion, or sacerdotal needs, instead of the simple, natural, childlike prayer for the daily necessaries of life.

The petition "thy kingdom come"—how we have twisted and expounded and spiritualized and futurized it. How does it read—"Thy kingdom come, thy will be done on earth as it is in heaven." Surely that is simple. As one American journal puts it, "Thy kingdom come, as in heaven, *so in Brownsville.*" That may sound sacrilegious, but Jesus was constantly shocking the false reverence and piety of the professed religious people of his day. Religion is not a cult. It is simply everyday living.

"Thy kingdom come," not in some future state in some far off world, and not in some vague way all over the universe, but thy kingdom come right here in Canada, in Manitoba, in Winnipeg, in Brownsville, in my own township.

● ● ●

There are great economic and moral and social evils that must be abolished. Further, it is not merely a case of getting rid of the weeds. Good grain must be cultivated in their place. Clean, wholesome recreation, satisfying labour, stimulating associations—all these must find a place in the renewed world. This means that business and politics and amusement must be made over.

What a change must come in the programmes of the churches and other agencies interested in the bringing in of God's kingdom!

Some years ago, when in charge of a mission located in a poor district in North Winnipeg, I was called upon to conduct the funeral of one of the children of the neighbourhood. We came to the cemetery; there was a long row of tiny baby graves; a number were fresh made, as scores of babies were being carried off during the hot weather. Here was the grave into which we were to lower the little body, and beyond it were a number of half-dug graves; their future occupants were not yet dead, but the grave diggers knew they were coming—disease was rampant, and they were keeping ahead of their work.

I read the well-known service, "For as much as it hath pleased Almighty God, in His wise Providence, to take out of the world the soul of the deceased . . ." And in my heart I said: "That is not true." I knew what had killed the baby —it was bad milk and bad housing. It was not fair to blame God for that of which we were guilty. It was not fair to tell the people that that was what God was like.

Next winter at a theatre meeting that I had instituted on Sunday evenings, we had one evening devoted to public health. The City Health Officer gave a lecture on how disease could be prevented. This was illustrated by means of moving pictures which showed how the fly developed, how it flew from the decaying refuse to the sugar bowl or from a spittoon to the baby's feeding bottle. It was a horrible exhibition—one saw snakes all night after it; but it was tremendously effective. Even the poor foreigners who could not understand English could understand the pictures.

But my church friends were shocked. Here was I, a minister of the Gospel, who had degenerated until I was running a moving picture show in a theatre on Sunday evenings! Well, to tell the truth, I sometimes was almost shocked at myself. But there came back to me the scene at the graveside the summer before. This was how the matter presented itself to me. If it was my religious duty to read the funeral service over the body of a dead baby, was it not as much my religious duty to try to save the babies alive?

Our church reports tell how many funerals the minister has attended during the year; I have never yet seen a report which told how many people's lives the minister had saved. "Ah," you say, "the church's task is to save souls." But in the church of the future, saving souls will, more and more, come to be understood as saving men and women and children. At least in this world souls are always incorporated in bodies, and to save a man you must have him body, soul and spirit. To really save *one* man you must transform the community in which he lives. No man lives, or can live, to himself.

So we have a bigger problem than we had imagined and one that is very practical: the making of good roads; the getting rid of weeds; the improvement of stock; the providing of a ball ground; the higher education of the young people:

a square deal for the stranger; better laws and better administration of law—all these are essentially religious, all are surely part of the work of bringing in the kingdom of God in your home district.

This, of course, does not mean that the church must make roads or provide ball grounds or give agricultural education or go in for politics or engage in co-operative enterprise. The church as an organization should, as a rule, keep out of these things. The church is not the only agency for the bringing in of the kingdom. Each agency has its own peculiar functions. Those of the church would seem to be to interpret, to inspire and to guide.

From J. S. Woodsworth, "Thy Kingdom Come," in Malcolm Ross (ed.), *Our Sense of Identity* (Toronto: The Ryerson Press, 1954), pp. 292-296.

KNOWLEDGE FOR THE PEOPLE

Far to the east of Winnipeg, at the University of Saint Francis Xavier in Antigonish, Nova Scotia, Father Jimmy Tompkins shared J. S. Woodsworth's concern for the lot of the working man. Inspired by the achievements of the Workers' Educational Association in England and by the credit unions and popular agricultural schools of Quebec, Father Jimmy sought an answer to the people's problems through a programme of adult education. His pamphlet, Knowledge for the People, *published in 1920, preached the virtues of community co-operation and self-help. From his ideas and initiative grew the famous Antigonish Movement of economic and social group action. Although Father Jimmy left the university for parish work, he was instrumental in founding such varied projects as producers' co-operatives, building societies, public lending libraries and literally hundreds of self-education groups.*

The brunt of his argument even then was for adult education: "Are we to wait until the field of popular education, *in social subjects*, is firmly usurped by charlatans and false prophets of every kind?" Now, after thirty years, when we read these words, we can feel that a prophet was speaking in *Knowledge for the People*:

There is a great need for leadership to crystallize the fluid desires of the public for educational progress of all kinds. The people everywhere are more insistent in demanding reasons for the faith that is in their institutions of learning. As never before, they are calling upon the colleges to serve 100 per cent of the constituency from which they secure their money and their students. This cannot be done, they say, unless the heart of the colleges beats with the heart of the whole community and especially with the heart of honest toil.

It is a law that popular governments and popular institutions, whether religious or secular, are subject to decay if they lose touch with the people. They may even become tyrannous if they fall into the hands of men immune from accountability, either because the people, whom they are supposed to represent and serve, have lost the will or the power through indifference to hold them to account. They are subject to decay also if they fail to adjust themselves to the changing needs of the times. In their decadence they not infrequently become the tool of a clique or class maintaining the semblance of life rather than the reality. These facts are painted large on the map of the world. Institutions for the whole people are not self-perpetuating machines set once and for all in perpetual motion. They are living organisms whose roots are in the people, and unless they draw from these roots the material of life, the tree will die, will be cut down and burnt.

This theme—the vital institution rooted in the needs of the people—was to become a permanent part of his educational philosophy, even at the risk of offending the educational esthetes who were appalled by the vulgarity of the people, by their susceptibility to sentiment, to being misled by demagogic leaders who admittedly may emerge in movements good in themselves. All this Father Tompkins knew well; he counted the sum total a much smaller liability than the liability of neglect, or of only the condescending contact. To him an institution must never become an isolated eminence.

Many years later three or four visitors were having dinner with him in the Reserve Mines parish house when the newspaper was brought in. It was reported in the paper that fire was threatening the buildings of a certain university. Father Tompkins' reaction was typical of him: "It wouldn't hurt much even if they were burnt out. Some of them should be burned down regularly every twenty-five years. It might help to bring them into contact with the people. It is better to be poor and suffer with the people than to be rich and live in an ivory tower."

At another time he said: "Our critics say you can't trust the people. I say Christ prayed for the people. When wrong things have been done, it is because leaders mislead the people. We must teach the people to know a fool when they see one."

The five last pages of *Knowledge for the People* were an even more pointed call to St. Francis Xavier University to initiate measures of adult education.

This pamphlet is concerned . . . with the problem of bringing some measure of useful education to the great majority who stand and must remain outside the walls of our colleges and academies.

A step he considered necessary was to call together in conference with university leaders the representatives of agriculture and industry. The co-operation of Government departments would be sought before "we set our hands to the work that cries to be done." The other great principle that he here inaugurated was that the people themselves must be consulted *directly and not through any agency.*

For us, what the people most need to learn must be what they most want to learn. Let there be the least trace of superiority or propagandism in our attitude, let the people once think of us as academic persons come to force our preconceptions upon them, and the undertaking is dead. But if it is understood that our desire is not to dictate, but to fill a want, to help and serve, we shall have their confidence from the start, and a welcome for our work that will of its own force carry it to triumphant success. This does not mean that we are to sacrifice truth and independence in the substance of what we shall teach, but merely that the people must be allowed to prescribe their own studies.

But how was such a plan—rather, such a dream—to operate? Who would go to work at it? Who, as he used to say, "would bell the cat"?

We need a handful of devoted men prepared to make this work their single interest, and to consecrate to it their whole time and energies for no compensation beyond daily bread if necessary.

He believed that they would be drawn largely from the priesthood at first, as he foresaw that the work would be arduous, exacting, full of disappointment and discouragement. He called for social-minded young priests: "There is need of special vocations." He raised the objections and then answered them: "Was this a priestly work? Less sacred, less priestly than the parochial ministry?"

We answer, in the first place, that this branch of education is a great work of charity—perhaps the most effective shape in which the spirit of charity can express itself in these times. ... True the priest's mission is the saving of souls and he can place no merely corporal work of mercy, however noble, before this. We grant this, but insist that this work, when undertaken by the representatives of the Church, is raised to a spiritual plane. It will save souls. The surest way to spiritual influence today, a way chosen by the Lord Himself in His life among men, is through corporal charity.

In conclusion, he affirmed that such a movement could be utilized as an antidote to materialism. And he quoted Grundvig, the Lutheran bishop, a teacher of the People's School in Denmark:

There is a divine purpose running through the ages . . . in union with which we may all work for the establishment of the Kingdom of God upon earth.

Thus in *Knowledge for the People* the first flaming arrows were prepared. Adult education was not new. Specific projects had been carried on. But the tendency was that after a time they deteriorated and disintegrated. They were sporadic. They did not have the organism of continuation. Father Tompkins wanted to create that.

From George Boyle, *Father Tompkins of Nova Scotia* (New York: P. J. Kenedy & Sons, 1953), pp. 81-84.

BIBLE BILL

The Great Depression brought into sharp relief the problems of farmers and industrial workers alike. With the economy of the country shaken to its foundations, many people looked to the churches for leadership in their hour of confusion. Ontario-born William Aberhart was already established as a popular radio preacher in Calgary when he discovered his answer to the economic question in the doctrines of Social Credit. Using his Prophetic Bible Institute as a base of operations he was able to win the support of Alberta for the new political doctrines, and in the process infused into the Social Credit movement a deeply religious strain that has remained a hallmark of the party he founded. John A. Irving has described the techniques of "Bible Bill" in the early days of Social Credit in Alberta.

To its devotees in Alberta the early years of the Social Credit movement will always remain its heroic period. In the absence of an authentic history, the activities of the years from 1932 to 1935 have been invested with such a legendary halo that today even those most deeply involved in the movement sometimes find it difficult to distinguish fact from fiction. For an understanding of the movement, it is essential, therefore, to provide as detailed an analysis as possible of the strategy and tactics by means of which it was initiated and developed. The materials for such an analysis include field interviews, mimeographed and printed leaflets, pamphlets, and newspaper reports.

It must be emphasized, also, that the Calgary Prophetic Bible Institute was the unique headquarters of the movement, and that every activity was personally supervised, if not always inspired, by William Aberhart. It is doubtful whether there could have been a successful Social Credit movement without Aberhart; it is equally doubtful whether he could have provided effective leadership without the resources of the Institute, over which he had undisputed control. Nor would the movement have grown so rapidly had it not been rooted in the religious following which he had built up during the previous twenty years. Further, the techniques used in developing the movement did not represent a departure from, but were rather continuous with, the methods of indoctrination for which he had long been famous in Alberta.

In its inception, the Social Credit movement may be best understood, therefore, not as a new movement but rather as an extension of an already well-established fundamentalist and prophetic movement. That Social Credit activities were considered from the outset as merely an extension of religious interests is evident from Aberhart's first move in publicizing his recently discovered idea. Sometime during the early autumn of 1932 (the precise date cannot be established), at a meeting of the Institute's Board of Management in the T-Kettle Inn on Eighth Street, he asked for and received permission to introduce Social Credit doctrines into his Sunday afternoon broadcasts. Those present on that half-remembered occasion seem to have viewed such a request as merely routine business of the Institute: did not Bible prophecy deal with certain aspects of man's economic needs? It was implicitly understood that any references to Social Credit would be religious and economic and not political.

Gradually, and with cautious reservations, Aberhart now began to weave Social Credit ideas into his addresses. The radio scripts are not available, but those who remember the broadcasts were apparently not aware of a sudden shift in the emphasis to which they had been accustomed. Social Credit ideas, Aberhart insisted from the beginning, offered a fulfilment of fundamentalist and prophetic Christianity. As his thoughts evolved during the autumn of 1932, his listeners noticed a gradual shading-off of a purely religious emphasis and a growing reference to economic problems.

Then he began to throw out challenging questions: Isn't the root of our economic troubles a shortage of purchasing power? Why couldn't Social Credit be applied to the solution of the problems of the depression, which was then entering its fourth grim year? He urged the people to decide *for themselves* after careful study of Social Credit ideas. Within a few weeks the new appeal began to interest even those who had scant respect for Aberhart's religious doctrines. Late in the fall, in response to an invitation, he held a public week-night meeting in the Canadian Legion Memorial Hall for the discussion of Gessell Scrip. At this, his first non-religious meeting in Calgary, Aberhart informed his audience that the Gessell plan was entirely unsatisfactory. He announced, further, that Social Credit alone offered hope. As a result of this meeting, at a time when both the prices of farm products and the wages of urban workers were falling to new low levels, and when thousands of families in Calgary were on relief, the idea that the depression might be due to a shortage of purchasing power began to be discussed in secular circles in Calgary, and especially among such groups of intelligentsia as the Knights of the Round Table and the Open Mind Club.

Towards the turn of the year interest in Social Credit had increased to the point where Aberhart, in response to numerous requests, announced that early in 1933 he proposed to offer at the Institute a series of public week-night lectures devoted to a systematic exposition of the writings of Major Douglas. It was emphasized that the enterprise would be strictly educational. As these lectures developed it was noticed that the content of Social Credit material in the Sunday broadcasts was increased and presented with more urgency.

From John A. Irving, *The Social Credit Movement in Alberta* (Toronto: University of Toronto Press, 1959), pp. 50-51.

BROTHER ANDRE

On the slopes of Mount Royal stands the monumental Oratory of Saint Joseph, visible for miles to the traveller approaching Montreal. From near and far pilgrims come

*to the Oratory, drawn by the miracles and memory of one
small and humble man, André Bessette. James A. Roy, a
Scot who spent most of his life teaching English at Queen's
University, wrote this sympathetic and moving account of
Brother André and of his own meeting with this modern
miracle-worker. Roy, a Protestant, made a sincere plea for
more faith and less self-assurance in this age of science and
scepticism.*

Possibly you have never heard of Brother André. Many
Protestants and, probably, some Roman Catholics have not.
I had not myself until a few months ago. But the fact remains that for many years Brother André has been a mighty
pillar of his faith and his miracle-working powers are
almost as ardently believed in by hundreds of thousands as
are the cardinal and fundamental doctrines of the Catholic
faith itself. Innumerable miraculous cures have been
ascribed to his mediation, but he vigorously denies that
these have been effected through any gifts or powers of his
own. He claims to be—as, in fact, he actually is—a humble,
ignorant disciple who lives not only in hourly fellowship
with the Unseen but who believes in the special interest and
friendship of St. Joseph, through whose intervention he
himself has been chosen as the instrument whereby the
works of God are made manifest.

Brother André was born on the 9th of August, 1845, of
French-Canadian parentage. His father was Isaac Bessette,
a carriage worker; his mother Clothilde Foisy. His parents
dying when he was still very young, the child received a
meagre education. He was in turn apprenticed to a boot-
maker and a baker, but his health proved unequal to the
demands made on it by these trades. Next he worked on
a farm; then, in the cotton mills in Connecticut. Returning
from the United States he was brought into touch with the
Brothers of the Holy Cross and, after a brief novitiate, he
was admitted to the Congregation of the Holy Cross in
1870 and became in religion Brother André. He remained
at the Boys' College at *Côte des Neiges* for forty years as
porter and messenger, and acted also as barber to the
school. From the beginning of his connection with the

Brotherhood the young religious impressed not only his superiors but all with whom he came into contact by his piety and his devotion to Saint Joseph. His reputation quickly spread, with the result that pilgrims began to flock to the institution to seek his help and counsel, until representations were made to the College authorities by relatives of the pupils, complaining of the danger of infection from the motley crowds that assembled to seek his mediation. The Public Health Authorities were aroused; an investigation was held; many grew alarmed lest the new cult should bring ridicule and discredit upon the cause of true religion, maintaining that the distribution of medallions and holy oil was grotesque and unauthorized. Archbishop Bruchesi was urged to stop the farce; a pavilion was erected for the accommodation of the pilgrims whom Brother André was permitted to interview during the hours when he was off duty. Opposition only increased the popular enthusiasm. A tiny chapel was next erected on Mount Royal in which a statue of Saint Joseph was installed. The first shrine, however, soon proved inadequate to house the ever increasing host of pilgrims and a new and larger one was presently built. But, in time, this also proved inadequate and now a magnificent new crypt has been erected, above which one day will rise the wonderful Basilica destined to be the lasting earthly memorial of the humble little Brother who sits quietly waiting his final summons in the *presbytère* of *Côte des Neiges*.

It is an amazing story, this story of faith and miracle-working. At first the Protestant feels baffled and sceptical, until he suddenly recalls the pointed Pauline query; "Why should it be thought a thing incredible with you that God should raise the dead?" "That," answers the sceptic, "is merely begging the question. Assuming that God can raise and has raised the dead, why should He think it necessary to assert Himself in these modern days by such ordinary and conventional prestidigitations as making the lame to walk, the deaf to hear and even the blind to see—through the intermediary of Brother André? Has the image of God grown so dim that it is necessary to recall Him to man by such childish demonstrations? Have we not outgrown the infancy of the mind? Do not fresh discoveries of science increase our wonder and awe of the Almighty, and our growing knowledge of ourselves reveal the lasting kinship with the Father? Is there a thinking man who is likely to have a loftier conception of God by the sight of a cripple suddenly throwing away his crutches, hobbling about on his withered shanks and proclaiming that God has spoken?" If miracles actually were performed in Apostolic times by persons who made claim to nothing but common humanity, there is no logical reason why we should deny the possibility of their happening today.

●　　●　　●

I met Brother André on only one occasion, when I drove with Father Gagnon to the Oratory at *Côte des Neiges.* After waiting for a short time in the reception room in the *presbytère* while the Father went to inquire whether I could be received, I was requested to step into a little room where I had my first sight of the thaumaturge. The room was bare and scantily furnished. Brother André was lying on the bed, clad in his cassock. My first impression was of a very old man. He struggled into a sitting position as I entered and, while the Father was explaining my presence, I had time to take cursory stock of him. His features are plain almost to ugliness and the skin seamed and creased with a thousand loops and wrinkles. His hair is white; his eyes are small and half concealed by their drooping eyelids, but full of kindliness and peace. Perhaps it was my imagination, but it seemed to me that there was the very light on his face that never was on sea or land. . . . I tried gently to push him back on the counterpane but he insisted on remaining as he was and talking to me. After talking for a time he seemed to grow suddenly tired and I helped him to lie down —a fragile wisp of a man whom you felt you might have broken in two like a withered branch. He lay for a little as if exhausted; then he took my hand in his again, murmured his blessings, and Father Gagnon and I withdrew quietly from the room.

For a moment there came into my mind the scene in the shop where two young men behind the counter sold trinkets and holy oil and crucifixes and souvenirs and picture post-cards and medallions of Saint Joseph, and I experienced a feeling almost of nausea. The saying of a cynical friend flashed suddenly across my mind: "A saint may be nothing but a whitewashed sepulchre and the charity of the phil-anthropist a mere cloak for the pride of humility." But one had only to think of the little man—of his work, the record of his life, one's fleeting contact with his personality—to be convinced that *he*, at least, was free of any taint of commer-cialism or the suspicion of self-exploitation. He is as humble today in that weather-beaten old cassock as ever he was, and will presently leave this world as poor as when he entered it. Brother André is sincere even if he may be mistaken. And who is to prove him in the wrong and by what code can he be so judged except by the arbitrary standard of individual opinion? Brother André dwells in close and vital contact with the hidden things of God. That is something worth while in an age when too many persist in the barren policy of getting and spending and laying waste their powers.

From James A. Roy, "Brother André," in Malcolm Ross (ed.), *Our Sense of Identity* (Toronto: The Ryerson Press, 1954), pp. 67-69, 72-73.

A DAY OF HIGH SOLEMNITIES

The union of the Congregational, Methodist and Presbyterian churches of Canada in 1925 marked a great step forward to Christian reunion, not only for Canada but for world-wide Christianity. For the first time major denominations representing distinctive traditions were joined as a single body. The example set in Canada has since been an inspiration to other lands.

The hopes of the "fathers" of this union and the aura of excitement surrounding the inaugural service of the United Church of Canada were captured in this eye-witness account of that dramatic event.

June the tenth stands as one of the greatest days in the history of Toronto, perhaps of Canada, certainly of American Christianity. Whispers had grown to growls at the idea of holding the inaugural service at Massey Hall. These had come from two sides. On the one hand many wanted a day of high solemnity within a church building, at least, for the service of worship. On the other hand hosts of people thought that they wanted to attend and would be shut out even from the great hall. When it was decided to engage the Arena many gasped, for there were sure to be two thousand empty seats or even more. What likelihood was there of getting eight thousand pepole to come to three services on a busy week day. For an evening demonstration it might be done, and has been done after gigantic efforts at publicity. But this was different—purely a religious appeal and all day long. No one hoped for a full house. Ticket holders were sure of their seats until fifteen minutes before opening, but no one would take chances of being near the limit. So we all got along in good time and as we crossed Yonge Street and the Metropolitan Church there seemed to be a lot of folk on the street all going the same way. At Cooke's Church one here and there dropped out of the stream, for here were the Anti-Unionists in their great demonstration, with delegates whose fares were paid to come from every part of Canada. But the stream grew denser and presently we ran into a solid column four deep. Surely these were some folk waiting for rush seats? But no, they were ticket holders and the column moved steadily towards the entrance of the great arena. How could we get in the line? There was just one way—to go back two blocks to the rear of the column and take our turn.

Presently we entered the vestibule and found ahead of us the vast open space. Climbing to the upper tiers one looked down on a marvellous sight. The eight thousand seats were filling rapidly until there was scarce a seat left. The audience was fully half men—indeed the front part of the floor was entirely filled with men. Down the steep slopes and over the vast floor space spread this sea of human forms, the women's hats lending some color and the outing suits of men relieving the darkness. But in the centre in front of the capacious platform was an open block of seats reserved. How few they seemed in the mass. Yet they were to accommodate the whole General Council, 350 strong. Behind them was hidden a good orchestra and above them a first rate choir. The hall was but slightly decorated as everything spectacular was to be eliminated. There were, however, some "artistic concealments," while from the great ribs of the roof hung the flags of all nations. In front of the speaker's desk was a tiny receiver of a radio and above, far up in the roof, was a set of seven horns—all designed to multiply the voice so that every word would be heard throughout the building.

Promptly at half past ten from the rear of the platform, Dr. Fricker rose and silently signalled his choir, the whole audience rising with them. A chord from the orchestra and then the stately opening notes of *Aurelia* gave voice to the processional hymn—"The Church's One Foundation." From the wide-open door emerged the council, headed by the two tall figures of Dr. S. D. Chown and Dr. George C. Pidgeon, Moderator of the Assembly, which was then passing out of existence. With them came Professor Warriner, chairman of the Congregational Union, and Rev. C. S. Elsey, Moderator of the United Churches, already organized to receive into the company of pioneers this main body. The processional awakened thoughts and memories. There came the noble and distinguished scholars and pastors sent across the seas by mother Churches in England, Scotland, South Africa, and China, all here to attest the world-wide interest and wistful thoughts of the larger Christendom which believes that the trail is being blazed out of the frightful ecclesiastical chaos which has been developing since the Reformation. There, too, in the procession were men scarred, not in person or in spirit, but in loss of livelihood through devotion to the cause. The First General Synod at Nicaea was glorified by the presence of those who, in the days not long gone by, had tasted the martyrs' sorrows and lost eye or limb for their Christian faith. So here were faces aglow, not with fanaticism, but with faith triumphant over fears. And in the procession, too, were the nine Moderators of past General Assemblies, each of whom had made his contribution to the opening of the great highway for the Lord. Of course, there were the delegates appointed by the Methodist Church, the Congregational Churches, and the Union Churches, but these had passed through no similar fires of pain—they came easily to the goal of their longings. Yet the three hundred and fifty men—yea, and a few elected women with them—marched calmly and without confusion to their places. The empty space on the floor and the platform were alike filled and all was ready for the opening.

•   •   •

It was in this setting that the United Church of Canada was formally constituted and consecrated. Opening formulae from the Book of Common Order asserted the purpose and spirit of the Church and then one by one the uniting bodies, through their heads, tendered the specific contribution which their experience had produced for the edifying of the body of Christ. Each gift was greeted by the whole body responding, "We glory in the grace given to us in this goodly heritage." And it was only fitting that this phase of the morning programme should culminate in an act of commemoration of the faithful, who in all ages have helped to prepare the day of the Son of Man. In this atmosphere, of disinterested devotion and Godward aspiration, Dr. Chown read the formula in which, after reciting the authority for the action, the United Church of Canada was proclaimed as being now a fact—it was exactly half past eleven when the historic words were spoken—and one by one the heads of the uniting bodies signed the declaratory act, each being accompanied as he signed by the standing of the whole body of his fellow churchmen in the olden days.

●　　●　　●

And then a strange new feeling came—"'Tis done, the great transaction's done." These fine fellows, whose endowments of grace and ability we have admired from afar off were now part of us. We were no longer waiting for the time when we should see each other across the walls of our garden. The middle wall of partition was broken down. Truly God is good to Israel and many a heart whispered its *Nunc Dimittis*. One old man especially who had long lived to see this hour saw it, and at once the meaning of life had been achieved and silently he passed suddenly away into the larger life of the unseen. Just what our three Churches were at this moment doing—passing quietly and without shock into the unseen, but assured future of richer life! What better voice could our soul find at this moment than the old paraphase, "O God of Bethel!"

From Ernest Thomas, D.D., "A Day of High Solemnities: The United Church of Canada Starts Its Work," *The New Outlook* (Toronto), June 17, 1925.

A CLAIM OF RIGHT

The United Church of Canada did not win undivided support from all members of the three uniting churches. For some years a swelling voice of opposition to union had been heard within the Presbyterian communion, and when the hour of decision was finally reached in 1925 about one-third of all Presbyterians registered their dissent from the decision of their General Assembly by withdrawing to form the continuing Presbyterian Church in Canada. Their reasons for rejecting union had often been stated, but they were recapitulated in the General Assembly on the very eve of union in the following "Claim of Right" signed by seventy-eight ministers and elders.

We the undersigned Ministers and Elders, commissioners to this fifty-first General Assembly of the Presbyterian Church in Canada, although feeling painfully the solemnity of our position, and deeply distressed in view of the impending separation, do nevertheless, in our own name, and in the name of all who may choose to adhere to us, hereby solemnly protest that,

Whereas the Presbyterian Church in Canada as a Church of Christ, composed of certain four Presbyterian Churches in the Dominion that entered into a Covenant of Union in 1875, and of such additional persons as since then have chosen to unite themselves with her, constituted upon (a) the Scriptures of Old and New Testaments as being the only infallible rule of faith and manners, upon (b) The Westminster Confession of Faith, and the Larger and Shorter Catechisms as her doctrinal standards, declaring how the Church interprets the teaching of the Scriptures on the several matters embraced in the documents, and upon (c) the recognized principles and practice of the Presbyterian Churches as laid down generally in "The Form of Church Government" and the "Directory for the Public Worship of God" as to her government and worship, all set forth in the Basis of Union in 1875;

It is her faithful adherence to the aforesaid standards of doctrine and worship, and forms of discipline and government, adequately secured unto her by the said Covenant of Union of 1875, that the real historical and hereditary identity of the Presbyterian Church in Canada consists, as well as her continuity as the lawful successor in this Dominion of the Reformed Churches of the Motherland;

And whereas the Basis of Union negotiated between the Methodist, Congregational and Presbyterian Churches contains very many features inconsistent with the standards of the Church secured unto us by the Covenant of Union of 1875;

And whereas the Ministers met in this General Assembly have come under a solemn engagement to maintain and defend the government of the Church by Sessions, Presbytries, Synods, and General Assemblies, and to follow no divisive course from the present order established in the Church;

And whereas the Elders met in this General Assembly have come under a solemn engagement, and still lie under it, to maintain and defend this government of the Church by Sessions, Presbyteries, Synods, and General Assemblies.

We do further protest that we cannot comply with the course pursued by the prevailing party, or acquiesce in their decision to merge the Presbyterian Church in Canada in another Church under the aforesaid Basis of Union;

And whereas the resolution adopted by the General Assembly of the Presbyterian Church in Canada held in the City of Winnipeg in 1916, approving of the said Basis of Union, together with all things since done to implement the said resolutions were beyond the power of that or any other General Assembly,

We do further protest that, notwithstanding the action of the Assembly in 1916, or any further action by the prevailing party in this Assembly, it shall be lawful for us, together with such other commissioners as may adhere to us, to continue in session in St. Andrew's Church, Toronto, on Thursday, June 11th, 1925, as commissioners to the fifty-first General Assembly of the Presbyterian Church of Canada, and there, in humble dependence on God's grace and the aid of the Holy Spirit, and maintaining with us the Confession of Faith and standards of the Church as hitherto understood, to adopt such measures as may be competent to us for the continuance of the Presbyterian Church in Canada, to the advancement of God's glory, the extension of the Gospel of our Lord and Saviour throughout the world, and the orderly administration of Christ's House, according to His Holy Word;

And finally, we do protest before the great God, the Searcher of all hearts, that we, and all those who shall adhere to us, are not responsible for this schism in the Church, or for any consequences which may flow from this enforced separation. In humble submission to His will, we give this our testimony. To Him we commend our cause, and we pray that in the days to come His richest blessing may rest upon the Church of our fathers, which Church we are resolved by His help to maintain.

From N. G. Smith, *et al, A Short History of the Presbyterian Church in Canada* (Toronto, 1965), pp. 88-89.

IN THIS SIGN CONQUER

In 1939 the churches of Canada were once more called on to provide spiritual guidance for Canada's fighting men in time of war. Padres from all the major denominations joined the three branches of the armed forces as members of the Canadian Chaplain Service. In every theatre of war where Canadians fought their padres were to be found beside the men in the thick of the battle. It is a tribute to their devotion and sacrifice that one of the sixteen Victoria Crosses awarded to Canadians during the Second World War was presented to Captain John Weir Foote, minister of the Presbyterian Church, for his gallant actions at Dieppe. The official citation for his V.C. is reproduced here. It requires neither explanation nor embellishment.

At Dieppe on 19th August, 1942, Honorary Captain Foote, Canadian Chaplain Services, was Regimental Chaplain with the Royal Hamilton Light Infantry.

Upon landing on the beach under heavy fire he attached himself to the Regimental Aid Post which had been set up in a slight depression on the beach, but which was only sufficient to give men cover lying down. During the subsequent period of approximately eight hours, while the action continued, this officer not only assisted the Regimental

Medical Officer in ministering to the wounded in the Regimental Aid Post, but time and again left this shelter to inject morphine, give first-aid and carry wounded personnel from the open beach to the Regimental Aid Post. On these occasions, with utter disregard for his personal safety, Honorary Captain Foote exposed himself to an inferno of fire and saved many lives by his gallant efforts. During the action, as the tide went out, the Regimental Aid Post was moved to the shelter of a stranded landing craft. Honorary Captain Foote continued tirelessly and courageously to carry wounded men from the exposed beach to the cover of the landing craft. He also removed wounded from inside the landing craft when ammunition had been set on fire by enemy shells. When landing craft appeared he carried wounded from the Regimental Aid Post to the landing craft through heavy fire. On several occasions this officer had the opportunity to embark but returned to the beach, as his chief concern was the care and evacuation of the wounded. He refused a final opportunity to leave the shore, choosing to suffer the fate of the men he had ministered to for over three years.

Used by permission of The Department of National Defence.

THE PADRE OF THE PUBS

The new world of the twentieth century—this world of rushing industry, of sprawling cities, of space-age miracles, of changing values—challenges the traditional ways of the Christian churches by offering unlimited opportunities to present the gospel message by new means and in new places. The churches are responding—perhaps responding too slowly to suit some—to these many-sided challenges, and one of the most notable responses is the break with the rigid concept of a parochial ministry. To combat the spiritual problems besetting modern society the modern churches have begun to provide special ministries. A unique experiment in Canada is the United Church's "padre of the pubs." Not without misgivings and some opposition, the late Arthur Packman was permitted to leave regular parish work and devote his full time to a ministry in the beverage rooms. So successful was his venture to reach and help outside the church that the post of "padre of the pubs" has become a recognized appointment within The United Church of Canada.

A good-looking, slightly inebriated girl sat across from us at a table in one of Toronto's posh night clubs. As we talked, she took furtive glances at a little slip of yellow paper she held under the table. She was obviously curious about the man who had given her the card: the man who sat beside me and was talking to her about her job, her home and her church.

The card read: "Rev. Arthur Packman. Your Personal Padre. *I would like to chat with you and help you if needed. . . . I have dedicated myself to this purpose.*" There was a telephone number where he could be contacted.

She was a member of the United Church, the girl said, but her escort was an Anglican. Neither had been very diligent in church attendance.

Earlier in the evening we had talked with the operator and two members of an exclusive club. All were United Church members; one attended regularly, one had been a church organist. All were perplexed about their faith and they fired innumerable questions at the "Padre of the Pubs," as Mr. Packman has become affectionately known in downtown Toronto.

I don't know if the padre solved any problems for them, but I suspect, from the tone of the conversations, that he started them thinking on things they hadn't bothered about for a long time.

These were just two encounters during my rounds of Toronto beer halls and taverns with Mr. Packman. He handed out dozens of his "personal padre" cards (a gift from a Scarborough print shop). Everywhere we went, people called him to their tables to talk, or waiters told him about people who wanted to see him. Not once did he approach anyone without an invitation. About three out of every five people we talked to said they "belonged to the United Church."

Mr. Packman has been making his nightly visits to Toronto taverns for four months. "It was really difficult to go into the first one, back on September 28," he says, "I walked up and down the street a couple of times before I got up the courage to go in. But I've been well received everywhere, by barmen, waiters and owners, and there are always plenty of people who want to tell me their troubles." He's made it a point to wear his clerical collar on every visit.

●　　●　　●

"I was very concerned about the great gulf between the church and the people, because of the forces at work within and outside man," the padre says. "That's why I entered this work. If it is true that 70% of our people drink, then the sooner the church goes out into the world the sooner the world will go out of the church."

Mr. Packman did a little of this work while in the pastorate. He was the first chaplain of a club in Belleville. "But you're not free enough in the pastorate," he says, "and you've got to be free. I see no reason why there can't be a few hand-picked men carrying on this type of functional ministry. But they must do it in the right spirit, because they love people—not going in as though they are talking to naughty people doing something they shouldn't."

"The beverage room is an established reality, and we are not going to get rid of it; in fact I don't know that that would be desirable. People are going to drink, no matter what happens. We must do something more than attack. We must form a basis on which we can work with these people, and we can only do it through friendship."

●　　●　　●

There are many who apparently share Mr. Packman's views. But there are others who violently disagree. One minister wrote, "No doubt you will soon be on the brewers' payroll."

There are some, too, who say that Mr. Packman's cordial reception from tavern operators is because they think his visits give their premises prestige. "That's not so," Mr. Packman says, "they thoroughly understand why I'm there.

But would it not be desirable to elevate the beverage room, give it prestige if you want to use that term, or do we leave it to become part of the underworld of our cities? Like it or not, the beverage room is here to stay."

And Jimmy Clemens, one of the operators of the Edison Tavern, told me over a cup of coffee and the din of rock and roll music, "we've been needing someone like him for a long time. He's no phoney: he's genuinely interested in people, and the people pour out their hearts to him. There are lots of lonely people, and people with troubles, who need someone to talk to, someone who cares and can help them. The padre is doing a wonderful work."

We met one such troubled person in a Jarvis Street bar which Mr. Packman was visiting for the first time. A gleam of recognition spread over the man's face as he saw us enter. The padre had taken him home, drunk, about 17 hours earlier. I asked the padre if it was the man's wife sitting beside him at the bar. "That's part of his trouble." Mr. Packman said, "he's married but that's not his wife." The man took sheepish glances at the padre several times as we sat at a table six feet away, then got up and walked out of the room. "He's left me and gone home to his wife," the girl told us a few minutes later.

Then there was a little Frenchman, a former Roman Catholic priest, in a noisy, smoke-filled beer hall; a stocky Italian youth, confused by the big city and in trouble with the police; a bartender, who said he was an alcoholic but had "stayed dry" for four years. "Yours is a tough job," he told the padre, "and I was glad to talk to you when you came in here. I haven't talked to many ministers, and you know where I would have told you to go if you had come to preach to me. . ."

And there were others.

●　　●　　●

"I'm not concerned with the fact that people drink," Mr. Packman says, "but I am concerned with why they drink and why they drink to excess. The cause of much of it is loneliness and inner conflict. These are the things that challenge me and make the ministry necessary."

He is hoping that this concern will be shared by others in the church, and that there will be more ministers to undertake such a ministry. "I'm pioneering now, but I hope and pray that this work can be put on a sound basis and be continued by strong, able and dedicated men."

From E. L. Homewood, "The Padre of the Pubs," *The United Church Observer* (Toronto), February 1, 1961.

THERE IS THE LORD

The modern movement for co-operation and understanding among all Christians took a long step forward with the election of Pope John XXIII in 1958. One of his strongest ambitions was to improve the relations between Catholics and non-Catholics. To promote this ideal other Christian churches were invited to send delegate observers to the great Ecumenical Council that opened at Rome in 1962.

The winds of change generated by that Council were wafted from Rome to Canada at a very opportune moment. In July, 1963, just five weeks after Pope John's death, the fourth World Conference on Faith and Order of the World Council of Churches met in Montreal. At the pressing invitation of the conference Cardinal Paul Emile Léger, Archbishop of Montreal, spoke to the members about the new ecumenical spirit, and joined his "separated brethren" in prayers for Christian unity. Never before had Catholic and non-Catholic come so close together beneath the cross in Canada. The presence and message of Cardinal Léger at that Conference encouraged the dynamic dialogue that is bringing the Canadian churches into ever deepening contact and understanding.

We acknowledge with gratitude the sincere desire and firm will of all who are gathered here to establish unity among "those who rejoice in being united in faith to the Lord Jesus."

We know that this desire for unity is inspired by the very Spirit of Our Lord for, according to the words of St. Paul, we have not received a spirit of slavery, to govern us by fear, but "a spirit of adoption which makes us cry out, Abba, Father."

We know also that the work of the Conference on Faith and Order has done much to spread this desire of unity throughout the Christian world. All who participate in the work of this conference become more conscious of their responsibilities in the presence of the divine will of the Lord who, before leaving them, repeatedly said to his apostles: "This is my commandment, that you should love one another, as I have loved you. This is the greatest love a man can show, that he should lay down his life for his friends." (John XV, 12-13).

This unity is a gift of God and a fruit of prayer, but it is also a goal towards which must be directed all the efforts of wills cleansed of egotism and enlightened by the findings of intelligent minds subject to the demands of faith.

Last year, the General Assembly of New Delhi formulated the following statement which was the result of the common study of theologians of different religious communions: "The unity of the church is made manifest when all those who are baptized in Christ Jesus and who acknowledge him as Saviour and Lord are led by the Holy Spirit to a total community, profess the same apostolic faith, preach the same gospel, partake of the same bread, unite in common prayer and are in communion with the entire Christian community in all places and at all times."

However, while we are able to recite together a common prayer for unity, we are forced to admit that even this unity is in jeopardy because of our hesitation to accept unity as the Lord willed it, because our prejudices set us up one against the other, because our ignorance is unable to penetrate the veil behind which are the unfathomable riches of Christ (Ephesians III, 8).

The Apostle Paul considered it his vocation to "publish to the world the plan of this mystery, kept hidden from the beginning of time in the all-creating mind of God" (Ephesians III, 9). This mystery, for Paul, is that the Christian is called to reproduce in this life, in his spirit and his flesh, the very acts of Christ, that is to say, his passion, his death and his resurrection. And to arrive at this unity, we need more than prayer, we need the Holy Eucharist. It is through communion with his Eucharistic Body that the Lord truly brings us unity by giving us his Spirit who shapes us in his image so that the Father may say in all truth, to each of the baptized: "This is my beloved son, in whom I am well pleased."

In this sense, the Eucharist appears as the centre and the source of the unity of the Church and the fecundity of its life.

I know well that these affirmations may not meet with the approval of all who are gathered here. In fact, the discussions which are taking place show us that the different churches do not have identical notions of the eucharistic mystery. It is because of these differences that we cannot yet celebrate together the eucharistic prayer of unity.

If the Roman Catholic Church affirms that the fraternity which exists between us is not the perfect fraternity which is wanted by the Lord and which is expressed in the communion of one Church, be assured that it does so in all humility and with the clear conviction of its responsibilities. . . .

• • •

The fraternal meetings of Roman Catholic theologians with theologians of other Christian Communions show clearly the truth of the statement made by an eminent member of the Reformed Church of France: "However serious may be that which divides us, that which unites us is greater still," for we are brothers, we have certitude of being united to Christ. St. Paul tells us that "By baptism, we have all become one being with Christ" (Romans VI, 5). This is our great consolation and the source of our joy. Our mutual affection, grounded on this union in faith, allows us to entertain in our hearts a hope that God cannot permit to be empty and illusory. Following the example of the Father of all believers, who hoped against all hope and believed that he would be the Father of many nations (Romans IV, 18), we are determined, yes, strengthened by divine promise, we are determined, without admitting the least trace of incredulity in the sturdiness of a faith which gives glory to God, to walk with gladness towards unity so that one day we may all sing together in all truth this chant of the Catholic liturgy: "Where there is charity and love, there is the Lord."

Is not this ecumenical gathering a sign of our common hope? May it also be the proof of our good will to live according to the truth, in all charity, so that we may grow in every manner towards the one who is the head, Christ, from whom the body derives its co-ordination and cohesion (Ephesians IV, 16).

Yes, it is in truth and in charity that we must carry out our task, for "truth without charity becomes intolerable and repels; charity, without truth is blind and does not endure" (Cardinal Bea).

This evening, I am happy to find at my side, brothers in Christ who experienced with as much intensity as I the unforgettable hours of the First Session of the Second Vatican Council. As we did then, so do we this evening, sense deeply the common bond of fellowship which draws us together in spite of our divisions. I know well, and so do all who are gathered here, that the road to complete unity will be long. But is not the family reunion of this evening, in the words of John XXIII, a "sign of the times"?

Yes, there was a man who was given to the Church whose name was John. He was given just enough time to extend his arms to all men of good will in a gesture of fraternal affection and to invite them to discover in his intentions and in his heart, rectitude and love. His last gesture was a blessing and those who were there fell on their knees in St. Peter's Square.

It is on their knees that men must continue their difficult search for peace. In a divided world, where blocs set themselves against each other, where peoples have become restless, Christians must search for truth, practise justice by respecting the rights of all men and seek to establish a climate of freedom which is necessary for men who want to live in charity.

If the Churches do not bring this peace to the world, if they do not give the witness of unity in Christ, the 20th Century may well lose its opportunity of salvation.

From Address of His Eminence Paul-Emile Cardinal Léger, Archbishop of Montreal, delivered at the Fourth World Conference on Faith and Order of the World Council of Churches, University of Montreal, July 21, 1963.

THAT ALL MAY BE ONE

One of the first fruits of the new spirit of religious co-operation in Canada is the imaginative Christian Pavilion built for Expo '67 by seven of Canada's Christian churches. The Christian Pavilion is distinctive in both concept and design, and is the first such joint undertaking in the history of Christianity. Symbol of this ecumenical age, the Christian Pavilion stands forth as a visible witness to the unifying influence of the cross in Canada.

Ecumenical dialogue has its own interesting and dramatic way of bringing the Christian churches together. Who, for example, could have imagined a few years ago that modest but regular ecumenical exchanges between a few Montreal priests and ministers would result in an ambitious centennial project, undertaken with the support of the Christian church of Canada?

This is precisely what has happened. As soon as the Canadian International Exhibition was announced as the main attraction for Canada's centennial celebrations, the small Montreal group of practical ecumenists dreamed up the idea of a common Christian pavilion. A discreet inquiry about the feasibility and acceptability of such a project won an instant and enthusiastic response from the officials of Expo '67.

The unusual thing about this project is not the participation of Christian churches in an international exhibition. Since the Second World War, Christian churches have participated in several international Exhibitions and Fairs. As someone has pointed out, the Christian churches spent nearly $20,000,000 for their pavilions at the recent New

York World Fair. We may recall that the Vatican pavilion at this fair made a great hit with its display of Michelangelo's Pieta.

Nor could it be considered strange for the Christian churches of Canada to take part in Expo '67. After all, the general theme of this important event for Canada and the world is Man and His World. With such a theme, it would be perfectly understandable that Christians of Canada would feel the need and urgency of taking part.

What marks the Christian Pavilion of Expo '67 as something special and unusual is its ecumenical dimension. Never before in the history Christainity have Christian churches joined forces to erect and operate jointly a common pavilion. No wonder the Faith and Order Committee of the World Council of Churches strongly endorsed the proposed project at their meeting in Montreal in 1963.

When representatives of the Roman Catholic, United, Anglican, Presbyterian, Lutheran, Baptist and Greek Orthodox churches can come together and, as Christians, agree on a common project for Canada's centennial celebrations, the ecumenical repercussions cannot be minimized. The Christians of Canada should be proud of their representatives who are making the Christian pavilion a reality. While Expo is open, the pavilion will stand out as a constant reminder of the need and growing possibility of Christian unity.

The building and operation of the Pavilion necessarily imposes a financial commitment, but not an unreasonable one. The projected cost is $1,300,000. The seven churches involved have already pledged 85 per cent of this amount, and it is expected that the balance will come from private sources. One official has calculated the cost of the average contribution based on the number of adherents of the participating churches; it comes to just seven cents per person.

Agreement on the architectural shape of the Pavilion was easily reached. The building, which in no way resembles or suggests a church or chapel, will have three levels as well as a garden and small administrative centre. Any controversy or criticism that has arisen revolves mainly about the theme of the pavilion, the actual presentation of the message.

One early suggestion of three courts, to represent fellowship, dialogue and contemplation, was rejected as being too traditional and not challenging enough. Finally chosen was an audio-visual presentation designed to involve the visitor, young or old, of one of many languages or cultures, in a memorable brush with up-to-date technical and disturbing effects. Sound, mirrors, light, motion pictures and space will aim at identifying the visitor with the presentation. The designers are striving for a spiritual impact that will provoke an inner response.

It is possible that the presentation of the Christian Pavilion will be a controversial one, i.e., so unusual as to dismay some and puzzle others. The authors of the presentation will only say "so much the better," for they do not want the novel experience to be dismissed lightly. They are seeking a strong reaction.

Explicitly, the Christian Pavilion wishes to raise relevant questions for the men and women of 1967. What is modern man? How does he see himself in this world? Can he get along well enough without God? Is he really self sufficient? The Christian Pavilion will let modern man see himself within the family, the community, the city, and today's mechanized society.

It will draw his attention to the problem areas of mankind in a range from family quarrels to atomic annihilation. No neat little answers will be handed out. But key questions will be asked within a framework of hope. In the Christian Pavilion Christ will be offered as the hope of the world.

Man, with all his problems, hopes and expectations, is the primary concern of the Christian faith. Since Expo '67 wants to show man his world, the Christian Pavilion wants to be at the heart of Expo, throwing out a challenge, an invitation to man to meditate on the human condition. But the challenge and invitation will be presented in an idiom that modern man will readily understand.

A stereotyped presentation of the gospel message would fall on deaf ears at Expo '67. The creators of the pavilion expect that a fresh, novel approach will arouse curiosity, interest and reflection, and that these will endure.

John O'Brien, of Montreal, the chairman of the building and program committee, has this to say about the desired impact of the pavilion: "In a world which is often without hope, we trust that modern man will begin to see Christ as the world's real hope. In a world with little love, it is hoped he will see Christ as the source of love."

If this message gets through, the seven participating churches will praise and thank God for the opportunity of serving their fellow men. They will seek no other reward or consolation.

In the common declaration signed by the Church representatives in December 1964, it is stated that through the Christian Pavilion the Christians of Canada "wish to express their love to their fellow men throughout the world and to alleviate the anxieties and to fulfill the expectations of our century by a common proclamation of the Gospel." It is an intelligent effort to show through architecture and an audio-visual presentation that Christ is present in all that is happening concerning "Man and His World."

From A. J. Macdougall, S.J., "Churches Unite on Expo Stand," *The Globe and Mail* (Toronto), March 12, 1966, p. 11.

ACKNOWLEDGMENTS

Grateful acknowledgment is given the following for permission to reprint excerpts in this collection: *The Voyages of Jacques Cartier* by H. P. Biggar, and the *Report* of the Public Archives for 1892, by permission of the Public Archives of Canada; Cambridge University Press and the Hakluyt Society for *The Three Voyages of Martin Frobisher in Search of a Passage to Cathaia and India by the North-West, A.D. 1576-78*, Richard Collinson (ed.); The Champlain Society for *History of New France* by Marc Lescarbot, W. L. Grant and H. P. Biggar (eds.), *Works of Samuel de Champlain*, H. P. Biggar (ed.), *Long Journey to the Country of the Hurons* by G. Sagard, G. M. Wrong (ed.), and *An Historical Journal of the Campaigns in North America* by John Knox; Little, Brown for *The Jesuits in North America, Montcalm and Wolfe, The Old Régime in Canada* by Francis Parkman; J. M. Dent & Sons for *History of Montreal* by Dollier de Casson, R. Flenley (ed.); *The Huron Carol*, J. Middleton (trans.), by permission of the Frederick Harris Music Company, Oakville, Ontario; University of Toronto Press for *The Social Credit Movement in Alberta* by John A. Irving, and *Social Development of Canada* by S. D. Clark; Prentice-Hall of Canada for Canadian Historical Documents Series, Vol. I: *The French Régime*, Cameron Nish (ed. and trans.); The Macmillan Company of Canada for *The Rise and Fall of New France* by G. M. Wrong; Doubleday & Company for *Hands to the Needy* by Sister Mary Pauline Fitts, copyright 1950, 1958, and *Mère Marie of the Ursulines* by Agnes Repplier, both reprinted by permission of the publisher; Department of Public Printing and Stationery for *Documents Relating to the Constitutional History of Canada, 1759-1791*, Adam Shortt and A. G. Doughty (eds.); The United Church of Canada for *Bulletin, 1958*, and *Nation Builders* by J. L. Murray, and "A Day of High Solemnities: The United Church of Canada Starts Its Work" by Ernest Thomas, in *The New Outlook*, June 17, 1925; The Society for Promoting Christian Knowledge for *The Life and Letters of Charles Inglis* by J. W. Lydekker; St. Francis Xavier University for *A History of the Catholic Church in Eastern Nova Scotia* by Father A. A. Johnston; William H. Elgee for *The Social Teachings of the Canadian Churches* (Ryerson); The Perkins Bull Foundation for *From Macdonell to McGuigan* by W. Perkins Bull; R. V. Harris for *The Church of Saint Paul in Halifax, Nova Scotia: 1749-1949*, as related by R. V. Harris; Flora McPherson for *Watchman Against the World* (Ryerson); Douglas Library Archives, Queen's University, for *Diary of William Bell* (MS), Vol. XIV; George E. Levy for